Financial breakthroughs and testimonials from recent students of the "Financial Freedom in 7 Weeks Plus" course:

"As a direct result of the Financial Freedom in 7 Weeks Plus course, we have a new mindset that will no longer allow the past to rob our future. God's financial plan is now our priority. We realize that the 'stinkin thinkin' of the world's system (easy credit rip offs and debt) is an absolute lie. The redeemed of the Lord can and should live like it."

--- ***Tim and Patricia Nichols***

"We finished the Financial Freedom in 7 Weeks Plus course the week before we got married. It was one of the wisest things we did. It resolved many issues we came across when consolidating our finances. It was a true blessing. It also started our marriage on the right track by establishing a solid biblical financial foundation. We highly recommend the 7 week focus group course to everyone."

--- ***Jim and Terry Dunlap***

"Today, we realize that we will be totally debt free in just 2 years. Thank you God, and thank you Bill and Maureen for this course. When we started this course we were $45,000 in debt and did not have the tools to work with. This to us is what we call a miracle."

--- ***Dan and Gayle Ford***

(Note: The Ford's served as leaders in training and recently led a 7-week focus group.)

"The Financial Freedom in 7 Weeks Plus course has completely changed our lives. Although we were only looking for answers to our financial difficulties, we received much more. Yes, we are now on our way to financial freedom. Spiritually, we learned God's will for our lives as a one-flesh couple. Our mindset has been transformed. We hope to be future focus group leaders for the teaching of this great ministry. Before we came to the first focus group session, we never had enough money to make ends meet. However we were not tithing. Then we made up our hearts and minds to be obedient and to tithe according to God's will. Today, we tithe properly, give offerings, save money, and pay all of our bills. It's our belief that once you truly open your heart to God, and remain obedient, the blessings will start coming even before you start to ask! We plan to continue to trust in God rather than man. May God bless you both, Bill and Maureen."

--- ***James and Vanda Nealous***

"The Financial Freedom in 7 Weeks Plus course gave us the tools to be better stewards of our money. We now pay more attention to small financial details. We've learned that it's not how much money we make that's important, but how we manage it. We now know where our money is being spent and how to better plan. Instead of ignoring a difficult situation, we face it. The weekly lessons taught us a great deal. We made a slight adjustment to our mortgage payment (it cut 5 years off the loan). We now pay it (half of a full monthly payment) every two weeks instead of once a month. Also as a result, we will save $20,000 in interest payments. Anyone who has self-employment income will definitely be blessed by the Guidelines for the Self Employed in chapter two. We really appreciate the Sitters' willingness to teach and train others."

--- ***Larry and Maria Dahlstein***

(Note: The Dahlsteins first served as leaders in training and progressed to lead a 7-week focus group. They have eight children, home school, and both spouses work multiple jobs — so what's your excuse?)

"After finishing the Financial Freedom in 7 Weeks Plus course, the Lord gave us a new understanding of how to steward our finances. The course also gave us hope and a vision of one day being totally debt-free!"

--- ***Richard and Sandra Martinez***

(Note: Richard and Sandra have led a focus group and they taught these principles both in English and Spanish-speaking churches. Before becoming leaders in training, they had no background knowledge in finances. We are so proud of what God is doing through their faithfulness. Their progress and growth proves the importance of the mentoring role leaders play when disciplining and training leaders in training.)

"Dear Bill and Maureen, When we attended your finance focus group we didn't really know what to expect. Our finances were in bad shape. Frankly, it was embarrassing to share. Thank you for being so compassionate and caring. The small group environment made it easy to be transparent. Thank you for showing us God's never changing principles. This has definitely helped us gain control of our finances. In addition, your course has been very effective in teaching us how to deal with debt. We are on the road to becoming DEBT FREE! We know where we stand, and we have a plan, thanks to you. In the name of JESUS we declare, in faith, that we are debt free! Thank you and may God bless you both."

--- ***Mike and Kathie Maloney***

"Before the course, my husband Bill and I were not on the same page. I was the one who did everything regarding our finances. I tried to give the financial responsibility to my husband, but he didn't want it. Now, we make financial decisions as a team."

--- ***Irene Rinehardt***

"The 7 week course taught us a lot more than just getting our stuff (finances) in order. What we have learned empowers us to leave a legacy for our kids and future generations. (It's like opening up a can of worms and seeing a cabinet full.) The good news is that the book offers Godly solutions."

--- ***Bill Rinehardt***

"This Financial Freedom in 7 Weeks Plus course showed me that God wants to be a part of my life and my finances. You have made a great step financially and spiritually by buying this book. Any thoughts of fear, stress, shame and not having enough time are clearly thoughts from the devil. The devil wants to keep God out of your financial life. The strongest and brightest light is from our Father. So, turn on the light, and let God govern your finances. He is ready to bless you and your family! In the 7-week focus group study, you will find faith, fellowship, and love. You will also receive an understanding of how to keep God in your bank account and the devil out. Go get it! You will learn practical financial applications based on biblical truths. These truths are essential for the rest of your life. The joy that comes from this class will elevate your spirit and strengthen your faith. Tithe to your Father, pray for guidance, share with your class, and do your homework. I thank God for his many blessings, for this class and for the incredible focus group leaders called to faithfully teach this life changing material."

--- ***Amelia Hartzel***

"The Financial Freedom in 7 Weeks Plus course was a major blessing to us. We are now applying the principles we learned in our daily lives. Before attending the class, Percy managed the finances. Now, we take time to plan short and long term financial goals.. This course taught us to work together as a one-flesh team regarding our finances. As we were participating in the course, we received a great breakthrough. God revealed to us that we were sowing good seed into bad ground. We repented and God brought about a great financial blessing, within days. Praise God!"

--- ***Percy and Daynelle Kimbrough***

"For about three years, my wife and I have been discussing/planning for my retirement from my second career. By December 2003, we want to be debt free, with the exception of (4 more years) our home mortgage. The Financial Freedom in 7 Weeks Plus course helped us finalize this plan in an organized manner. We had been exposed, at one time or another, to most of the principles, but never in a neat package. The course forced us to accurately list all our liabilities and assets. Thus, giving us a

true picture of our financial position. It also helped us formulate a family-spending plan that will allow us to succeed with our plan. At first we were overwhelmed, but as we neared the end of the 7-week course all the pieces of the puzzle started to fall into place. The greatest impact on us was that our hearts were forever changed towards finances (God's money). The course made Psalm 37:4 a reality in our lives: 'Delight yourself in the Lord and He will give you the desires of your heart'."

--- ***Tony and Blanca Chapa***

"As leaders of multiple Financial Freedom in 7 Weeks Plus focus groups, we have been encouraged to see God's faithfulness. Lives are being continuously changed because the curriculum targets the root of financial problems. In the focus groups we led, we witnessed breakthroughs from one end of the spectrum, such as tithing for the first time, to the other, with group members literally burning credit cards! Christians now have a road map to financial freedom."

--- ***Sam and Sheryl Porter***

"This course provided financial principles that we found are easy to both understand and apply in our daily lives. The small focus group (meeting in a friendly home environment) put us at ease. We are both self-employed and we especially benefited from the Guidelines for the Self-Employed (chapter two). We learned how to calculate "increase" and our tithe, even though our real estate income is very irregular."

--- ***Ed and Margaret Marotta***

Testimonies from Fiji

The beautiful country of Fiji is made up of several islands and is located to the east of Australia. Through Marriage Ministries International, Bill and Maureen forged an incredible friendship with Matai and Mei Niumataiwalu. He works at a radio station and she is a homemaker and mother of 3 fine sons. In addition to serving as National MMI Leaders, and while simultaneously leading a 14-week *Married for Life* group, Matai and Mei started and led a Financial Freedom in 7 Weeks Plus focus group. The group was comprised of pastors, a fisherman, a businessman, and their spouses. The results were excellent and we are encouraged that more focus groups are planned for the very near future. The following statements are some of the encouraging testimonies from Fiji:

"We have been tremendously blessed because finance was an area we did not often discuss as a family. Sitting down and planning financially are major breakthroughs for us. Traditionally, we gave to the extreme extent being 'tomorrow takes care of itself'. As a result, our family was occasionally deprived of their basic needs. We thank God that we can now pass on to our children, and to future generations, a Godly financial legacy. As we prepared to teach the 'paradigm shift' concept, God showed us that a married couple must unite as one flesh, and renew their minds with His Word, in order to receive His promises.

In Exodus 20:2, His word gave us insight into the Lord's will for us. Egypt was a house of bondage because Pharaoh had enslaved and mistreated God's people. We, too, have been brought out of a house of debt bondage through Christ and the renewing of our minds. Like the Israelites, we have to enlarge and expand our thinking to be ready for God's plans to come to pass. We're excited at what God is doing. We pray for continuous breakthroughs in the Financial Freedom in 7 Weeks Plus project because we believe many families around the world will be blessed by it."

--- ***Matai and Mei Niumataiwalu***

"We own a small fishing business. The 7- week focus group, led by Matai and Mei, taught us a great deal by using God's Word as the standard. We now communicate better, pray better, pray together and love one another more intensely. After undertaking this course, we are now working together on our daily spending plan which has enabled us to pay off some of our

debt. We foresee big financial breakthroughs in our home. The course, as a whole, has helped us to become much better stewards at home and in church."

--- ***Jeremaia and Erima Varni***

"Bula (greetings), we have had the special privilege of serving as leaders in training, to Matai and Mei. This was the first time the Financial Freedom in 7 Weeks Plus course was taught in Fiji. The course has been a huge blessing to our family. We went into it expecting to be blessed in the area of finance and came out blessed in all areas. We realized that, in the area of finances, we had excluded God. Once we acknowledged this and allowed him to start ministering to us in this area, it became a spiritual stepping-stone. Through this course we have learned to be faithful, not only with finances, but with all the wonderful blessings from Abba Father. It has also brought about a spiritual revival in our lives. We thankfully praise God for taking us up to another level. Bill and Maureen, we thank God for you and your continuous commitment to give of what He has given you. We pray that as you continue to sow into the lives of others "Our Heavenly Father will bless you abundantly."

--- ***Wade& Janelle Gibson & family***

I WHOLEHEARTEDLY RECOMMEND THIS BOOK.

"In today's economy, consumers face a dizzying array of purchase decisions and financial choices. Each of us is constantly bombarded by advertising messages telling us that to be complete, we must have one more product. And shopping networks, Internet buying, and catalogs make it possible to max out our credit cards without even leaving home!

Yet, most of us have very little preparation or teaching regarding making decisions that lead to prosperity rather than to financial doom. This reality is reflected by the record amount of consumer debt and the massive number of personal bankruptcies.

You can find help! The Bible is full of answers that can help you be free to do what God has called you to do. Bill and Maureen Sitter have organized many of the scriptures and Biblical concepts in a step-by-step set of instructions that all of us can follow to escape the financial rat race and live a purpose filled life. Their focus group course, Financial Freedom in 7 Weeks Plus also identifies factors creating financial bondage and shows how to break that cycle.

This course should be a part of the ministry of every church in America and around the world."

Dr. A. Clyde Vollmers
Professor Emeritus
Minnesota State University, Moorhead
Professor of Business
Northwestern College

FINANCIAL FREEDOM

IN 7 WEEKS PLUS

A Bible-Based Course For Financial Breakthrough

FINANCIAL FREEDOM

IN 7 WEEKS PLUS

A Bible-Based Course For Financial Breakthrough

By Bill & Maureen Sitter

Published By Bill & Maureen Sitter

Published by:
Bill and Maureen Sitter

To Order This Book
Please Visit Our Website For Instructions
www.debtfreelegacy.com

Contact Authors @
Bill and Maureen Sitter
23995 Bat Cave Road, Suite #200
San Antonio, Texas 78266
Toll Free: 1-800-392-9410
Fax: 210-651-5562
E-mail: bill@jordansitter.com
Website: www.debtfreelegacy.com

Scripture quotations are from several versions of the Bible, and are designated with appropriate abbreviations.

Editing Support by: Cindy Kreiner and Heather Mills

Cover Graphics by: Joyce Shoemaker
E-mail: facesdm@wwdb.org

ISBN 0-9727246-0-5

CONTENTS

ABOUT THE AUTHORS

Bill and Maureen Sitter have been married for over forty years. As one flesh, they have shared a strong desire to help people become debt free. This seven-week course Financial Freedom in 7 Weeks Plus is the outgrowth of several years of training, counseling and mentoring adults. The focus of their efforts has always been to show others that God's Word, the Bible, provides clear instructions that will ensure true financial freedom.

The course clearly acknowledges that God wants His people to prosper (3 John: 2), while the devil only desires to kill, steal and destroy (John 10:10). Based on these two key truths, the course provides Christians with God-given instructions on how to use God's weapons in order to attack and defeat the devil. Prayer, praise and spiritual warfare are key ingredients.

User friendly forms and *examples* are clearly woven throughout the course in order to equip all course graduates with the practical financial tools needed to develop a flexible family spending plan and a cash flow control system.

Back to our authors. Maureen and Bill met at Western Maryland College (now McDaniel College) where they both received their undergraduate degrees. They have two children, Chris and Cassidy. Bill also served in the US Army-Infantry and achieved the rank of Captain. He went on to build a successful business career in the U.S., Europe and the Middle East. In addition, he has served as President, Chief Operating Officer, and General Manager of companies in the Midwest and in Texas. At the age of 50, Bill was the honor graduate of his MBA class at Our Lady of the Lake University, in San Antonio, Texas. Since 1990, Bill has owned a small and successful business, Jordan-Sitter Associates (www.jordansitter.com). The vision statement expresses the firm's commitment to honoring Jesus Christ and to Godly stewardship principles.

In the past several years, Bill and Maureen have had the privilege of conducting a number of small *Financial Freedom Focus Groups* using the material presented in the book. They have also trained group leaders in various churches and have provided oversight to groups in the U.S. and overseas.

Because the Word of God is absolute and true, those who have sincerely and genuinely applied the material in the book have achieved success. (See "financial breakthroughs and testimonials from recent students," in the front of this book.)

For several years, the Sitters have encountered people who are desperate for Godly practical financial instruction. Demand from the U.S. and other countries like Fiji, left Bill and Maureen with no other option but to publish the material.

Financial Freedom in 7 Weeks Plus also serves as a workbook (manual) for the Financial Freedom in 7 Weeks Plus course, which is ideally presented in small *focus groups*.

PREFACE: NOTES TO THE READER AND A DISCLAIMER

If you or your family are feeling the bondage of heavy debt, and if you have a desire to be financially free God's way, then we believe this book and the seven-week *focus group* study will be a blessing. We have witnessed lives being changed as the light of hope and truth from God's Word is applied. Your life can be changed too. The book equips you with *user-friendly* practical forms and simple methods (that require only a pencil, a basic calculator, and a commitment to change).

There are not enough pages in one book or enough time in a 7-week small group course to include everything about personal finances. In addition, there is insufficient space to (even begin to) scratch the surface regarding business financial management issues. This book and the 7-week course are not intended to provide any specific accounting or legal advice regarding investments, tax regulations, insurance, or otherwise. As they advance on the exciting road to financial freedom, we encourage our readers to seek wise council regarding specific financial transactions and to pray for guidance from God's Holy Spirit.

Focus group leaders are instructed not to allow any group members to engage in sales activities or provide specific investment or other financial advice. This course is designed to highlight what God's Word says about financial matters and to provide practical techniques for the development of a total *family financial freedom plan.* Once these basic principles are understood, and when a positive monthly cash flow is achieved, then... and only then... can an individual be ready to pursue specific financial opportunities.

ACKNOWLEDGEMENTS

Michael and Marilyn Phillips head a powerful worldwide ministry called Marriage Ministries International. MMI (www.marriage.org) has wonderfully impacted our marriage of 40+ years. A few years ago, Michael and I (Bill) were engaged in a long conversation in which I confidentially shared our goal for giving a very large amount of money, in our lifetime, to God's work. The amount seemed really big to me but Michael did not flinch. He remarked that it was a good goal, but he could see us doing something that would lead many others to true financial freedom, so they could give a hundred or more times the figure I had mentioned. (Note: MMI is changing their name to: The University of the Family.)

Maureen and I would like to thank MMI for the Married for Life 14-week course, for the principles we learned, and for the constant encouragement we received in continuing our teaching and training of others to be financially free. Additionally, we found the MMI small weekly group format to be very effective. We also encourage our Financial Freedom in 7 Weeks Plus focus group leaders to incorporate the (MMI) leaders-in-training concept. The "Focus Group Leaders' Instructions" (chapter ten) also recommends several meeting guidelines which are patterned after MMI.

Through MMI, we met many wonderful leaders. Dr. Clyde and Kathy Vollmers have been faithful friends, and a constant encouragement to this project. We plan to collaborate with them on future projects.

Rick Faulk, Ph.D., has been a key contributor (we met via MMI). We are forever indebted to him. Thanks Rick for allowing us to edit and utilize the material regarding breaking curses, blockages and strongholds (chapter nine).

We would like to thank our church, Eagles Nest Christian Fellowship (soon to be Summit Christian Center of San Antonio), for providing the avenue we so greatly needed in our teaching and training of hundreds of students and many small group leaders. We would also like to express our thanks personally to Pastor Rick and Cindy Godwin and to many of the senior staff for supporting this ministry. We would also like to thank Alan Vincent who provided encouragement and advice at an important phase of this project.

Dr. Wayne Gordon is a good friend and church Elder. It was his initiation of a Kingdom Finance Class that jump-started our desire to teach and train people to live debt free. The seminar was based on Ron Blue's excellent Master Your Money Workbook. Even though the paperback workbook is out of print, we encourage everyone to search for a copy, and utilize it as a reference.

Special thanks go to our friend Heather Mills who provided excellent administrative support; she has been a special blessing. To our friends Joyce Shoemaker, Cindy Kreiner and Debbie Clay, thank you all for assisting with the artwork, editing and typing. God bless you all.

We would also like to express our deep appreciation to the many volunteer leaders that have used this material to lead small 7-week focus groups in their homes. Not only have they been a blessing to the individuals who have completed the focus groups, but they have also helped us refine the material and the f rms in ur n g ing quest in creating the ultimate — financiall user-friendl — b k and c urse.

We also pay tribute to the scores of authors and teachers who have influenced our lives, and to the individuals who ignited the initial spark that led to this book and course. (In the reference section we name just a few of the many excellent sources of information.) To the following, thanks and may God richly bless you in your efforts: Larry Burkett and Crown Ministries; Ron Blue; Kenneth Copeland Ministries;

Mary Hunt; T.D. Jakes, Sr.; Marilyn Hickey Ministries; and Terry Savage. Additionally, there are a host of excellent authors who provide practical financial advice from a "non-spiritual" perspective (in our opinion). We find their books helpful, if filtered through the Word of God. Robert Kiyosaki, David Bach and Suze Orman are a few such authors.

Finally, a special thanks to our family and our Associates at Jordan-Sitter Associates. Thank you for your support and for understanding how very important this project is to us and to others.

INTRODUCTION & COURSE OVERVIEW

INTRODUCTION

We are excited for you and your family as you embark on the road to debt-free living and as you seek God's way to true financial freedom.

This book can be used as a personal study guide if you have self-discipline and commit faithfully to completing the seven weekly homework assignments. However, we strongly recommend that the material be used in a small *focus group* setting with seven consecutive weekly sessions of two to two and a half hours each. Ideally, these groups are led by trained leaders with leaders-in-training (LITs) serving as assistants.

Chapter ten provides several guidelines for effective leadership. We encourage local churches and ministries to implement this course with their members. The church covering provides proper (headship) authority and accountability and presents an opportunity for the church to train and authorize small group leaders. We further recommend that the church designate a Financial Freedom Coordinator who will receive weekly reports and periodically visit groups, in order to monitor teaching effectiveness, to provide a measure of financial leadership accountability, and to encourage all participants and the group leadership teams.

COURSE OVERVIEW

- **THERE WILL BE SEVEN WEEKLY SMALL FOCUS GROUP MEETINGS** with the leadership of dedicated and caring leaders and assistant leaders. Ideally, the leaders should be trained and covered by (and accountable to) a church or ministry.

- **PRAISE, PRAYER & SPIRITUAL WARFARE** will be taught and employed in each session. The intimacy of a small group provides prayer support and comfort in a secure environment. A home setting is ideal but another private meeting place is acceptable.

- **WEEKLY HOMEWORK ASSIGNMENTS** are designed to lead group members, step by step, in understanding what God means by prosperity and how to achieve true financial freedom. Practical exercises are shared weekly (during homework sharing time), but no one is obligated to share confidential specifics with the group.

- **A SERIES OF USER-FRIENDLY FORMS** are provided. There are easy to understand examples of how Bob and Mary Jones "did it wrong" and eventually "got it right." These examples are great tools as you complete your own forms each week.

- **A PRIVATE ACCOUNTABILITY SESSION** is held with the leadership team approximately 30 to 45 days after week seven. (This is when each student or couple meet privately with the leaders for a full review.) At this time, the leaders hold the student/couple accountable for completing all forms, which are individually reviewed and discussed. The accountability sessions last approximately 90 minutes and are strictly confidential.

- **APPROXIMATELY 200 SCRIPTURE REFERENCES ARE CITED** in this book using several different translations of the Bible. Participants are encouraged to dig deeper into God's precious Word and to seek the guidance of the Holy Spirit.

- **THERE IS A HUGE NEED FOR FOCUS GROUP LEADERS** and those who feel called to this role will be encouraged to step forward for future training.

- **A LEGACY OF FINANCIAL FREEDOM IS THE GOAL.** We believe that God is a generational God and He expects us to pass on a legacy of true financial freedom to all those we encounter in the years to come.

- **WWW.DEBTFREELEGACY.COM** is a website that has been reserved to provide exciting information in the future. We invite you to pray with us that we will be able to develop and use this website to provide additional tools that will help others achieve true financial freedom and pass on that legacy.

"PLUS" DEFINED

According to the Worldbook Dictionary "PLUS" is defined as: *"added to", "more than", and "in addition to".* So what does "PLUS" mean in our Financial Freedom in 7 Weeks Plus course? Actually there are seven (7) "pluses" involved in this course, especially for those who participate in a 7-week *focus group.* We pray you will fully employ the following seven "pluses" (or tools) to achieve all of God's blessings.

1. **God's Word** provides the foundation for this program. The deeper you dig into Scripture, the bigger your "plus" will be. And, the more you will have added to living a victorious life for Christ.

2. **Prayer** is a part of every *focus group* (opening and closing), and should be integrated into the start of every homework session. Married couples learn the incredible power of prayer in agreement.

3. **Praise and Worship** is critical to the course. Even though time is short for each weekly session, every *focus group* opens with praise and worship which sets the tone and invites the Holy Spirit.

4. **Spiritual Warfare** is taught and is used in every session. You will learn that the devil is the enemy, and his mission is to kill, steal and destroy. You will learn how to fight and defeat the devil in the power of Jesus' name. This type of warfare should be employed in every financial planning and homework session. Spiritual warfare will set in-place a positive life changing pattern.

5. **Pastoral and Group Covering** is strongly recommended. It is also recommended that this material be taught in a 7-week *focus group* format, with the blessing and covering of a local church or ministry. This establishes order and provides covering by a spiritual authority. Additionally, it is vitally important that the *focus group* leaders and leaders-in-training form a support and prayer covering team. The leadership team also encourages the entire *focus group* to cover each other in prayer.

6. **Accountability** is built into the course by requiring all *focus group* members to report/share during weekly homework sharing time. In order to graduate, each group member must also complete a follow-up session with the leadership team, (approximately 30 to 45 days after week 7).

7. **Effort and Discipline.** Yes, you will ultimately get out of this course results in proportion to the effort and discipline you apply to this program. We know that a legacy of true financial freedom is worth your very best — so, give it all your effort!

CONGRATULATIONS

You just embarked on God's path to true financial freedom.
We wish you Godspeed.

— *Bill and Maureen Sitter*

CHAPTER 1
(WEEK 1)

"Beloved, I wish above all things that thou mayest prosper and be in health, even as thy soul prospereth."
3 John 2 (KJV)

Foundation Principles For Finance

CHAPTER 1 *(WEEK 1)*
FOUNDATION PRINCIPLES FOR FINANCE

Welcome to chapter 1 and week 1 of the Financial Freedom in 7 Weeks Plus course. By arriving at this point, you have taken a gigantic step towards financial freedom. Congratulations!

We have prepared this book primarily as a guide or workbook for a seven-week small focus group study. If you do not have access to a group, you still have a right to expect success if you are diligent in applying this Bible-based material.

If you are not in a focus group, please disregard the Leaders' Notes throughout this book. These notes are specific instructions for those leading small groups.

LEADERS' NOTE – Before proceeding introduce the Focus Group Leaders and Leaders in Training. Warmly welcome the participants to the group. They've made a big step by getting this far.

I. WHY WILL THIS COURSE WORK FOR YOU?

You may have tried other financial courses without lasting results. If you commit to this Financial Freedom in 7 Weeks Plus course, you will reap good fruit because:

- **EXCITEMENT, HOPE & BREAKTHROUGH** are the key thoughts for the entire course. By being here you are taking a huge step toward building the Godly legacy spoken of in Jeremiah 29:11 — *"For I know the plans I have for you, declares the Lord, plans to prosper you and not to harm you, plans to give you hope and a future." (NIV)*

- **GOD'S WORD** provides clear instructions for us concerning finances. His Word will not return void if we speak, believe and act on it.

- **PRAYER & SPIRITUAL WARFARE** are absolutely vital elements of this course and set the pattern for future financial planning and action steps. As strongholds are broken and you pray for wisdom and courage to change, the Holy Spirit will guide you to freedom.

LEADERS' NOTE — We recommend that you select an appropriate (not too long) praise song to sing at the beginning of each session. Create a handout with the lyrics (in large type) for each participant. Have the music ready and play it fairly loud. Exhort all to participate.

After the song, lead the group directly into prayer and then spiritual warfare.

Follow this pattern at each weekly session.

II. SUCCESS ESSENTIALS

To receive God's blessing in your finances, it is essential that you open each session with:

- **A SONG OF PRAISE** as instructed in Psalm 100:4 — *"Enter into His gates with thanksgiving, and into his courts with praise: be thankful unto Him and bless His name." (KJV)*

- **PRAYER** *(with group joining hands)* — Pray for **God's blessing** and the **leading of His Holy Spirit.** Also pray specifically for each participant.

- **SPIRITUAL WARFARE —** The devil uses "money problems" to destroy marriages. In fact, financial pressure is the #1 cause of divorce and marital stress. To defeat the enemy, God has given believers more than 1,000 verses of Scripture. Therefore, right now, in Jesus' mighty name, bind Satan and his demons from hindering this course. Proclaim victory!

LEADERS' NOTE — At this point, please ask all participants to introduce themselves. Take only one to two minutes (per individual or couple). As part of their introduction, participants should share what they expect to accomplish as a result of this course.

III. WHERE ARE WE HEADED IN THIS 7 WEEK COURSE?

- **FINANCIAL FREEDOM GOD'S WAY** is the ultimate aim.

- **A COMPLETE FAMILY SPENDING PLAN** concept is incorporated in this course. It emphasizes: (1) goal setting, (2) biblical giving, (3) debt elimination, (4) living expense projections, (5) monthly cash flow, and (6) cash control techniques. This **Flexible Spending Plan** approach puts you in control and is far superior to a budget plan imposed by others.

- **A GODLY LEGACY** is perhaps the most exciting aspect of this course. **Imagine being able to** model, teach and pass on a legacy of true financial freedom to future generations. The thought of *changing your world* should provide more than enough motivation for you to diligently complete every lesson, homework assignment and your own spending plan forms.

  3 John 2 — *"Beloved, I wish above all things that thou mayest prosper and be in health, even as thy soul prospereth." (KJV)* **God wants us and future generations to prosper.**

IV. WEEKLY PROTOCOL & ORDER OF MEETINGS

> **LEADERS' NOTE** — Now is a good time to highlight the protocol for your weekly meetings, to include any special house rules *(such as parking areas, etc).*
>
> We encourage you to write a letter to each participant at least two weeks prior to Week 1 of your group to confirm: date, time, directions, address and phone number, and any special instructions.

- **STEWARDSHIP** is a critical key to this course. Time is short for each session, so all group members must strive to be excellent stewards of their time and talents. If you do not have a clear understanding of the times, dates, costs, offering, or other details concerning this course, please ask your leaders. Groups should start on time and never exceed the maximum allotted time of two to two and one half hours.

- **CONFIDENTIALITY** is essential. You should only disclose what you desire to share. The group members should not discuss each other's situations outside of the sessions.

- **PRAYER SUPPORT** is absolutely vital. Please pray for each group member and for your leadership team. Your leaders will be praying for you.

- **MINIMIZE DISTRACTIONS** by turning off cell phones, pagers and beepers. Also, please note that childcare is normally not provided. Please do not bring children (including infants), visitors or guests to the meetings.

- **WEEKLY OFFERING** — We strongly encourage the group's church or ministry covering to authorize a weekly offering. These offerings provide an excellent opportunity to develop good habits of Biblical giving. We suggest the offering be in the form of "sowing alms" as taught in chapter two/week two. Proverbs 19:17 says, *"He who has pity on the poor lends to the Lord, and He will pay back what he has given." (NKJ)* The early test groups of this course had great success with alms being designated for the benevolence fund of the sponsoring church. We suggest using checks for offerings so there is no cash to handle. To provide accountability for handling money, a weekly report should be signed by one of the leaders and one of the assistant leaders. *(A sample form can be found in chapter ten.)*

- **FULL 7-WEEK COMMITMENT** — Normally, <u>no</u> make-up sessions are planned. This course compresses a great deal of information into seven weeks. We are counting on your complete commitment, and we are confident that God will honor your faithfulness.

- **FOLLOW-UP SESSION 30 to 45 DAYS AFTER COURSE COMPLETION** — To help make sure you understand and begin to implement financial freedom principles, your leaders will meet with you for a private 90-minute "follow-up" session (30 to 45 days) after the completion of the course. **It is the student's responsibility to call the leaders to schedule the session.** This meeting will give you a measure of accountability as you press on towards financial freedom. (See chapter eight for details.)

- **HOMEWORK** — There will be homework for each week. *(For married couples, homework must be done together.)* The devil will try hard to put up blockages, so start early in the week and keep up your prayers and spiritual warfare. This is essential!

- **WHAT SHOULD YOU BRING TO EACH FOCUS GROUP** — Please bring: (1) your Financial Freedom in 7 Weeks Plus book, (2) a Bible, (3) pencils and pens, (4) highlighters, (5) a small cordless calculator, and (6) your completed forms and homework. Also **remember your checkbook for the offering!**

- **ORDER OF MEETINGS** — This course consists of seven weekly focus group meetings, averaging two to two and one half hours per session. There will be one short break for beverages only. Group leaders are responsible to provide a weekly meeting/attendance report and a report of weekly offerings to the church or ministry coordinator. (Leaders see chapter ten.)

Following is the recommended schedule of activities for each weekly focus group session:

1. **Praise God!** — Open promptly at the scheduled time with one hope-filled praise and worship song. Leaders will select the song and provide typed lyrics to each group member each week.

2. **Prayer and Spiritual Warfare**

3. **Announcements**

4. **Homework Sharing** — Led by leaders or assistants *(normally by the part of the leadership team which is not teaching the week's lesson).* Limit sharing to two minutes per individual or four minutes per couple. If married, both spouses should comment — no preaching!

5. **Offering** — Prayer and offering basket. *(Various group members may be asked to pray over the offering.)*

6. **Break** — 10 to 15 minutes maximum. Beverages only and restroom break.

7. **Lesson** — Taught by group leaders (or assistant leaders). No interruptions! Your leaders will answer questions after the teaching. *(Please limit questions to clarification of the lesson.)*

8. **Preview Homework**

9. **Prayer and Dismissal by Leaders**

10. **Special Prayer** — If you would like special prayer, you may meet briefly with your leaders after the session. Please, however, be respectful of your leaders' time. *(They have post session reports to complete.)*

> ***HELPFUL TIPS***
>
> ★ **COPY BLANK FORMS (located in Chapter 15)**
>
> *You'll need 6 complete sets plus your originals.*
>
> ★ Use highlighters and take lots of notes.

V. FINANCIAL BATTLE SPIRITUAL PREREQUISITES

You may have already experienced *Salvation, Baptism,* and *Baptism of the Holy Spirit.* You may also already practice powerful principles of covenant with God and, if married, with your one-flesh mate. However, since our desire is for you to have access to God's very best, we will briefly touch on these vital principles before going deeper into the course.

> **LEADERS' NOTE** — If you are teaching these financial principles to those who have not experienced *Salvation, Baptism,* and/or *Baptism of the Holy Spirit,* we encourage you to include these essential steps so your students will be fully armed for victory. Leaders should be ready with scripture and God-given boldness.

➢ SALVATION

1. **Admit you are a sinner.** *(Romans 3:23)*

2. **Repent and turn away from sin and submit to God.** *(Luke 13:5 and Acts 3:19)*

3. **Believe and confess out loud that Jesus died for you and paid the price for your sins.** *(John 3:16)*

4. **Ask God to save you.** *(Romans 10: 9 and 10 and Romans 10:13)*

5. **Ask Jesus Christ to be Lord of your life.**

6. **Give Him thanks, praise and glory for your new birth.**

7. **Pray a prayer of salvation.** Leaders may wish to lead the following type of prayer for focus group members to receive Jesus Christ. *(This can also be done after the session concludes.)*

   Heavenly Father, I confess that I am a sinner and I repent of all my sins. I know that Jesus Christ died for my sins and was raised from the dead. Jesus is my only source of eternal life and I ask Him to come into my life and to be my Savior and the Lord of my life. Thank

you God for now I am a new creature. I ask for your powerful grace to help me live for you. Amen!

➢ BAPTISM

1. God's Word gives a clear command for new believers to be baptized. *Acts 2:38 — "Then Peter said to them, Repent, and let every one of you be baptized in the name of Jesus Christ for the remission of sins; and you shall receive the gift of the Holy Spirit." (NKJ)*

2. Leaders may wish to recommend baptism by the covering church or ministry. However, we believe that any true believer can baptize another.

➢ BAPTISM OF THE HOLY SPIRIT AND BEING FILLED WITH THE HOLY SPIRIT

In his book, The Holy Spirit, the Reverend Billy Graham provides a powerful teaching on how the Baptism of the Holy Spirit activates God's power in our lives. *(See reference Chapter 11 for details.)* On page 67, the author reinforces the scripture in *Acts 2:38. "I have become convinced that there is only one baptism with the Holy Spirit in the life of every believer, and that takes place at the moment of conversion. This baptism with the Holy Spirit was initiated at Pentecost, and all who come to know Jesus Christ as Savior share in that experience and are baptized with the Spirit the moment they are regenerated. In addition, they may be filled with the Holy Spirit; if not, they need to be."*

1. God wants to give the gift of the Holy Spirit. *(Luke 11:13)*

2. Sin can block our receipt of this powerful gift. Repentance can unclog the blockage.

3. Billy Graham encourages believers to submit to God and walk in faith with the knowledge that we have the amazing power of the Holy Spirit living inside us.

4. Now that we are baptized with and filled with the Holy Spirit, we should confidently pursue God's will for our lives and expect to receive his promises as we obey his Word.

➢ POWER OF PRAYER IN AGREEMENT

Matthew 18:19 — "Again I say unto you, that if two of you shall agree on earth as touching anything that they shall ask, it shall be done for them by my Father, which is in Heaven."

Amos 3:3 — "Can two people walk together, except they be agreed?" (KJV)

➢ SPIRITUAL WARFARE

Ephesians 6:12 — "For we wrestle not against flesh and blood, but against principalities, against powers, against the rulers of the darkness of this world, against spiritual wickedness in high places." (KJV)

Put on the Whole Armor of God as described in Ephesians 6:10-18.

➢ COVENANT

1. Covenant with God means living with Jesus Christ, not apart from Him, and this covenant entitles believers to receive God's covenant blessings. *(See or read aloud Ephesians 2:1-22 NAS)*

2. Covenant with your spouse **must be restored or God will not hear your prayers.** ***Malachi 2:13-14 (NIV)*** *"Another thing you do: You flood the Lord's altar with tears. You weep and wail because he no longer pays attention to your offerings or accepts them with pleasure from your hands. You ask "Why?" It is because the LORD is acting as the witness between you and the wife of your youth, because you have broken faith with her, though she is your partner, the wife of your marriage covenant."*

- **OBEDIENCE**

Obedience to God is required if we expect to receive His covenant blessings. God forgives and He gives abundant grace. However, we must never fool ourselves.

Galatians 6:7 — "Be not deceived, God is not mocked: for whatsoever a man soweth, that shall he also reap." (KJV)

LEADERS' NOTE — Now is a great time to put the gift of giving into practice with the weekly offering. Please keep the following tips in mind:

- Choose a powerful giving scripture and have someone read it aloud.
- Explain where the offering will go and how checks should be prepared.
- Have someone pray over the offering and ask God for a 100-fold (10,000%) increase, as described in Matthew 13:23.
- Collect the offering. *(Count and record money after the group dismisses.).*
- After the offering, take a 10 to 15 minute restroom and beverage break.
- Reconvene promptly! (Limit session to 2 ½ hours max.)

Remember, God loves a cheerful giver! *(2 Corinthians 9:7)*

VI. BIBLICAL BUILDING BLOCKS FOR FINANCIAL VICTORY

The following principles from God's Word will serve as invaluable building blocks as you continue to pursue financial victory. Time restraints allow only a brief mention, and each principle merits further study.

- **HOPE** — In Jeremiah 29:11 **God promises a good plan for us.** 3 John 2 clearly tells us that God means for His covenant people to prosper and be in health: *"Beloved, I wish above all things, that thou mayest prosper and be in health, even as thy soul prospereth." (KJV)*

- **CONVICTION IS GOOD BUT CONDEMNATION IS EVIL** — Romans 8:1 says, *"There is therefore now no condemnation to them which are in Christ Jesus, who walk not after the flesh, but after the Spirit."(KJV)* Satan will try to heap shame and guilt on you to keep you from financial victory. Acknowledge that such condemnation is from the devil and refuse to accept any part of it.

For Married Couples

Protect your one flesh and war against division.
Always support and edify each other.

- **PROSPERITY** — We saw in 3 John 2 that God wants us to prosper. **In this course, prosperity is defined as having enough resources (money, time, talent and health) to accomplish everything God has called us to do.** In contrast, the world's view of prosperity is often "the one who dies with the most toys wins."

- **WE HAVE A MANDATE TO FUND GOD'S WORK (EVANGELISM)** — God wants us, as members of the body of Christ *(His church),* to prosper so we can fund the Great Commission, given to all believers in *Matthew 28:19-20 — "Therefore go and make disciples of all nations, baptizing them in the name of the Father and of the Son and of the Holy Spirit, and teaching them to obey everything I have commanded you. And surely I am with you always, to the very end of the age." (NIV)*

- **GOD OWNS EVERYTHING** — *"Everything in the heavens and the earth…" 1 Chronicles 29:11 (LB). "The cattle on a thousand hills,"* which means all of the cattle and everything else, *Psalm 50:10 (NIV).*

- **THE POWER AND ABILITY TO GET WEALTH COME FROM GOD** — Deuteronomy 8:18 *says, "but thou shalt remember the Lord thy God: for it is He that giveth thee the power to get wealth, that He may establish His covenant which He swore unto thy fathers, as it is this day." (KJV)* This leaves no place for pride or greed. Instead, we should humbly thank God for all we have or will ever have.

- **WE ARE REQUIRED TO BE FAITHFUL STEWARDS** of the resources God entrusted to us *(money, skills, abilities and time).* Matthew 25, the *parable of the talents,* clearly demonstrates this principle. In it, we learn that the amount we are given is not what counts. Instead, our faithfulness with the resources entrusted to us is the key. We encourage you to read this parable out loud and reflect on what you should do, with His grace, in order to hear the wonderful words of Jesus Christ: *"Well done, good and faithful servant; you were faithful over a few things, I will make you ruler over many things. Enter into the joy of the Lord." (Matthew 25:23, KJV)*

- **BRANCH MANAGER CONCEPT — God expects us to be excellent stewards of the "three Ts": our time, our God-given talent, and our treasure.** Just as a bank branch manager must give account to the bank president, we are accountable to God for our stewardship. Good stewardship requires us to: (1) give cheerfully of our tithes, offerings and alms; (2) save; and (3) faithfully provide for our families. These subjects will be covered in depth in the following weeks. For immediate references, you can study *Malachi 3:8-12, Matthew 23:23,* and *2 Corinthians 9:6-11* (on giving); *Proverbs 6:6-8* and *Proverbs 21:20* (on saving); and *1 Timothy 5:8* (on providing for a family).

- **GOD INSTRUCTS HIS PEOPLE TO PLAN**, and we are foolish if we fail to plan. *Proverbs 21:5 says, "The plans of the diligent lead to profit as surely as haste leads to poverty." (NIV)* This course will teach you how to write clear and Godly goals *(Habakkuk 2:2).* We see in *Proverbs 29:18, "Where there is no vision, the people perish." (KJV)*

- **WE MUST LEARN TO TRUST HIM WITH OUR (HIS) RESOURCES**, especially money. As we trust Him with our physical and our eternal lives, we must trust Him with our finances. *Matthew 6:24* tells us: *"No one can serve two masters. Either he will hate the one and love the other, or he will be devoted to the one and despise the other. You cannot serve both God and money." (NIV)*

- **HONESTY IS ABSOLUTELY REQUIRED** in order to walk with God and to receive the blessings He wants to give us as covenant believers. If we cheat, steal, and lie, we act foolishly and have no right to expect to receive from God. In *Matthew 5:23-24*, Jesus tells us that: *"if you are offering your gift at the altar, and there remember that your brother has something against you, leave your gift there before the altar and go; first be reconciled to your brother, and then come and offer your gift." (RSV)*

  Earlier, we saw that *"God is not mocked."* So we better not make him angry by expecting answers to prayer while flaunting sin in His face.

  <u>EXAMPLE:</u> Shortly after Bill (co-author of this course) got saved, God gently began to expose his past sins — as if peeling off layers of an onion. As Bill dealt with these past transgressions it provided him with a good testimony of honesty, repentance, seeking and receiving forgiveness. It also provided him the opportunity to witness for Jesus. The key is, when God reveals your transgressions, repent and take action to admit and correct them. Then, move forward with His amazing grace.

- **THE KNOWLEDGE OF GOD'S TRUTH WILL SET US FREE** — free from the bondage of debt, free from the curse of poverty, and free to prosper God's way. *John 8:32 — "And you shall know the truth and the truth shall make you free." (NKJ)*

- **A DEEP RESPECT FOR THE ALMIGHTY GOD** is often referred to as "<u>fear of the Lord</u>." *Deuteronomy 5:29 — "Oh that they had such a heart in them, that they would fear Me, and keep all My commandments always, that it may be well with them and with their sons forever!" (NAS)*

- **DEBT IS NOT SIN,** but God's Word says only bad things about debt. <u>It is a sin not to repay debts</u>, and in chapters (weeks) three and four, you will learn how to realize God's plan for debt-free living.

- **MONEY IS NOT THE ROOT OF ALL EVIL,** nor is it evil at all. <u>Greed is evil and is based on the love of money</u>. *1 Timothy 6:10 — "For the love of money is a root of all kinds of evil. Some people, eager for money, have wandered from the faith and pierced themselves with many griefs."* (NIV)

  In *Hebrews 13:5* we are told: *"<u>Keep your lives free from the love of money</u> and be content with what you have, because God has said, never will I leave you; never will I forsake you." (NIV)*

- **GOD DOES NOT NEED "OUR MONEY."** What He longs for is a <u>right heart attitude</u>.

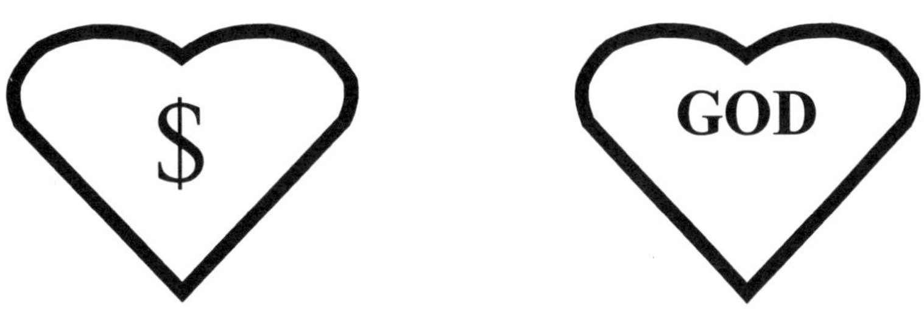

We must never try to use money to manipulate God into giving us what we want. He wants us to love him deeply. So deeply that we would desire to learn His instructions and be fully obedient to His word! *(Over 1,000 scriptures relate to financial instructions.)*

- **ALL FINANCIAL DECISIONS ARE SPIRITUAL DECISIONS** — if God is at the center of our hearts and at the center of all our planning. For these seven weeks, we will seek Him, find Him and draw on His biblical wisdom.

VII. BREAKING FINANCIAL CURSES & STRONGHOLDS

Many born-again, spirit-filled believers are struggling in the area of finances and do not know why. They may even be tithing, giving offerings, and sowing alms, and still not achieving anything that resembles Godly prosperity. There are many evil spiritual curses, hexes and vexes that often attack in the area of finance. These could be keeping believers from victory. We will briefly discuss strongholds and negative life patterns. We will also learn that spiritual warfare is the key to victory.

- **CURSES** may be brought on by negative words spoken about us by others, or even by ourselves. Some other sources of curses are:

    1. Belief in false gods
    2. Involvement in idolatry, witchcraft and the occult
    3. Withholding tithes and freewill offerings
    4. General sin, sexual sin, and marital unfaithfulness
    5. Not honoring our parents
    6. Generational curses

- **OTHER FINANCIAL BLOCKAGES** result from:

    1. Not being sensitive to (cherishing) our spouse
    2. Not forgiving others or ourselves
    3. Strongholds and negative life patterns

- **FIVE ESSENTIAL STEPS FOR BREAKING CURSES & STRONGHOLDS**

    1. Renounce involvement. We urge you to identify and name curses or strongholds and confess them to God *(and if you are married, also confess them to your one-flesh mate).* Lean on Jesus for strength: see *John 14:6 — where our Lord tells us, "I am the way, the truth and the life." (KJV)*
    2. Repent and confess your sin. *1 John 1:9 "If we confess our sins, He is faithful and righteous to forgive us of our sins and to cleanse us from all unrighteousness." (NAS)*

3. Ask Jesus to take back the ground you gave to the enemy, the devil. In *Psalm 23:3,* we see that: *"He restoreth my soul." (KJV)*

4. Bind the enemy in Jesus' name then loose God's blessings by faith in the power of His Word and in Jesus' name. *Matthew 16:19 — "I will give you the keys of the kingdom of heaven; whatever you bind on earth will be bound in heaven, and whatever you loose on earth will be loosed in heaven." (NIV)*

   Now boldly proclaim that *2 Corinthians 5:17* is true and that you are *"a new creature; old things have passed away; behold all things are become new." (KJV)*

5. Walk as a child of light, a child of God. Practice *Romans 12:9-13*, which exhorts us to display genuine (Godly) love, and to hold fast to what is good. If we do fail, then we need to dust ourselves off, repeat the process, and thank God for His abundant grace and mercy.

- **REFERENCE MATERIAL** for a deeper understanding of breaking curses and strongholds is located in chapter nine entitled *Breaking Curses, Blockages & Strongholds.* We encourage you to study and pray about the information that is presented. *(Our special thanks go to our friend Rick Faulk, who gave us permission to edit and use his powerful material.)*

LEADERS' NOTE — Breaking curses and strongholds are vital parts of the journey to achieving true financial freedom. Take time to show students the material in chapter nine, and encourage them to study it this week.

VIII. PREVIEW OF FORMS & EXAMPLES

LEADERS' NOTE — Now take about 10 minutes to briefly show the forms and examples that will be used during this course. This will help each person grasp where the "mechanics" of the *Spending Plan* are headed. Please follow the order indicated below.

Your goal should be to only briefly orient the participants to the examples and forms. Take care not to go too deep. (Provide assurance that this material will be gradually introduced in future sessions.)

- **EXAMPLE #1** — The forms marked Example # 1 feature a fictitious couple, Bob and Mary Jones. Example #1 is their situation prior to their completion of the Financial Freedom in 7 Weeks Plus course. As you will learn in the next several weeks, Bob and Mary needed to make several changes.

- **EXAMPLE #2** — A quick look at Example # 2 *(one full year after course completion).* It shows what Bob and Mary were able to accomplish (without an increase in income) after applying God's wisdom to their family's financial plan. Both examples will prove helpful as you prepare your own forms.

- **BLANK FORMS** — Each of you will learn how to use every form (that is why there are blank forms for you to copy and use). You will start working on these forms as the weeks progress. For now, we just want you to have this brief overview. The forms are *user friendly* and they will *work* if you use them correctly.

- **GOD DESIRES US TO DEVELOP RIGHT ATTITUDES ABOUT FINANCES.** This course will stress proper *heart attitudes*. As important as the *mechanics* are, please remember the key lies in our willingness to seek, learn and apply God's wisdom to our own finances.

HELPFUL TIPS

To complete each of these forms in the coming weeks, you will need some financial records. Now is a great time to start organizing files and records. We also encourage you to pay by check, whenever possible, to create a record of your spending. Saving receipts will also be beneficial.

IX. WEEK 1 CONCLUSION

We have covered a great deal of biblical truths in this week's session. For some, this can be compared to drinking water from an open fire hydrant! For others, this may be a good review.

We know you are dedicated to success, and we are counting on you to do three things:

1. Extra study and prayer
2. Completion of all of your weekly homework
3. Ask your leaders questions before or after class

LEADERS' NOTE — Please acquaint group members with the Week One Homework and explain that there will be a brief time for homework sharing, every week, by each group member.

Close the group in a 3-part prayer including:

- Thanksgiving
- Binding the devil and loosing blessings (Spiritual Warfare)
- Jabez Prayer — 1 Chronicles 4:10 "*Jabez cried to the God of Israel, saying, Oh that You would bless me and enlarge my border, and that Your hand might be with me, and You would keep me from evil so it might not hurt me! And God granted his request.*" (Amplified)

(Read the powerful book *The Prayer of Jabez by Bruce Wilkinson*, for excellent insight into being all God wants you to be.)

PLEASE PRAYERFULLY DO YOUR HOMEWORK!

CHAPTER 1 (WEEK 1) HOMEWORK
FOUNDATION PRINCIPLES FOR FINANCE

1. **OPEN IN PRAYER.** *(If you are married, pray together.)* Thank God for His grace, mercy, and the financial breakthroughs that are coming soon.

2. **DO SPIRITUAL WARFARE** in order to kick the devil out, and to block his deceitful interference in this homework session and throughout this course.

> ***IMPORTANT!***
>
> Steps 1 and 2 should become standard operating procedure for every homework and financial planning session, and before and after each weekly focus group session. This is vital!

3. **REJOICE!** Pat yourselves on the back. You have already taken a huge step in ensuring a Godly financial legacy. This is a big step…way to go!

4. **COMMIT TO SUCCESS.** Start by reading, signing and dating the one-page form entitled *Commitment Statement,* which reinforces your promise to complete this 7-week program. There is real power in making a written commitment, so please consider this as the first element of this week's homework assignment.

> **Note:** *The Commitment Statement* form is on the following page. Please, do **not** skip this step.

COMMITMENT STATEMENT

Financial Freedom in 7 Weeks Plus

Written commitments are powerful. So, we now encourage you to make a written, dated and signed promise to faithfully complete this Financial Freedom in 7 Weeks Plus course. Furthermore, we ask that you be accountable for the completion of your private review session with your focus group leaders, 30-45 days after week seven. We are absolutely confident that faithful completion of this program will get you started on the path to true financial freedom. This plan is built upon God's own instructions, from His Holy Bible! You will be equipped to pass-on a legacy of freedom from debt to your family, friends and future generations.

You would not sign-up for sports lessons, cooking classes, or a university program, and then take-on conflicting obligations. This seven week program will consume two to two and one half hours of focus group time each week, plus some travel time and an average of two or more hours each week for homework. So, clear your schedule and commit to this life-changing seven week program. You'll be glad you did.

Good news. Once you have mastered the flexible *spending plan* concept, you can probably keep your financial management up to date by spending only 60 minutes a week on your records. Eventually, this process will become routine. Do not delay! Read, sign, and date the commitment form below.

Note to Married Couples: You must both complete and sign this form to work as a one-flesh couple.

I (we) ________________________ &________________________, really desire to seek God's wisdom regarding how to properly steward His resources: time, talent, and money. By promising to faithfully complete these lessons, homework assignments, and the post-course (private) review/accountability session, I (or we) commit to completing this course by investing effort, prayer and spiritual warfare throughout this learning process.

Signed: ______________________________ & ______________________________

Date: ______________________________

5. **PRAYERFULLY CONSIDER TAKING COMMUNION** to reinforce your commitment. Prior to communion, repent of any lingering sins (we recommend you read 1 Corinthians 11:23-30) and prepare yourself to remember Jesus' beautiful sacrifice. This will make any future financial sacrifices seem insignificant by comparison. Communion is a way to reinforce your covenant with God, and to your spouse (if you are married).

6. **BREAKING CURSES.** If the teaching on breaking curses "hit a nerve", then we encourage you to read Rick Faulk's excellent material in chapter nine. Then, do your own biblical study on this topic. You have Jesus' authority to bind satanic curses and loose God's blessing. **Take authority over your situation in Jesus' name.**

7. **REVIEW THE LESSON.** This course is very compressed. In week one, we laid several key biblical principles. We encourage you to review any principles that need clarification. Use your Bible *(a concordance will help),* and look up specific references. Ask the Holy Spirit to reveal its true meaning. James 1:5 instructs us to ask God if we lack wisdom (understanding), and God will give it to us.

8. **PAY BY CHECK.** Soon you will be developing a complete *spending plan.* It is generally easier to construct spending history records if bills are paid by check. Consider using checks for all possible expenditures — at least for a few months. *(This is not absolutely required, but good records are very important, so start now.)* Also, begin saving receipts.

9. **BREAKTHROUGHS.** Each weekly homework assignment will include a *breakthrough form.* You are expected to record all (small and large) breakthroughs, and report them in next week's homework sharing time. All group members will celebrate your breakthroughs... so don't forget to give God the credit!

BREAKTHROUGHS!

FINANCIAL FREEDOM COURSE - RECORD YOUR WEEKLY TESTIMONIES

NAME: ______________________ & ______________________

DATE: MONEY, CAREER, GIFTS/INHERITANCE, & OTHER

______ ______________________________________

______ ______________________________________

______ ______________________________________

______ ______________________________________

10. **LIST VALUES & GOALS.** In his popular book, Smart Couples Finish Rich, David Bach suggests that couples should start the goal-setting process by listing five key values, and then, developing goals and subsequent action steps with completion dates. This process works equally well for individuals. His book makes very good reading, but for now, we ask you to pray and list your top five values. (*Examples might be: security, making a difference, spirituality, fun, health, power, family, independence, growth, adventure, friends, and creativity.*)

BASIC VALUES & GOAL SETTING

FIVE TOP VALUES

A. ______________________________

____

B. ______________________________

____

C. ______________________________

____

D. ______________________________

____

E. ______________________________

____

Now comes the fun part! List at least five goals you would like to achieve in the next one to five years. It is okay to dream — these are your faith goals. Below, list the goals and set your timetable in years, anywhere from one to five years, (do this for each goal). It is OKAY to have different timetables (dates) for each goal.

GOAL A ______________________________

____

____

____

by (date) ____________________

GOAL B ____

____

____

____

by (date) ____________________

GOAL C ____

____

____

____

by (date) ____________________

GOAL D ____

____

____

____

by (date) ____________________

GOAL E ____

____

____

____

by (date) ____________________

> **Note:** Be prepared to share 1 or 2 key values & related goals with next week's focus group.

CONGRATULATIONS: You have completed one seventh of the course…way to go!

CHAPTER 2
(WEEK 2)

"Now this I say, he who sows sparingly shall also reap sparingly; and he who sows bountifully shall also reap bountifully. Let each one do just as he has purposed in his heart; not grudgingly or under compulsion; for God loves a cheerful giver. And God is able to make all grace abound to you, that always having all sufficiency in everything, you may have an abundance for every good deed;"
2 Corinthians 9: 6-8 (NAS)

Biblical Giving

LEADER'S NOTES – WEEKLY PROTOCOL

- Praise Song – A great way to start!
  Suggest Typed Lyrics and Upbeat Music
- Prayer – Led by a Leader or LIT
  Recommend Group Holding Hands
- Spiritual Warfare – in Jesus' mighty name
- Homework Sharing – Normally led by LITs
  Led by Leaders if LITs are Teaching this Week
  Time Control and Equal Sharing are Keys
- Sharing of Weekly Breakthroughs
  Brief but Builds Hope – Celebrate!
- Weekly Offering Time – Opportunity to Sow
  Have a Focus Group Member Pray First
  Put Faith into Action!
- 10 Minute Break
  Beverages & Restroom
- Call Group Together
- Weekly Lesson
  Taught by Leaders or LITs
- Homework Preview
- Dismiss in Prayer – Holding Hands
  Entire Session Should Average 2 to 2 ½ Hours
- Leaders and LITs Complete Weekly Report

CHAPTER 2 (WEEK 2)
BIBLICAL GIVING

I. WHAT GOD'S WORD SAYS

As covenant-keeping Christians, we need to learn what God's Word says about resources, tithing and giving beyond the tithe. Here are some basic principles from His Word that will help us to participate in His work here on earth.

- **GOD OWNS EVERYTHING** and He is our only source of resources.

1. *Psalm 50:10-11 — "For every beast of the forest is mine, and the cattle upon a thousand hills. I know all the fowls of the mountain, and the wild beasts of the field are mine." (KJV)*

2. *1 Corinthians 10:26 and Psalm 24:1 — "For the earth is the Lord's and all it contains." (NAS)*

3. *Deuteronomy 8:18 — "But remember the Lord your God, for it is He who gives you the ability to produce wealth and so confirms His covenant... " (NIV)*

STEWARDING THE "THREE T'S"

Once Christians truly believe that God Almighty owns everything and is their only source of the "three Ts" *(treasure, talent and time)*, it will be easier for them to accept His instructions in the area of stewarding His resources.

- **THE TITHE IS TEN PERCENT OF OUR INCREASE** and is commanded (of believers) as a minimum to be consecrated to the Lord. It is to be the first ten percent of our income, or increase, which represents the *first fruit* of what God has given us. This *first fruit* honors God. Christians pay their tithes and cannot tithe more or less than ten percent. We will also examine giving freewill offerings and sowing alms.

1. Believers who give God their tithe payment of ten percent have a right (a promise) to expect God to open heaven's windows, pour out blessings and rebuke the devourer on their behalf.

   Malachi 3: 8-12 is so powerful that we encourage you to read several Bible versions of it. The following is from the NAS translation under the heading *You have robbed God — "Will a man rob God? Yet you are robbing me! But you say, 'How have we robbed thee?' In tithes and offerings. You are cursed with a curse, for you're robbing me, the whole nation of you! 'Bring the whole tithe into the storehouse, so that there may be food in My house, and test Me now in this,' says the Lord of hosts, 'if I will not open for you the windows of heaven, and pour out for you a blessing until it overflows.' 'Then I will rebuke the devourer for you, so that it may not destroy the fruits of the ground; nor will your vine in the field cast its grapes,' says the Lord of hosts. 'And all the nations will call you blessed, for you shall be a delightful land,' says the Lord of hosts."*

2. When Abraham won the great victory (with God on his side), he immediately tithed ten percent of everything to Melchizedek, the High Priest of God. *Hebrews 7:1-4 — "For This Melchisedec, king of*

Salem, priest of the most high God, who met Abraham returning from the slaughter of the kings, and blessed him; To whom also Abraham gave a tenth part of all; first being by interpretation King of righteousness, and after that also King of Salem, which is, King of peace; Without father, without mother, without descent, having neither beginning of days, nor end of life; but made like unto the Son of God; abideth a priest continually. Now consider how great this man was, unto whom even the patriarch Abraham gave the tenth of the spoils." (KJV)

3. *Proverbs 3:5 (KJV)* — tells us that if we acknowledge God, He shall direct our paths. In Proverbs 3:8-10, we see the blessings we can receive by this dependence on God: *"This will bring health to your body and nourishment to your bones. Honor the Lord with your wealth, with the first fruits of all your crops; then your barns will be filled to overflowing, and your vats will brim over with new wine." (NIV)*

4. In *Malachi 3:10*, God actually tells us to *"test Him"* or *"prove Him"* with our tithing. This is incredible — our Lord God instructing us to test him by paying our tithes. This verse should absolutely convince us of His promise to deliver the blessings that tithing produces for God's followers.

➢ JESUS COMMANDS BELIEVERS TO TITHE...NEW TESTAMENT

1. Jesus reinforced the tithing principle in the New Testament, thus eliminating the notion that tithing was just an Old Testament concept or practice. *Matthew 23:23 — "Woe to you, teachers of the law and Pharisees, you hypocrites! You give a tenth of your spices — mint, dill and cumin. But you have neglected the more important matters of the law — justice, mercy and faithfulness. You should have practiced the latter, without neglecting the former." (NIV)*

   Luke 11:42 provides another reference of Jesus reinforcing the ten percent tithe.

2. Jesus used agricultural explanations in His teachings because His audience was made up of farmers and shepherds (they were key producers in the economy). Today, most of us earn the majority of our income from jobs or businesses that are not directly related to agriculture. However, just as the farmer traded his hard work for "increase", we trade hours at work for our "increase." So, the concept of paying a ten percent tithe on our increase is left unchanged. We pay our tithes in money, while the farmer used grain, fruits or cattle. The bottom line is that God gives us our increase, and the paying of tithes is a timeless requirement for all believers.

FAILING TO TITHE IS PLANNING TO FAIL

When God gives believers His promises, they are typically double edged. By paying our full ten percent tithes, we are in line for the promised blessings. Failure to be obedient, puts us under a curse, and opens us and our family to attacks from the devourer.

➢ **WE SHOULD GIVE FREEWILL OFFERINGS** — this is beyond our payment of the ten percent first fruits tithing. It is important to grasp this concept of freewill offerings (beyond the tithe). So, let us explore scripture.

1. Matthew 28:18-20 says, *"Then Jesus came to them and said, 'All authority in heaven and on earth has been given to me. Therefore go and make disciples of all nations, baptizing them in the name of the Father and of the Son and of the Holy Spirit, and teaching them to obey everything I have commanded you. And surely I am with you always, to the very end of the age'." (NIV) Jesus'* command to His first disciples was a clear command to all believers that comprise the body of Christ. As we give freewill offerings to evangelistic ministries who teach the gospel, we invest in the Great Commission. In his book, The Laws of Prosperity, Kenneth Copeland talks about *Investing in the Gospel.* He is referring to Christians funding the Great Commission.

2. In *MARK 10:29-30 (NIV),* Jesus also promised his disciples that, if they sacrificed for Him and for the spreading of the gospel, they would reap a hundred fold return in this present age and in the age to come.

3. In *1 Corinthians 9:14,* the Apostle Paul tells believers that, God intends for them to support those who preach the gospel. *"Even so the Lord ordained that they which preach the gospel should live of the gospel." (KJV)* In the Amplified version, the word *live* is translated *"get their maintenance."*

FUNDING THE SALVATION MESSAGE

It should be clear to the 21st century Christian that it takes large amounts of money to fund the salvation message to all the world — via missionaries, evangelists, satellite TV or translated Bibles. You are obliged to pray about your freewill offerings so you can participate in such endeavors. Seek good soil and invest in spreading the gospel as part of your *biblical giving plan.*

In *Mathew 28:19 and 20,* Jesus commands believers to spread His Word. This is often referred to as "The Great Commission."

- **WE SHOULD SOW ALMS TO THE POOR**. Alms, today is more commonly known as *charity.* It is defined as sowing monies to those who are in real need (the poor, widows and orphans).

1. *Proverbs 19:17 — "He who is gracious to a poor man lends to the Lord, and He will repay him for his good deed." (NAS)*

2. *2 Corinthians 9:6* tells us about sowing generously (or sparingly) and reaping abundantly (or sparingly). In verses *8-15 (NIV),* we see that God promises rich blessings for those who distribute their gifts to the poor. By sowing alms, we put powerful words into action. These Godly deeds touch the hearts of hurting people. As a product of our sowing, God also promises to multiply our seed and make us prosperous so we can sow more. What a blessing! He blesses us so we can faithfully bless His children — not just believers, but all in real need.

3. *Luke 12:33-34 — "Sell your possessions and give to charity; make yourselves purses which do not wear out, an unfailing treasure in heaven, where no thief comes near, nor moth destroys. For where your treasure is, there will your heart be also." (NAS)*

4. *Proverbs 22:9 — "A generous man will himself be blessed, for he shares his food with the poor." (NIV)*

5. Believers are also instructed to support widows so the church is not burdened (*1 Timothy 5:16)*.

> ***WHERE SHOULD YOU SOW ALMS?***
>
> There are many places to sow alms. The benevolence fund at your church merits consideration, and the Holy Spirit will show you others.

- **WE ARE TO GIVE CHEERFULLY** and He promises an excellent reward. Paying tithes, giving offerings and sowing alms should all be times of excitement, joy and thanksgiving for us.

  1. *2 Corinthians 9:6-8 — "But this I say, He which soweth sparingly shall reap sparingly; and he which soweth bountifully shall reap also bountifully. Every man according as he purposeth in his heart, so let him give; not grudgingly, or of necessity; for God loveth a cheerful giver. And God is able to make all grace abound toward you; that ye always having all sufficiency in all things, may abound to every good work." (KJV)*

  2. In *Matthew 6:1-2,* God warns us to give our alms secretly (anonymously) because if we trumpet (boast about) our giving before men, we will get no reward from God.

- **GOD CALLS US TO EXCEL IN THE GRACE OF GIVING.** In 2 Corinthians 8:7, we see that God actually provides grace for giving, and believers are called to excel in using this gift. "*But just as you excel in everything — in faith, in speech, in knowledge, in complete earnestness and in love for us — see that you also excel in this grace of giving.*" (NIV)

  Our respected friend, Alan Vincent, produced two excellent audiotape series, which provide powerful biblical financial foundations, including teaching on "the grace of giving". (Money Talks and Prosperity) See the reference section, chapter 11, for instructions on how to obtain these via Outpouring Ministries.

II. MAINTAINING A GOOD ATTITUDE

How we handle paying our tithes, giving freewill offerings, and sowing alms clearly reflects the attitude of our heart. Here are some ways to help you develop and maintain a good heart attitude.

- **DECIDE TO TRUST GOD.** We have to decide to faithfully trust God and not to put our faith in things or money or self. Because, as *Luke 16:10-13* says: *"He who is faithful in a very little thing is faithful in much; and he who is unrighteous in a very little thing is unrighteous also in much. If you therefore have been unfaithful in the use of unrighteous mammon (money) who will entrust the true riches to you... No servant can serve two masters... you cannot serve God and Mammon." (NAS)*

  In their book, Wealth Riches and Money, Craig Hill and Earl Pitts explain that the spirit of mammon, or greed, is very real. This ungodly spirit must be fought by Christians who are in bondage to it.

- **UNDERSTAND THAT GOD DOES NOT NEED YOUR MONEY.** All money belongs to God, and it is His divine plan to use His covenant people as instruments to bless others. He wants us to serve as His conduit so that as He blesses us, we faithfully and cheerfully bless others.

- **GIVE YOUR BEST.** We need to seek God and show our obedience to Him by faithfully tithing, giving of our freewill offerings, and sowing alms. After all, it is absolutely impossible to out-give God! *Luke 6:38 says, "Give, and it shall be given unto you; good measure, pressed down, and shaken together, and running over shall men give into your bosom. For with the same measure that ye mete withal it shall be measured to you again." (KJV)* This is only one of the many reminders of sowing and reaping.

- **GIVE CHEERFULLY.** As we see in *2 Corinthians 9:6-11*, the pattern is for us to be generous and cheerful givers. We cannot fake this because the Lord knows our heart.

- **PUT FAITH INTO ACTION.** Faith in the Bible's accuracy/truth is critical. Even more importantly God wants us to put that faith into action. In *James 2:14-17*, we are instructed to put faith into action by providing food and clothing to our brothers and sisters that are in need. Kind words do not feed or clothe the needy of this world.

  In *Matthew 25:34-40*, Jesus promises a "kingdom" inheritance for those who feed the hungry, give drink to the thirsty, provide shelter to strangers, give clothes to the needy, and visit the sick and the imprisoned. Action is an essential key. It shows that our heart is seeking to please God by giving our time, resources and money to God's people.

- **ASK GOD TO SEARCH YOUR HEART.** If you are willing to submit to God and really desire to be led by the Holy Spirit, you should pray this prayer *from Psalm 139:23-24 — "Search me, O God, and know my heart; test me and know my anxious thoughts. See if there is any offensive way in me, and lead me in the way everlasting." (NIV)*

- **BE THANKFUL.** We need to be thankful and excited about the opportunity that God has given us to pay tithes, give offerings and sow alms, (We need to be thankful at having been blessed by God with resources and excited about what we expect God to do as He multiplies our seed.)

WATCH IT GROW!

Pray to God, water the seed with His Word and He will multiply your gifts. Using scripture, ask the Lord to supernaturally bless the church, the needy, the evangelists who spread the gospel and the missions (where you have sown in faith). Then, step back and see what God will do with seed that was sown in faith and in obedience — seed that is represented by your tithes, freewill offerings and alms.

Remember...He is the same God, today, yesterday, and forever... who fed the thousands with just a few fish and loaves of bread *(Matthew 15:32-38).*

III. WHERE DO OUR TITHES, OFFERINGS AND ALMS GO?

- **TITHES GO TO THE LOCAL CHURCH.** Your ten percent tithe is paid (as a first fruits obligation to God) to the church where you are spiritually nourished. *Malachi 3:10 says "Bring ye all the tithes into the storehouse, that there may be meat in mine house and prove me now herewith, saith the Lord of hosts, if I will not open you the windows of heaven and pour out a blessing that there shall not be room enough to receive it."* (KJV) God goes on to promise that for our obedience, He will rebuke the devourer and protect our crops.

  If your local church is fulfilling God's action plans for the body of Christ, then you need to be a reliable supporter by paying your tithes. Of course, you are also to give of your time, your talents, and your material goods (which all come from God).

  You may also feel led by the Holy Spirit to give additional offerings to your church for special needs like missions or building projects.

- **FREEWILL OFFERINGS GO TO THOSE MINISTRIES THAT SPREAD THE GOSPEL.** This may be through your local church and/or through evangelistic ministries or foreign missions.

- **ALMS GO TO THE POOR AND NEEDY.** There are many ways to help the poor. You could give to your church benevolence fund, or you could give to organizations such as the Salvation Army, Red Cross, Homeless or Inner City Ministries. Let God lead you.

SOW IN GOOD SOIL...EXPECT HEAVENLY MATH

In *Matthew 13:23,* the parable of the sower, we are told that seed sown in good soil produces crops at a rate of 30, 60, or even 100 fold. This is supernaturally fantastic because it equates to a 3,000%, 6,000% or 10,000% increase. Therefore, you should diligently evaluate the places where you intend to give offerings and sow alms. Prayer and wise counsel will result in God's Holy Spirit leading you to commit to a *biblical giving plan.* Then, with an attitude of thanksgiving, you can put the plan into action by cheerfully, purposely, and abundantly giving out of your resources.

God expects us to be good soil, and He expects us to give and sow into good soil. We would not knowingly invest our savings into faulty banks or bad stocks. Likewise, we should investigate any ministry's fruit before investing God's offerings and alms. In America, charitable organizations are required to prepare financial accountability statements. We urge you to check out and pray about your giving. Avoid *emotion* as the basis for giving. Seek God's wisdom and Godly counsel to get the 100-fold return. Then when you sow, expect a huge return as God multiplies your seed in His kingdom.

Covenant couples need to pray together and reach agreement on where these additional offerings and alms should be sown.

IV. DEVELOPING A GIVING PLAN

Later on in this course, we will discuss spending and savings plans. Now, we will concentrate on a giving plan in order to plan for tithes, offerings and alms. To simplify the *Projected Income And Biblical Giving Form* (chapter 15), we have provided one blank line for the tithe, one line for freewill offerings, and another line for alms.

➢ **TITHES MUST BE GIVEN WHEN YOU RECEIVE THE INCREASE.** This may mean weekly, twice a month or monthly. But it should not be delayed, for example, until the end of the year or at tax time.

1. We need to remember that gifts, inheritances and other pleasant financial surprises are also part of the "increase" and are very much subject to tithing.

2. Interest earned is also an "increase" and is subject to the tithe.

3. If we accept the fact that all we receive comes from God, then we are obliged to tithe from the full amount (the gross amount) of our pay. Yes, your employer will deduct for income taxes, social security, and perhaps, for health insurance and retirement. And, yes, the paycheck you cash is your take-home pay (net pay). However, if we only give to God from our net pay, are we clearly putting Him after the government, and after our health insurance and other benefits and taxes?

4. A tax refund is not an increase. In fact, the government is simply returning some of your money without interest. Sadly, consistent large tax refunds reflect poor stewardship!

5. **Caution:** If you do experience a financial crisis, we urge you not to even think about refraining from tithing. It is at these very moments that we especially need to have God right in the center of our finances!

➢ **PLAN IN ADVANCE TO GIVE OFFERINGS & ALMS.** Beyond the tithe, our plan should also include the giving of freewill offerings and the sowing of alms. Thus, a giving plan means that "we plan in advance to give" versus "looking in our pockets for some extra cash."

GIVING EXAMPLE

A simple example can be demonstrated by our fictional couple, Bob and Mary. Their combined gross monthly income is $4,000. If they have prayed and agreed to tithe (10%) and to give an additional amount of offerings and alms equal to 2% of their gross, then the calculations are as shown below.
Remember, this is just an example:

Gross monthly pay.........................	$ 4,000
Less all payroll deductions................	$ 500
Net (take-home) pay........................	$ 3,500
Tithes to church (10% of gross)........	$ 400
Offerings and Alms (2% of gross).....	$ 80
Total Tithes, Offerings & Alms...	**$ 480**

- **BE OPEN TO GIVE FOR SPECIAL URGENT NEEDS.** Since God intends for us to be conduits to bless others, we need to be available (as the Holy Spirit leads) to give for special urgent needs. *1 John 3:17-18* tells us that — *"If anyone has material possessions and sees his brother in need but has no pity on him, how can the love of God be in him? Dear children, let us not love with words or tongue but with actions and in truth."* (NIV) This scripture reminds us that we can give possessions as well as money.

- **USE ALL LEGAL TAX DEDUCTIONS.** In America, the federal income tax code allows certain deductions for charitable giving. It is definitely prudent to use all legal tax deductions. In fact, doing so indicates good stewardship of God's resources. However, there may be times when God leads you to give to people in need who are not connected to a tax exempt charity. This gives you a great opportunity to pray and to seek God's wisdom. If you feel led to give, then you should give…regardless of tax benefits.

- **BE CREATIVE.** You can address the act of giving and sowing alms in many creative ways. For example, a large "blessing box" can be used for family members to deposit good used items (such as clothes, toys, and school supplies). A special savings or checking account can also be opened just for offerings and alms. As you pray, the Holy Spirit will guide you regarding the best place and time for these gifts. Regular additions to this fund will ensure ample resources are available, when the family is ready to bless someone.

- **ALWAYS REMEMBER GOD'S INSTRUCTIONS.** You should not be surprised if a non-believing accountant, CPA or budget counselor advises you against tithing and giving beyond the tithe. We need to seek God's instructions, not worldly counsel or the popular opinions of the world. Jesus gave us a model to follow in the *parable of the good shepherd, John 10:1-10.* Our Lord tells us that if we are His sheep, we will hear His voice and follow Him. We will not follow the thief (devil) who wants to steal, kill and destroy. *(Also see John 10:27-28.)*

LEADERS' NOTE – For a visual aid, use a small piece of flexible pipe to demonstrate a conduit. The conduit should be plugged up with papers labeled: "not tithing," "curse of poverty," "greed," "disobedience." (As you put coins in the conduit, make sure you clearly demonstrate the blockage that "greed" and "disobedience" have caused. Then, slowly remove each piece of paper. At the same time, please read the specific cause of the blockage. Then, once again, demonstrate how the removal of the blockages has allowed the coins to flow through the conduit.)

- **PRAY AND AGREE.** For married couples, praying together and coming into agreement regarding tithes, offerings and alms will please God. It will therefore provide a firm foundation like that of the house built upon the rock in *Luke 6:48.*

- **PLEDGES – BE GUIDED BY THE HOLY SPIRIT, NOT MANIPULATED.** The discussion of pledges to churches, ministries or missions is a sensitive topic. We recommend that before you commit to a pledge, you pray and seek the Holy Spirit's guidance.

Below, we provide some thoughtful suggestions regarding pledges:

1. Remember, pledges are a serious matter because you are committing to a financial obligation.

2. Couples must agree on all financial obligations (this definitely includes pledges) which represent one-flesh decisions.

3. Do not submit to manipulation or any kind of pressure. Rather, be led by God. Ask Him and patiently listen. You may need to wait on His timing before rendering a decision.

4. Remember, pledges are not part of the tithe. They are freewill offerings.

5. We agree, with Alan Vincent, that it is best to pledge only an amount you can actually give within one week's time. In other words, fulfill the pledge immediately, in full, or as soon as funds can be transferred from one of your accounts to a checking account. We feel it is not prudent to presume on the future by promising to give (pledging) funds you do not have.

6. Never write post-dated checks, and avoid using credit cards (high interest debt), as part of your giving plan.

7. Fulfill your obligations. If you made a pledge (not through manipulation) in good faith, then fulfill your promise.

CAN'T AFFORD TO GIVE?

If the whole concept of paying tithes, giving offerings, and sowing alms is brand new to you, your first reaction may be: "I simply cannot afford this." In the natural (in your own strength), you are correct. However, if you sincerely seek Gods wisdom regarding the "increase" He has so graciously given you, then trust God and act in faith (remembering that He does not call us to do things without providing the necessary resources). Purposeful and sacrificial giving shows that you are truly seeking after God's own heart.

Philippians 4:19 — "And my God will meet all your needs according to His glorious riches in Christ Jesus." (NIV)

V. MAKE A FAITH STATEMENT

Our willingness to pay tithes, give offerings, and sow alms (freely and cheerfully) into God's kingdom makes a strong statement of faith to the world. It lets believers reflect the true light that God wants the world to see.

GOD CONSIDERS MONEY TO BE IMPORTANT, AND THAT IS WHY THERE ARE MORE THAN 1,000 OLD AND NEW TESTAMENT SCRIPTURES ON MONEY, WEALTH, STEWARDSHIP AND OTHER RELATED TOPICS.

➢ **TEACH & TRAIN YOUR CHILDREN.** God's plan is for parents to teach and train their children in the Word of God. Since there are so many scriptures devoted to finances, it is important for us to teach them to our family. *Proverbs 22:6, 7 and 9 — "Train up a child in the way he should go, even when he is old he will not depart from it. The rich rules over the poor and the borrower becomes the lender's slave. He who is generous will be blessed for he gives some of his food to the poor."* (NAS)

1. What better way to train our children to be good stewards than to involve them in the family tithing and giving plan! We can also show them how to apply God's financial principles with their allowance and financial gifts. Don't we all wish that we had learned these Godly habits as children?

2. Larry Burkett founded an excellent ministry called Christian Financial Concepts. It recently merged with Crown Ministries. The new Crown Financial Ministries (www.crown.org) provides wonderful resources for children: "My Giving Bank" *(a three compartment bank to teach children three and older how to separate giving, saving and spending)*, a fun "Money Matters for Kids" board game *(featuring Larry the Cat) and* a host of training books and workbooks for teens. *Call 866-424-4000 to request a resource catalog, or to receive a free newsletter, or to learn more about related radio programs sponsored by Larry Burkett.* (As always, we encourage you to filter and test all teaching with God's Word.)

➢ **BE FAITHFUL STEWARDS.** Earlier, we defined prosperity *as "having enough resources to accomplish everything that God has called us to do."* If we use our God-given resources wisely, then we have a right to expect Him to be pleased with us — as seen in the *parable of the talents. Matthew 25:21 — "Well done, good and faithful servant! You have been faithful with a few things; I will put you in charge of many things. Come and share your master's happiness!" (NIV)*

VI. DEVELOPING YOUR OWN PROJECTED INCOME AND BIBLICAL GIVING PLAN

This week's homework involves your completion of a two-part form labeled: *Projected Income and Biblical Giving*. This is a vital step because it directly involves God in your financial freedom plan.

Throughout the upcoming weeks, you will be studying examples #1 and #2. (Bob and Mary Jones, our fictional couple). Bob and Mary are a family of four. Bob works while Mary has chosen to stay at home and raise their two children.

The example #1 form is dated June 30, 2000. It represents Bob and Mary's financial situation before they started the Financial Freedom in Seven Weeks Plus group course. As you might suspect, Bob and Mary needed some help. However, they were eager to learn and improve their finances.

Example #2 represents Bob and Mary's financial picture on August 30, 2001 (this is approximately one full year after they completed the course). As you study example #2, you will see the changes made by the Jones in order to get on the road to financial freedom.

Remember, these are just examples. Everyone's financial situation is unique. However, it is still helpful to study examples in order to learn how to develop a financial freedom plan.

EXAMPLE #1 – BEFORE COURSE

PROJECTED INCOME AND BIBLICAL GIVING

(Example #1 - Before Course)

NAME(S): Bob and Mary Jones — Date: June 30, 2000

Projected Income

	Amount Paid Monthly	Mo. x 12 =Subtotal for Yr.	Amount Paid Other Than Monthly	Total Annual Amount	Total Annual Amt. Div. by 12 = Avg. Mo. Amt.
Sources:					
Gross wages: husband	$4,000	$48,000		$48,000	$4,000
Gross wages: wife					
Dividends					
Interest					
Rents (cash flow)					
Business Income/"Increase"					
Pensions & annuities					
Other					
TOTAL GROSS INCOME:	**$4,000**	**$48,000**		**$48,000**	**$4,000**

Projected Giving

	Organization	Amount Paid Monthly	Mo. x 12 =Subtotal for Yr.	Amount Paid Other than Monthly	Total Annual Amount	Total Annual Amt. Div. by 12 = Avg. Mo. Amt.
10% Tithe	Church	$350	$4,200		$4,200	$350
Freewill Offerings	Missions	$10	$120		$120	$10
Alms						
Other	Misc. Charities			$600	$600	$50
Other	United Way	$5	$60		$60	$5
Other						
TOTAL GIVING:		**$365**	**$4,380**	**$600**	**$4,980**	**$415**

Once the income is determined, the next step is to determine where it goes. Begin with giving. Project your giving for the year by considering each organization you support. This can be from pledges, percentages of income, past giving, or specific giving goals. You may want to check your actual giving to date and then project what you plan to give for the rest of the year.

NOTE ON USING THIS FORM: This form will help you arrive at an average monthly amount which is crucial for your spending plan and cash flow management. Record the monthly amount in the first column and then multiply by 12 months for a yearly subtotal. In the third column, record amounts that do not occur every month. Add columns 2 and 3 together to get the total annual amount for column 4. Finally, divide the total annual amount by 12 to get the average monthly amount. Do this for each line item.

Let's study example #1. The top of the form is where the Jones family projected their income for the next 12 months. Bob gets paid $4,000 once a month so the form is easy to follow. His annual income ($4,000 x 12 months) equals $48,000. Since he has no other income beyond the monthly paycheck, the monthly average ($48,000 ÷ 12 months) equals $4,000. If there were any other sources of family income, it would have been added in an appropriate column.

Projected giving (the bottom half of example #1) depicts the normal giving pattern of the family on a monthly and a yearly basis. You can follow the math and you will see that the average monthly giving was $415. You can see that some of the giving was done on a consistent monthly basis, while some giving was placed in the other than monthly column.

- **WHY MONTHLY CALCULATIONS?** We know that not everyone is paid, or gives, or pays bills on a monthly basis. However, experience has shown that a monthly spending plan works. A weekly plan is too short, while quarterly or annual periods are just too long to control.

- **WHAT IF I GET PAID 26 TIMES A YEAR?** Many people receive paychecks every two weeks and this equates to 26 pay periods per year. We strongly recommend that you arrive at an annual amount (bi-weekly check x 26) and then divide the annual income by 12 months, so you can plug it into the monthly calculations of all forms used in this course.

Let's return to Bob and Mary's giving in example # 1. You will note that their "tithes" of $350 do not represent a ten percent tithe of gross income. Remember, this was the Jones's situation before they took this course. Example # 2 will properly depict their corrected tithing.

LEADERS' NOTE: Take time to let your *focus group* digest examples # 1 and # 2. Show how all columns are filled out and take time to clarify any questions regarding the forms.

EXAMPLE #2 – 1 YEAR AFTER COURSE

PROJECTED INCOME AND BIBLICAL GIVING

(Example #2 - After Course)

NAME(S): Bob and Mary Jones — Date: August 31, 2001

Projected Income

	Amount Paid Monthly	Mo. x 12 =Subtotal for Yr.	Amount Paid Other Than Monthly	Total Annual Amount	Total Annual Amt. Div. by 12 = Avg. Mo. Amt.
Sources:					
Gross wages: husband	$4,000	$48,000		$48,000	$4,000
Gross wages: wife					
Dividends					
Interest					
Rents (cash flow)					
Business Income/"Increase"					
Pensions & annuities					
Other					
TOTAL GROSS INCOME:	**$4,000**	**$48,000**		**$48,000**	**$4,000**

Projected Giving

	Organization	Amount Paid Monthly	Mo. x 12 =Subtotal for Yr.	Amount Paid Other than Monthly	Total Annual Amount	Total Annual Amt. Div. by 12 = Avg. Mo. Amt.
10% Tithe	Church	$400	$4,800		$4,800	$400
Freewill Offerings	Missions	$5	$60		$60	$5
Alms	Benevolence	$5	$60		$60	$5
Other	United Way	$5	$60		$60	$5
Other						
Other						
TOTAL GIVING:		**$415**	**$4,980**		**$4,980**	**$415**

Once the income is determined, the next step is to determine where it goes. Begin with giving. Project your giving for the year by considering each organization you support. This can be from pledges, percentages of income, past giving, or specific giving goals. You may want to check your actual giving to date and then project what you plan to give for the rest of the year.

NOTE ON USING THIS FORM: This form will help you arrive at an average monthly amount which is crucial for your spending plan and cash flow management. Record the monthly amount in the first column and then multiply by 12 months for a yearly subtotal. In the third column, record amounts that do not occur every month. Add columns 2 and 3 together to get the total annual amount for column 4. Finally, divide the total annual amount by 12 to get the average monthly amount. Do this for each line item.

Notice: example #2 shows no change in Bob and Mary's income.

Now, their giving plan reflects a proper ten percent tithe of $400 per month. This is the first check the Jones write each month. They rearranged their giving plan in order to ensure that they give additional freewill offerings and also sow alms. The family, as a whole, discussed the allocation of all offerings, alms, and any other charitable donations. Now, with a *Biblical Giving Plan*, they have every right to expect God to lead the way to financial freedom.

VII. SUMMARY – BIBLICAL GIVING

- **GOD'S WORD IS CLEAR** about paying our tithes (ten percent), giving additional freewill offerings (to spread the gospel), and sowing alms (for the needy).

- **GOD DOES NOT NEED OUR MONEY** but He calls us to be good stewards.

- **EVERYTHING WE HAVE AND ALL WE WILL EVER EARN IS NOT OURS.** It all belongs to God, who is our only provider.

- **BIBLICAL GIVING IS EXCITING AND ENJOYABLE** when we get our hearts right with God.

- **CHEERFUL GIVING BY COVENANT BELIEVERS** demonstrates God's power to the world, and blesses believers and non-believers alike.

- **WE WILL SEE OTHERS MOVE TO A LEVEL OF FINANCIAL VICTORY.** As Christians teach God's wisdom on giving and demonstrate these very principles in their own families and businesses, we will see others move to a level of financial victory. God is a BIG GOD, and He wants us to be abundantly blessed.

- **PUT GOD IN THE CENTER OF YOUR FINANCES.** Your *Biblical Giving Plan* allows you to put God in the center of your hearts and your *Family Financial Freedom Plan.*

LEADERS NOTES:

- <u>Self-Employed</u> — group members need to dig-in to the following pages in order to understand the basics of: revenue, increase, and calculation of tithes. Leaders should assess the focus group's needs and decide whether to present this material or not.

- <u>Homework</u> for week 2 follows the *Special Guidelines for the Self-Employed.* Please preview the homework prior to dismissing the group.

Special Guidelines For The Self-Employed

(Optional, but <u>recommended for all</u>)

These special instructions are provided for individuals or families who earn some or all of their income from self-employment.

The primary purpose is to help individuals understand what is income or "increase" due to self-employment. Once the amount of the income or increase is determined, then it is easy to calculate the ten percent tithe.

Our experience, to date, has shown that this information has helped many individuals learn more than the calculation of their tithe. They gain a basic understanding of revenue, costs and income (or increase) from a business activity.

<u>This basic material can also be used to train and bless young entrepreneurs.</u>

LEADERS' NOTE – Leaders, you need to decide whether or not this material will be covered during the study of the course. This information has been very well received. However, you may need to allow additional time for class and homework discussion in order to properly teach and discuss the material presented.

<u>I. KEY TERMS</u>

- **GROSS REVENUE** — This is the total dollar volume produced by the business. Think of it as total sales or gross sales or gross receipts for a given time period, whether it be weekly, monthly or annually.

- **BUSINESS EXPENSES** — These are various expenses related to the self-employment activity. Examples of expenses might be the cost of: products, supplies, advertising, postage, business calls, business transportation, depreciation expense relating to business equipment, special uniforms, safety equipment, accounting services, child care, and so on.

LEADERS' NOTE – In order to explain these concepts, begin by reviewing examples # 3 and # 4. Exclude the following: salary to the owner, or spouse of the owner, of a family-owned business, personal cost of health insurance, income taxes and retirement account deductions.

➢ **INCOME OR INCREASE.** For this course, income or increase is determined by subtracting business expenses from gross revenue.

Gross revenue	$____________
Less business expenses	-$____________
Income or Increase	$____________

➢ **TITHE.** This is a ten percent first fruits offering given to God and is determined by multiplying any income or increase by ten percent. It is to be the first ten percent of a Christian's increase and should therefore be the first check of the week or month. In other words, <u>the tithe should be paid as soon as possible</u> after the increase is received from God, who is the giver of all increase.

Income or increase	$____________
x 10% or 0.10	
Equals the tithe	$____________

➢ **RATIO OF INCOME OR INCREASE TO GROSS REVENUE.** This percentage ratio is determined by dividing last year's income or increase by last year's total gross revenue.

Annual income or increase ÷ annual gross revenue = __________% ratio.

This percentage ratio is easily converted to a numerical decimal value by placing a decimal point in front of the first digit. For example, 50% = .50 or 0.50. Some people prefer using percentages while others like doing math with numerical decimal values.

This ratio of income to gross revenue shows you how much of the prior year's gross revenue resulted in income or increase. For example, if the ratio was 70% or 0.70, then for every $1,000 of gross sales, the business produced $700 of income. If the ratio was 30%, then for every $1,000 of sales, the business reaped a $300 increase.

WHY DO WE NEED LAST YEAR'S RATIO OF INCOME TO GROSS REVENUE?

Because a self-employed person can use this ratio (from last year) to estimate the increase for the new year. It is easy to estimate the amount of income or increase as revenue is received during the new year, and this makes it easy to estimate and pay the tithe each week or each month.

II. EXAMPLES

Let us study two examples of self-employed businesses. Study the numbers, and remember that your group leaders will help with questions after you have reviewed both examples. Because of time constraints, this may require extra homework time and effort. However, if you are self-employed, it is completely worth the effort to seek God's instructions on stewardship.

➢ EXAMPLE #3 – A SELF-EMPLOYED COUPLE'S LAWN & TREE SERVICE

If all or part of your income is derived from self-employment, then the two key questions are: *"What is your real increase?"* and *"How do you calculate your tithes?"*

Since these questions are very common, let us examine a family-owned business scenario that involves George and Jane Smith. Their sole source of income is a family-owned and operated lawn and tree service. The business is run from their residence, and occasionally employs part-time or seasonal employees. We will keep the example basic in order to convey key principles.

This type of business has seasonal fluctuations in revenue, so we will take a look back at the year 2000 in order to help the Smiths develop a *Biblical Giving Plan* for the new year, 2001. Their total gross revenue (gross receipts) for 2000 added up to $95,000. In the following calculations, we will look at their business expenses in order to determine their actual income or "increase" for the year.

Total Business Revenue (Gross Receipts):	$95,000
Less Business Expenses:	
Salaries paid to helpers (employees)	$30,100
Cost of mowing and trimming equipment (depreciation)	$ 4,300
Gas, oil and consumable supplies for mowers, etc.	$ 1,700
Business use of 2 pickups and trailers	$10,000
Business phone line in home	$ 400
Postage, stationary and business cards	$ 250
Total Expenses	- $47,000
The Smith's income (increase) for 2000:	$48,000

Now, we have current data to help the Smith's determine a ratio of income, which will be used to estimate their "increase" and their tithing for the year 2001.

Their gross business revenue was $95,000. But after deducting legitimate expenses paid to run the business ($47,000), we see that their actual income or "increase" was $48,000. So, we divide the gross revenue of $95,000 into the income or increase of $48,000 and the result is:

$48,000 ÷ $95,000 = 50.5%

For this example, let's be conservative (favor God) and round the percentage up to an even 51%. This means that for the year 2000, approximately 51% of the total revenue was actually income or "increase" to George and Jane. To double-check the numbers, we can multiply the gross revenue of $95,000 by 51%. We will get an estimate of $48,450 as the income or "increase." By safely rounding up the percentage (from 50.5% to an even 51%), we are favoring God as we calculate the *biblical giving* for the new year.

To convert this percentage ratio to a decimal value, put a decimal point in front of the first number. For example, 51% = 0.51. This simplifies the math calculations.

Now that George and Jane know the ratio (51% of gross revenue), they can start the new year with a ratio that will help them determine their ten percent tithe.

In example #3, let's assume that their first week's total business revenues for the new year (2001) added up to $2,000. They can estimate that their income or increase will again be 51% of the gross revenue. So, for the first week of January 2001, they multiply their gross revenue of $2,000 by 51% to get $1,020 as a safe estimate of their income or increase for the week.

$2,000 x 0.51 = $1,020 increase

Their family tithe would then be ten percent of $1,020 or $102. Since the tithe is always a "first fruit" offering, the $102 check to their church should be their first check of the week.

$1,020 x 0.10 = $102 tithe

Freewill offerings and alms, above the tithe, should be prayerfully determined by George and Jane. They are encouraged to include their children in the decision process.

For the balance of this year (2001), the Smiths can use the same ratio, (51%) of gross revenue, to estimate their increase and their tithe. At the end of the year, they should again calculate the ratio and use the new ratio (percentage) for next year's (2002) estimates. If they learn that their income (increase) for 2001 was actually more than 51% of their revenue, then a one-time tithe check would be appropriate, to correct the shortfall.

If it turns out that their new ratio (percentage) actually fell below 51%, we suggest they not try to deduct some amount in order to downwardly adjust the tithe. Remember, it is impossible to outgive God.

➢ EXAMPLE #4 – ONE SPOUSE HAS A PART-TIME, IN-THE-HOME BUSINESS

Today, in many families, one spouse earns supplemental income with a part-time sales business operated from the home. Cosmetics, plastic products, and miscellaneous home supplies, may be representative of these types of small businesses. For many couples, questions arise such as "just how much of the gross sales revenue (or sales volume) is income or "increase" and "how are tithes calculated on this portion of the family income?"

We will label this Example #4 and refer to it as *Ann's In-Home Business*. Several facts are provided about Ann's business for last year (2000). In example #4, we ask you to calculate her increase and her tithe for the first week of this new year (2001).

Ann's Gross Revenue or Total Sales For Last Year (not including sales tax):	$10,000
Her Actual Yearly Business Expenses Were:	
Cost of Products Sold	$ 5,000
Promotional Gifts For Customers	$ 500
Supplies and Postage	$ 100
Advertising	$ 200
Business Use of Vehicle	$ 400
Long Distance Business Telephone	$ 50
Meetings and Training Events	$ 600
Child Care/Baby-sitting	$ 250
Total Expenses	$ 7,100

Calculate Ann's annual income/increase: $__________

Calculate the ratio (percentage) of income or increase to gross revenue using the formula below:

Annual income $________ ÷ Annual revenue of $________ = __________% (ratio)

Convert the percentage ratio to a decimal value by placing a decimal point in front of the first digit of the percentage (for example: 50% = .50).

Ann's percentage ratio of _______% converts to 0.________ decimal value.

Now you have calculated Ann's ratio of income or increase of her gross revenue for the past full year (2000). How would you advise Ann to calculate her income or increase, and her tithe, for the very first week of this new year? In this example, Ann's first week's product sales were $200. You can use the following steps to provide the information Ann needs:

Week one sales of $________ x (decimal value of income to gross sales ratio) 0.______ = $______________ which is her income or increase for week one of 2001.

Ann's tithe for the week would be ten percent or 0.10 x the estimated weekly increase of $______________ which = $______________ (tithe).

Remember, Ann's freewill offerings and alms are above the ten percent tithe, and no set formula applies.

III. DO YOUR OWN CALCULATIONS

If you own your own business, or if either spouse has some income from self-employment, then it is essential that you calculate your increase as part of the homework for week two. You can develop a simple form using example #3 or #4 as a guide or use the blank form provided on the next page.

- Use your information from last year.
- List your gross revenue.
- List all business expenses; do not include a salary to either spouse.
- Deduct total business expenses from gross revenue to get your income or increase for last year.
- Divide gross revenue into your income or increase to get a ratio (percentage or decimal value).
- Now you have a ratio to help you estimate what your increase is on any new revenue for this new year *(see examples)*.
- Once you know how to estimate your increase, your tithe is ten percent (or 0.10) of the increase.
- Freewill offerings and alms are above the ten percent tithe.

Blank Form For Self-Employed "Increase" Calculations

(A) Gross Revenue: $________________

Less Business Expenses:

(Item)	($ Amount)

(B) Total Business Expenses - $________________

(C) Income or "Increase" (Gross Revenue Minus Total Expenses) $________________

(D) Divide Gross Revenue Into Increase (C ÷ A = Ratio) ______________% ratio

(E) Convert ratio to decimal value by placing decimal point in front of % first digit ______% = 0.______

> **Note:** Now that you know your ratio, use it to calculate your actual *increase*, each time you receive self-employment revenue. Once you know your *increase*, multiply it by ten percent (0.10) to calculate your tithe. Remember to include additional freewill offerings, and alms, in your *biblical giving plan*.

- **PERMISSION TO COPY THIS BLANK FORM. The authors encourage owners of this book to copy and use this blank form for personal use. Remember, only blank forms and blank report forms may be photocopied, and only by book owners for personal use.**

CHAPTER 2 (WEEK 2) HOMEWORK

BIBLICAL GIVING

Use the Projected Income and Biblical Giving Form:
Blank Form located in Chapter 15.

1. **Create An Action Plan!** Now is the time to put our knowledge of biblical giving into an action plan. Look at the one-page form entitled *Projected Income and Biblical Giving.* ***(We recommend making a minimum of six extra copies of all blank forms found in Chapter 15 for future use.)***

   Examples #1 and #2 show how our couple, Bob and Mary Jones, completed their forms before and after the course. Use these as a guide.

PROJECTED INCOME AND BIBLICAL GIVING

NAME(S):______________________ Date: ______________

Projected Income

INCOME SOURCES:	Amount Paid Monthly	Mo. x 12 =Subtotal for Yr.	Amount Paid Other Than Monthly	Total Annual Amount	Total Annual Amt. Div. by 12 = Avg. Mo. Amt.
Gross wages: husband					
Gross wages: wife					
Dividends					
Interest					
Rents (Income Less Expenses)					
Business Income/"Increase"					
Retirement Funds					
Other					
TOTAL GROSS INCOME:	$	$	$	$	$

Projected Giving

	Organization	Amount Paid Monthly	Mo. x 12 =Subtotal for Yr.	Amount Paid Other than Monthly	Total Annual Amount	Total Annual Amt. Div. by 12 = Avg. Mo. Amt.
10% Tithe						
Freewill Offerings						
Alms (Poor)						
Other Charities						
Other Charities						
Other Giving						
TOTAL GIVING:		$	$	$	$	$

Once the income is determined, the next step is to determine where it goes. Begin with giving. Project your giving for the year by considering each organization you support. This can be from specific giving goals, percentages of income, or past giving records. You may want to check your actual giving to date and then project what you plan to give for the rest of the year.

NOTE ON USING THIS FORM: This form will help you arrive at an average monthly amount which is crucial for your spending plan and cash flow management. Record the monthly amount in the first column and then multiply by 12 months for a yearly subtotal. In the third column, record amounts that do not occur every month. Add columns 2 and 3 together to get the total annual amount for column 4. Finally, divide the total annual amount by 12 to get the average monthly amount. Do this for each line item.

2. **Fill out the Projected Income form in pencil.** Be conservative regarding income estimates. Round off numbers and avoid decimal points. These are estimates, so do not expect perfection. For couples, it is essential that this is done together and understood by both.

3. **Review the income projections for accuracy.** *(Be certain both spouses understand and agree.)*

4. **Now progress to the Projected Giving form** on the bottom of the same page. (Note: the one page form projects income at the top and giving at the bottom.) Pray about your *Biblical Giving Plan.* (*Again, couples must be in agreement for a plan to work.*)

5. **Complete the *BIBLICAL GIVING PLAN*.** Start with the tithe as ten percent of your gross income. Most often, the tithe will go to your church. Remember, the tithe needs to be your first expenditure in order to be the first fruit offering God requires.

   Additional freewill offerings may go to a number of ministries. Alms may be sown into your church benevolence fund or to missions and other charitable organizations. Freewill offerings may also go to your church for special activities or building funds. It is acceptable to designate where we give our offerings and sow our alms. However if we are paying our tithes into our church, then we should not attempt to designate or control how our trusted church leadership uses the tithes; after all it's God's money.

6. **Write your names on the top of the *Projected Income and Biblical Giving Form* and date it for your records.** You will develop revised plans in the future, but this first plan is a big step. *Congratulations*!

7. **Keep the completed form handy.** You will use it again as part of your complete *Spending Plan*, later in the course.

8. **Bring the completed form to the next session and be prepared to share:**

   a. What steps did you take in completing the form?

   b. How did God work in the process?

c. Problems encountered, and how you overcame them.

d. What will you do differently when you do this next time?

9. **Self-Employed Individuals and Families with any Self Employment Income** should study the *Special Guidelines for The Self Employed.* Then, they need to complete all the appropriate forms and be prepared to give a very brief recap to the group. Ask the leaders for special assistance if necessary.

10. **Fill in your *Breakthroughs* Form for week two.** Thank God for small and large breakthroughs and be prepared to share with your group during week three.

BREAKTHROUGHS!

FINANCIAL FREEDOM COURSE – RECORD YOUR WEEKLY TESTIMONIES

NAME: ______________________________ & ______________________________

DATE:	MONEY, CAREER, GIFTS/INHERITANCE, & OTHER
______	____
______	____
______	____
______	____
______	____
______	____
______	____
______	____
______	____

CHAPTER 3

(WEEK 3)

"The rich ruleth over the poor, and the borrower is servant to the lender."
Proverbs 22:7 (KJV)

Freedom From Debt Principles

LEADER'S NOTES – WEEKLY PROTOCOL

- Praise Song – A great way to start!
  Suggest Typed Lyrics and Upbeat Music

- Prayer – Led by a Leader or LIT
  Recommend Group Holding Hands

- Spiritual Warfare – in Jesus' mighty name

- Homework Sharing – Normally led by LITs
  Led by Leaders if LITs are Teaching this Week
  Time Control and Equal Sharing are Keys

- Sharing of Weekly Breakthroughs
  Brief but Builds Hope – Celebrate!

- Weekly Offering Time – Opportunity to Sow
  Have a Focus Group Member Pray First
  Put Faith into Action!

- 10 Minute Break
  Beverages & Restroom

- Call Group Together

- Weekly Lesson
  Taught by Leaders or LITs

- Homework Preview

- Dismiss in Prayer – Holding Hands
  Entire Session Should Average 2 to 2 ½ Hours

- Leaders and LITs Complete Weekly Report

CHAPTER 3 (WEEK 3)
FREEDOM FROM DEBT PRINCIPLES

OVERVIEW

In week 1, we learned that God has a lot to say about how we steward His resources. In fact, over a thousand Old and New Testament scriptures provide wisdom on how we are to be good stewards. Last week in chapter two, we learned God's basic ingredients to a recipe for financial freedom, namely: tithes, offerings, and alms. <u>Now,</u> we are ready to <u>kick the devil out of our life</u>.

There is freedom in the Word of God. *John 8:31 and 32 — "If ye continue in my Word, then are ye my disciples indeed; And ye shall know the truth and the truth shall make you free."* (KJV) It is important to start this section with the confidence that your debt situation is not at all hopeless. God is not embarrassed by your indebtedness, but He does want to free you from debt bondage. We applaud you for wanting to learn how to smash the debt cycle.

LEADERS' NOTE – We suggest creating a larger visual of the following graphic to display every week for the remainder of the course. It represents a *PARADIGM SHIFT.* Use it to emphasize the importance of shifting our world-view of debt to God's view (a totally debt free life for us…His children).

Hint: The visual shows two dimes (a pair of dimes) shifting.

<u>I. FOUNDATIONAL TRUTHS</u>

It is imperative that we shift our world-view about debt, to God's financial perspective.

- **GOD HAS A GOOD PLAN FOR US.** *Jeremiah 29:11 — "For I know the thoughts and plans that I have for you, says the Lord, thoughts and plans for welfare and peace and not for evil, to give you hope in your final outcome."* (Amplified) We also learn that if we pray to God, He will hear us and heed our prayers. Additionally, God promises to deliver us from captivity. <u>For those who have been or are now in debt bondage, debt is definitely a form of captivity</u>.

- **PROSPERITY DEFINED** – Having all the resources (time, talent and money) we need to accomplish what God has called us to do.

- **WE MUST LISTEN AND LET GOD'S WORD GUIDE US.** *Proverbs 19:20 —"Listen to advice and accept instruction, and in the end you (we) will be wise."* (NIV) Also be encouraged that the Holy Spirit wants to guide you, *Psalm 119:105 —"Your Word is a lamp to my feet and a light for my path." (NIV)*

- **YOU SHOULDN'T FEEL CONDEMNED FOR BEING IN DEBT.** *Romans 8:1* says, *"There is therefore now no condemnation for them which are in Christ Jesus, who walk not after the flesh, but after the (Holy) Spirit." (KJV)*

- **OUR PRAYERS MUST HAVE GODLY MOTIVES AND LINE UP WITH GOD'S WORD.** *"You ask and do not receive, because you ask with wrong motives, so that you may spend it on your pleasures." James 4:3 (NAS).* This scripture makes it clear that Our Lord is not interested in lavishing wealth on us for pure pleasure.

II. PREPARE YOUR HEART AND MIND

Wisdom from God's Word will help you gain freedom from debt's burdens.

- **ENVISION A DEBT-FREE LIFE.** Imagine you have no past due bills, no car payments, and no big mortgage payment due each month. You are totally debt free, free to serve others and God. God wants you to bless people with your time, talents and abundance. *Ephesians 3:20* tells us, *"Now to Him who is able to do exceedingly abundantly above all that we ask or think according to the power that works in us, to Him be glory in the church by Christ Jesus to all generations, forever and ever. Amen." (NKJ)*

- **BELIEVE THAT DEBT FREEDOM IS NOT JUST A DREAM.** After all, there were no bill collectors in the Garden of Eden. Clearly, God did not intend for His covenant people to be in debt bondage!

- **FORGIVE YOURSELF FOR PAST ERRORS** and let God do a new thing. *Isaiah 43:18-19 —"Remember ye not the former things, neither consider the things of old. Behold I will do a new thing; now it shall spring forth; shall ye not know it? I will even make a way in the wilderness, and rivers in the desert." (KJV)*

- **UNDERSTAND THAT DEBT IS NOT SIN, BUT NOT REPAYING DEBT IS SIN!** *Psalm 37:21 — "The wicked borrows and does not pay back, but the righteous is gracious and gives." Romans 13:8 — Keep out of debt and owe no man anything except to love one another; for who loves his neighbor — who practices loving others — has fulfilled the Law (relating to one's fellowmen), meeting all its requirements." (Amplified)*

FOR MARRIED COUPLES

You need to understand that your spouse is <u>not</u> the enemy…the devil is the enemy!

Your marriage vows most likely included promises to *"love, cherish and obey, in sickness and in health, and for richer or for poorer."* Since you promised each other and God to stick together, you need to deal with the difficult subject of debt…together!

Agreement in prayer can activate God's promises, and agreement is essential for a couple to accomplish something this important. *Amos 3:3 (KJV)* says: *"Can two walk together except they be agreed?"* And *Matthew 18:19 (AMP)* states: *"Again I tell you, if two of you on earth agree (harmonize together, together make a symphony) about — anything and everything — whatever they shall ask, it will come to pass and be done for them by My Father in heaven."* Jesus, reminds us of the power of praying together in agreement.

III. BAD CONSEQUENCES OF DEBT

Note: If you are currently experiencing severe strain related to finances, you can provide your own examples.

WILL MORE MONEY SOLVE DEBT PROBLEMS?

It is a serious mistake to assume that "more money" will remove debt problems. Individual's who tend to overspend typically continue to purchase (even more) on credit as their income increases. <u>Once the burden of debt is removed and habits are changed, people can focus on Godly goals and run their lives in a financially stress-free manner</u>.

- **POVERTY** — *Proverbs 21:17 — "He who loves pleasure will become poor; whoever loves wine and oil will never be rich." (NIV)* God does not say that prospering is bad; in fact, He wants his covenant people to prosper. However, if we seek pleasure before God, we can be easily tempted to go into debt. Unfortunately, this keeps us from <u>truly prospering</u> (which we previously defined as *"<u>having all the resources we need, to do what God has called us to do</u>").*

- **THE RICH WILL RULE OVER YOU** — *Proverbs 22:7 — "The rich ruleth over the poor, and the borrower is servant to the lender."* (KJV) If you have ever owed money to another person, then you know the relationship changes. There is no real joy in being in debt, and God wants His covenant people to have joy.

- **PRESUMPTION CONCERNING THE FUTURE** — Going into debt, especially if we do not have a guaranteed way to repay, presumes upon the future. In *James 4:13-15* we are warned not to presume upon God, but rather to make Him the center of our planning process, for ourselves or for our businesses. *"Come now, you who say today or tomorrow, we shall go to such and such a city, and spend a year there and engage in business and make a profit. Yet you do not know what your life will be like tomorrow. You are just* *a vapor that appears for a little while and then vanishes away. Instead, you ought to say, If the Lord wills, we shall live and also do this and that." (NAS)*

WHY NOT GO INTO DEBT?

If you have a "steady job," you might question how taking on sizable debt could presume on the future. Stop and reflect on your ability to repay it if you lose your job or suffer a serious disability. Also, if you have counted on the equity in your home to provide collateral for a debt, think about your status if the home market values decline in your neighborhood. These are heavy issues to ponder... before going in debt.

- **A DAMAGED CHRISTIAN WITNESS** — How Christians conduct their financial affairs is very important. What reaction do you have to someone who claims to run a "Christian business" if that person is consistently late in paying bills, abuses employees with sub-standard pay and/or poor working conditions, and operates from shoddy offices or with broken-down vehicles? *Proverbs 22:1 — "A good name is more desirable than great riches; to be esteemed is better than silver or gold."* (NIV) We know that having consistently past-due bills or declaring bankruptcy damages our potential Christian witness to our family and to the world. Conversely, as we learn and apply kingdom financial principles, the world will be much more interested in what we have to say about salvation.

NO CONDEMNATION

Now is a great time to recall Romans 8:1—"There is therefore now no condemnation to them which are in Christ Jesus, who walk not after the flesh, but after the Spirit." (KJV) Let God's wisdom teach you, convict you to change, and heal you. Do not allow the devil to hang guilt, shame or condemnation on you!

IV. DEBT MORTGAGES YOUR FUTURE

EXAMPLE

Consider a $100,000 home mortgage at 6.75% interest.

Payments over 30 years	$ 648.60
Total House Payment	$233,959.00
Total Amount of Interest Paid (*nearly*)	$134,000.00

For a $200,000 home, the payments and mortgage costs are doubled.

- **DEBT OBLIGATES YOU TO MAKE PAYMENTS FROM MONEY NOT YET EARNED.** This obligation can keep people from fulfilling other important obligations and from doing some of the activities God intends.

- **DEBT MAY FORCE PEOPLE TO LOWER LIVING STANDARDS** due to the heavy burden of payments. There is nothing wrong with some belt-tightening of the budget. (Soon you will learn to forget the "budget" concept and focus on a flexible *spending plan* concept.) However, this may even cut into some essential needs, and God does not like that at all. *1 Timothy 5:8 — "But if any provide not for his own, and especially those of his own house, he hath denied the faith, and is worse than an infidel." (KJV)*

- **DEBT ADVERSELY AFFECTS MARRIAGES.** It is widely accepted in American Christian circles that <u>the clear number one cause of marital separation and divorce is financial stress</u>. <u>Financial stress is cited in 50% to 80% of divorce situations</u>, (far more often than problems with intimacy or any other area). Most of the stress is related to severe debt pressure.

FOR MARRIED COUPLES

Divorce is not part of our Heavenly Father's divine plan for covenant marriages. In the first chapter of Genesis, God made it very clear that we are to take dominion over the earth. Being in serious debt would hardly indicate dominion. So, let's learn how to fight debt and get the victory God intends for His covenant couples to enjoy…true financial freedom.

V. A CLOSER LOOK AT DEBT

By understanding what debt is and how people get into it, we can start gaining wisdom that will help us break out of the debt cycle.

- **DEBT DEFINITION** —According to the American Dictionary of the English Language, Noah Webster defines debt as: "that which is due from one person to another, whether money, goods or services; that which one person is bound to pay or perform to another."

Webster adds that "when you run in debt you give to another power over your liberty." This reminds us of *Proverbs 22:7 — "The rich rule over the poor, and the borrower is servant to the lender." (NIV)*

> **KEEP THE FAITH!**
> Many of you are probably struggling to imagine living debt free. We encourage you to nourish and water this debt-free faith vision as you complete this course.

- **FROM DEBT TO CRISIS** — Debt becomes a serious problem for people when they incur debt with no sure way to repay. A family crisis occurs when we default on our debts, and that is when our borrowing becomes sin. *Psalm 37:21* warns us that the wicked borrow and do not repay; and *Romans 13:8* tells us to owe no man except to love him.

- **SURETY IS DEBT RELATED** — It takes place when we incur an obligation without the means to repay it. Then, we risk losing some or all of our assets. *Proverbs 22:26-27 — "Be not one of those who strike hands and pledge themselves or those who become security for another's debts. If you have nothing with which to pay, why should he take away your bed from under you?" (Amplified)*

  Surety is a very serious concept. In *Hebrews 7:22,* we see that by His death on the cross, the shedding of His blood, and His resurrection from the dead, Jesus made himself *"surety of a better testament."* (KJV) There is no evidence in the Bible for us to take surety lightly. It obligates us, and our families, to make good on the debts of another.

> **BE WARY OF CO-SIGNING**
>
> Co-signing notes for others makes you fully responsible if they default. By co-signing, you are helping others obtain credit they do not deserve. In any event, know that you are promising to pay the debt in full if the co-signer defaults.

VI. WHAT GETS US INTO DEBT?

- **EASY CREDIT** has allowed us to get in deep messes. In the first half of the 20th century, it was not easy for people to get deeply mired in debt because easy credit was not available. So, people were more likely to save for major purchases and pay cash on delivery.

Now, in the new millennium, the concept of delayed gratification (putting off buying things we desire and buying now only the things we really need) has given way to a "buy now and pay later" mentality. The message relayed by television, radio, and billboards, is aimed at our flesh. The message goes something like this: "buy now, you deserve it… or… surely, with your income, you can afford our easy payment plan of just a few dollars a month."

- **FEEDING "GREED" vs. "NEED"** — Are we <u>focusing on consumption</u> (what we desire) rather than what we need and can afford? A preacher once referred to the advertising spirit in today's society as the god of "DIS". These messages bombard us daily — making us feel <u>dis</u>satisfied or <u>dis</u>content with what we have. As a result, we are tempted to covet many things for the wrong reasons (such as keeping up with the neighbors, or showing off to impress others).

SOME HONEST QUESTIONS TO ASK:

Remember this is not a time for blame or condemnation, but rather a time of self-examination so you can gain victory over debt bondage. Couples should discuss these questions together.

1. Am I buying a home that is more than I can afford?
2. Does the car I drive reflect a good use of God's money?
3. Do I buy the latest gadgets, appliances or fancy clothing on credit when I have better places to use the money?
4. Do I get carried away with sports equipment, entertainment or hobbies?
5. Am I inclined to eat out far too often, or do I go to restaurants I really cannot afford?
6. Am I forsaking Biblical principles of tithing plus giving of freewill offerings and sowing alms because there is no money left at the end of the month? In other words, do I put God last on my priorities list because I run out of money?

VII. THE IMPORTANCE OF BALANCE

- **ENJOYING PROSPERITY WITHOUT GREED** — God does not say that we are not to enjoy nice things. The Bible is full of examples in which He prospered His faithful servants, including Abraham, Joseph, Job and many others. However, in *Luke 12:15*, Jesus warned: *"Watch out! Be on your guard against all kinds of greed; a man's life does not consist in the abundance of his possessions."* (NIV) In modern terminology, Jesus exploded the popular myth of *"whoever has the most toys, in the end, wins."*

- **IMPORTANCE OF CONTENTMENT** — The Bible is loaded with references to poverty as a curse. God wants to bless His people and He calls us to seek balance in our lives. Paul spoke of contentment in *Philippians 4:11 — "...for I have learned in whatever state I am, therewith to be content." (KJV)*

- **FLEE FROM TEMPTATION** — New Christians may not realize how easy it is to open themselves to debt's temptation. Just as the trolling fisherman pulls his fishing lure through the water to attract and hook the fish, we are trolling for debt (openly asking for it), when we window shop, watch a shopping channel, or check out fancy catalogs "just for entertainment." We need to flee from temptation and stay focused on the goal of being debt free.

VIII. CREDIT CARD ABUSE

- **CREDIT CARD DEBT IS THE WORST** — Credit card debt *(and other consumer loan debt)* has risen to astronomical proportions. Of all types of consumer debt, credit card debt is the worst. In fact, credit card abuse has led to a plague of debt bondage for believers and non- believers.

> **STARTLING REALITIES**
>
> Many American families deal with credit card balances of $7,000 to $50,000 or much more, with compound interest rates of 18% to over 23%.
>
> Most people have no concept of actually paying off the card balance each month. As a result, the interest charges often amount to considerably more than the actual purchase price of the item.
>
> **MANY AMERICANS CARRY AND USE AN AVERAGE OF 7 CREDIT CARDS!**

- **CREDIT CARD PURCHASES OFTEN LEAVE NO LASTING VALUE** — Unfortunately, many credit card purchases become ways to finance goods or services that have no lasting value, such as meals, vacations, clothing or other rapidly depreciating items. Therefore, a person often ends up paying off a credit card debt for an item that has absolutely no remaining value.

> **A QUOTEABLE QUOTE**
>
> *In his book, Dollars and Sense, Wilson J. Humber used the following quote to discuss the problem with excessive card use.*
>
> **"A credit card is a means of buying something I don't need, at a price I can't afford, with funds I don't have, from people who aren't polite, so I can impress people I don't know."**

- **CREDIT CARDS "MAKE" US SPEND UP TO 35% MORE,** even if we never pay a dime's worth of interest! Several prominent Christian financial teachers and writers have carefully studied this subject. They agree that an individual spends between 25% to 35% less if he or she does not use credit cards. Imagine having one third more spendable money each and every month. Studies show that we are far less apt to make spur-of-the-moment purchases if we have to write out a check or pay in cash. In other words, if we have the discipline to use a check or to pay in cash for purchases, we may save one third on our monthly expenditures. With such savings in mind, it is best to "go with the green" – use checks or cash, and only use them for planned expenditures.

  If you continue to regularly use "plastic" be on guard against impulse buying!

- **PRAY ABOUT USING CREDIT CARDS** – Everyone should pray about the use of credit cards. For couples, honesty is the essential key in gaining financial freedom. If there is a life pattern of card abuse, you should consider not using cards at all or consider establishing strict guidelines. Don't forget to ask God to give you the grace and wisdom to change.

BE CREATIVE TO BREAK OLD HABITS

Some people lock their credit cards in a safety deposit box to avoid overuse while others freeze their cards in a large Tupperware bowl. (Imagine praying about an expenditure, and then having to thaw the card out before purchasing the item!)

NOTE – *In the next chapter, we will develop an action plan and discuss specific strategies for accelerated repayment of credit card debt.*

IX. COMPOUND INTEREST – A BLESSING OR A CURSE?

- **ONE OF THE WONDERS OF THE WORLD** – Compound interest has been referred to as one of the wonders of the world. Unfortunately, many do not understand compound interest. Once we grasp the concept, we will see that compound interest can be good by working for us, or it can be a curse, working against us. Jesus, in the *parable of the talents (Matthew 25:14-27)*, characterized the wicked and lazy servant as the one who failed to put (invest) some of his master's money in the bank so it could have at least earned interest.

- **WHAT EXACTLY IS COMPOUND INTEREST?** Compound interest means the initial amount, borrowed or saved, earns interest that is added to the principal to get a new balance. Then, the new total amount earns interest, and the process of compounding is repeated for the term of the agreement. The higher the compound interest rate is, the faster the balance increases. Let's use a basic example... *(you may prefer to use interest tables or a financial calculator).*

- **If the starting amount, or the principal, is $2,000 and the compound annual interest rate is 18% (not far off from many of today's credit card rates), the following table shows us the effect of compound interest.** Utilizing the chart below, let's assume that no additional principal payments have been made and no withdrawals have been deducted. Remember, compound interest applies to any financial transaction, whether it is a debt or an investment.

Year	Principal $	Interest @ 18%	Balance at Year End
1	$2,000	$360	$2,360
2	2,360	425	2,785
3	2,785	501	3,286
4	3,286	591	3,877
5	3,877	698	4,575
6	4,575	823	5,398
7	5,398	972	6,370
8	6,370	1,147	7,517
9	7,517	1,353	8,870
10	8,870	1,597	10,467
15	10,467	1,884	12,351
20	46,424	8,356	54,780
25	106,206	19,117	125,323
30	242,974	43,735	286,709
35	555,866	100,056	655,922
40	1,271,687	228,904	$1,500,597

- This is a simplified example and the numbers have been rounded off to whole dollar amounts. But WOW! Starting with just $2,000, this amount grew to over $10,000 in just ten years. The increase (miracle growth) came because the principal at the start of each year was added to the interest earned during the year. The next year's starting principal amount was the combination of the two. Then, the larger amount earned interest and the process continued.

GOOD NEWS OR BAD NEWS?

If this $2,000 (in the compound interest example) is an investment, the resulting total is very good news. If it is a debt balance, the news is terrible. When the calculations are run for 20 or 30 years, we observe a very steep increase. At the end of 40 years, the balance is over $1.5 million. Wow!

Unfortunately, it is very easy to find credit cards that carry compound rates of 18% or higher. It is far more difficult to find investments with sure rates of return that are anywhere near this high.

If you have high interest rate debt and you accelerate the payoff schedule by making more than the minimum payments, you are in effect making an investment at that "guaranteed" rate. This is very important. If you pay-off (early) an 18% credit card balance, you have made the equivalent of an 18% guaranteed investment! So, before looking for speculative investments, invest in yourself by paying-off credit card balances and any other high interest debts.

- **THE EFFECT OF COMPOUND INTEREST** — *Note: The following graph displays the same numbers you just observed. For many people, seeing this dramatic compounding effect in a graph provides a clearer picture than just seeing the numbers in a table form. Because of the scale of the graph, it is difficult to show that the graph actually starts at $2,000 on the vertical axis, and increases to $1.5 million (refer back to the table for correct values, year-by-year).*

THE GRAPH DEPICTS GROWTH OF $2,000 AS THE STARTING VALUE COMPOUNDED @ 18 % FOR 40 YEARS

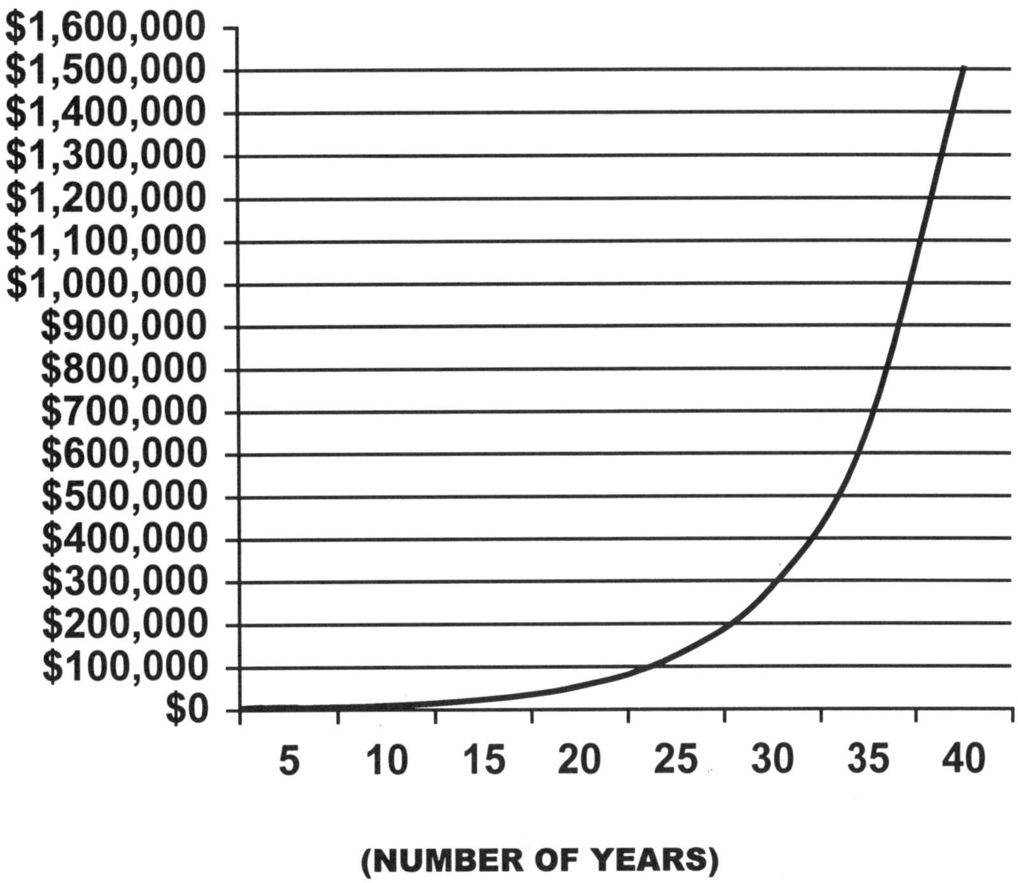

X. SUMMARY – FREEDOM FROM DEBT PRINCIPLES

- **GOD HAS A GOOD PLAN FOR YOU** *(Jeremiah 29:11)*

- **THE KNOWLEDGE OF COMPOUND INTEREST** should help you be good stewards of the resources God has given you. We can see that **compound interest can be either a blessing or a curse**. Prudent people should position themselves only for the blessing side of compound interest. (Let the miracle growth work for you!)

- **UNDERSTANDING DEBT PRINCIPLES** is essential to developing a plan for debt freedom.

- **GOD DESIRES TO SHARE/IMPART HIS WISDOM TO US.** He knew that Christians in the 21st century would be severely tempted by the bondage of debt, and that Satan would strive to use debt to destroy their testimonies and even their marriages. The more we seek His ways, the easier it will be to make this Godly "paradigm shift" to financial freedom.

WITH GOD ALL THINGS ARE POSSIBLE!

(Matthew 19:26)

LEADERS' NOTE – At this time, give the focus group a brief preview of the forms and examples that will be used in this course. You did this in week 1. So, by now, the group should be getting more familiar with the forms and examples. Note, they are only examples. They are only a guide.

- Example # 1 features Bob and Mary Jones before they learned the lessons of this course.

- Example # 2 shows how much their situation changed and improved (approximately one year after they successfully completed the course).

Be encouraged, you are on the right path!

CHAPTER 3 (WEEK 3) HOMEWORK

FREEDOM FROM DEBT PRINCIPLES

1. **Pray and attack the devil with spiritual warfare,** putting-on the whole armor of God. Getting free from debt's bondage requires honesty and transparency. You will need to explore your own debt portfolio and determine what if any patterns trapped you into bondage. Satan is cunning and he will attempt to turn this time into a blame and guilt session. Use *Ephesians 6:10-18* and *Romans 8:1* as a guide to your prayer and warfare.

2. **Communion is also recommended as a reinforcement of your covenant with God. If married, take communion together as a one-flesh couple.** (Be sure to repent of any sin, prior to communion.)

3. **For married couples, you must agree/desire to get out of debt. This is absolutely essential.** Openly discuss debt. Then, you need to discuss how debt is affecting your relationship with one another and your relationship with God.

   a. Is there agreement on getting out of debt?

   b. How will being debt free improve your relationship with:

      1) Each other?

      2) Your family?

      3) With God?

4. **Identify Supportive Scriptures.** Go back through the teaching outline and select two scriptures that especially help you understand the perils of debt. List them below and prepare to discuss one of them with the group.

   a. (first scripture)

   b. (second scripture)

5. **Review Compound Interest.** Compound interest is a very important principle that can work for you/against you. (Review the explanation of compound interest.)

   a. Be sure you understand how compound interest works. Explain it to someone else. *(For couples, explain it to your spouse or your children.)*

   b. How has compound interest worked against you?

   c. How is compound interest working for you? Or how do you envision compound interest being a positive factor in your household?

6. **Set Faith Goals.** In Week 1, you prepared some very broad goals. Now, use the blank forms provided *(after you've made 6 extra copies)* to set your goals. The form entitled Financial Vision & Faith Goals can be used for 1-year, 3-year, or 5-year goals. You decide what target period to set and state the target date (month and year) after the word "by" ____ at the top of the form. Pray, dream and enjoy setting your faith goals. Be prepared to discuss some of these goals next week. ***This multi-page blank goals form can be found in chapter 15.***

7. **An Annual Letter to Your Spouse or Dependents.** In June of 1998, Bill Sitter (co-author) got a shocking surprise. A hospital visit for "tests" ended with a seven-heart bypass surgery. God did an amazing healing work, as only He can. However, Maureen took some comfort in knowing that Bill periodically updated a letter outlining the family's actual financial position. The letter provided approximate balances of banking and investment accounts. It listed key contacts: CPA, lawyer, investment broker, family, and especially who to lean on for spiritual advice. It also discussed: wills, insurance and funeral instructions.

   No one enjoys reflecting on what life will be like if one spouse dies. This can be especially stressful if the main income provider dies first. So, we urge you (if you have a spouse or any dependents) to consider writing this annual "financial status" letter. Give it to your mate (or oldest dependent) and keep a copy. Then mark your calendar to update in a year. This is a big step in the process of being a "good and faithful steward".

8. **Record Financial & Other Breakthroughs. Be ready to give God the Glory during Next Week's Sharing Time.**

BREAKTHROUGHS!

FINANCIAL FREEDOM COURSE – RECORD YOUR WEEKLY TESTIMONIES

NAME: ______________________________ & ______________________________

DATE: MONEY, CAREER, GIFTS/INHERITANCE, & OTHER

_____ ____

_____ ____

_____ ____

_____ ____

_____ ____

_____ ____

_____ ____

CHAPTER 4
(WEEK 4)

"Let no debt remain outstanding, except the continuing debt to love one another, for he who loves his fellowman has fulfilled the law."
Romans 13:8 (NIV)

"Praise the Lord, O my soul, and forget not all His benefits...who redeems your life from the pit...who satisfies your desires with good things so that your youth is renewed like the eagle's."
Quotes taken from Psalm 103, Verses 2-5 (NIV)

Freedom From Debt Action Plan

LEADER'S NOTES – WEEKLY PROTOCOL

- Praise Song – A great way to start!
  Suggest Typed Lyrics and Upbeat Music

- Prayer – Led by a Leader or LIT
  Recommend Group Holding Hands

- Spiritual Warfare – in Jesus' mighty name

- Homework Sharing – Normally led by LITs
  Led by Leaders if LITs are Teaching this Week
  Time Control and Equal Sharing are Keys

- Sharing of Weekly Breakthroughs
  Brief but Builds Hope – Celebrate!

- Weekly Offering Time – Opportunity to Sow
  Have a Focus Group Member Pray First
  Put Faith into Action!

- 10 Minute Break
  Beverages & Restroom

- Call Group Together

- Weekly Lesson
  Taught by Leaders or LITs

- Homework Preview

- Dismiss in Prayer – Holding Hands
  Entire Session Should Average 2 to 2 ½ Hours

- Leaders and LITs Complete Weekly Report

CHAPTER 4 (WEEK 4)
FREEDOM FROM DEBT ACTION PLAN

REVIEW CHAPTER 3 – "Freedom From Debt Principles"

In chapter 3, you learned about a Godly paradigm shift (from the world's acceptance of debt as okay to a heavenly view with no debt bondage).

We know that debt is not sin, but failure to repay it is. We hope you will learn to hate debt and refuse to stay in the hideous cycle of debt bondage!

I. GET YOUR HEART RIGHT

Ask the Holy Spirit to help you have the right attitude so you can break out of the bondage of debt.

- **PRAY** (together if married) and ask God for wisdom. Believe that our Father in Heaven will give you good gifts (good answers) if you ask *(Matthew 7:11).*

- **BE TRANSPARENT ABOUT LIFE PATTERNS** that have led you to a destructive debt cycle. Ask God to deliver you and your family from all poverty curses.

  1. <u>With Christ in our lives we all have the power and the responsibility to renew our minds</u>.

  2. Often Christians accept a poverty mentality as a sign of spirituality. This is not God's plan, so break off that curse of poverty!

- **BE QUICK TO REPENT** over past abuses and lack of financial discipline. God already knows all about them and you should know He will forgive you if you admit and repent. In the Lord's Prayer, we are commanded to forgive each other. This is not an option but a direct command. So, forgive yourself (and your mate if married). Failure to forgive others or yourself holds you in debt. God wants His people free!

- **DARE TO DREAM** of financial freedom. Declare your vision openly. As *Habakkuk 2:2* instructs: *"... write the revelation and make it plain... "* (NIV). Remember, *Proverbs 29:18* tells us that *"where there is no vision, the people perish... " (KJV).*

- **GET INTO AGREEMENT WITH GOD'S WORD.** There is power in agreement. So, couples need to agree in prayer, and seek a freedom from debt plan. Non-married group members are encouraged to find a Godly partner, who shares their financial freedom goals. Pray in agreement and cover each other with prayer and spiritual warfare. *Matthew 18:19 — "Again, I tell you that if two of you on earth agree about anything you ask for, it will be done for you by my Father in heaven."* (NIV) This scripture is a promise from Jesus to us.

➢ **BE COURAGEOUS!** Your new biblical view of debt and credit will not be accepted by the world. The world is caught up in consumerism and focused on self-satisfaction. *1 John 2:16-17 — "For everything in the world — the cravings of sinful man, the lust of the eyes and the boasting of what he has and does — comes not from the Father but from the world. The world and its desires pass away, but the man who does the will of God lives forever." (NIV)*

FOR MARRIED COUPLES

You should always support each other and avoid playing the guilt and blame game. Satan wants couples to argue over financial problems. Ask God for grace for you and for your mate.

God assigned roles for both, the husband and the wife. Read *1 Peter 3:1-7* (together and out loud) and ask the Holy Spirit to help each of you assume your proper role. Seek and value your spouse's counsel.

II. FIRST STEPS

If you are a covenant Christian with a debt problem and you are willing to repent, then you are clearly ready to develop a get out of debt plan. Here are some key steps.

➢ **HONOR GOD WITH YOUR GIVING AND INVITE HIM TO BE PART OF ALL YOUR PLANS.** We have established that God owns everything and He is the only source of increase *(see Psalm 50:10-11 and Deuteronomy 8:18.)*. Therefore, your debt repayment plan must not exclude what His word says pertaining to the acts of tithing, freewill offering and alms. If you want God to bless your plan, you must honor him with your giving.

➢ **WHERE ARE YOU NOW?** Many people do not have a true picture of their debt status. A ***Debt Repayment Schedule*** form makes it easy to list all your current debts. Knowing your financial situation will relieve considerable stress, and that is a good start.

➢ **BOB AND MARY'S DEBTS – EXAMPLE #1.** Let's take a look at our fictional couple, Bob and Mary Jones. Before they enrolled in a focus group, Bob and Mary obtained their financial records in order to complete the ***Debt Repayment Schedule*** form shown in example # 1.

IMPORTANT NOTE

The *Debt Repayment Schedule* should include all debts with the exception of the primary home mortgage. The mortgage obligation is a debt and must be included as a liability when you complete the *Inventory Your Liabilities* form. However, the mortgage payment is not included on this form because it will be included in the monthly housing expense category when you complete the *Living Expenses* form.

DEBT REPAYMENT SCHEDULE

NAME(S): Bob and Mary Jones (Example #1)
DATE: June 30, 2000

	LENDER	$ BALANCE	$ MONTHLY PAYMENT	INT. %	REMAINING PAYMENTS	PAY-OFF DATE
1	Credit Card A	4,000	67	18.0	300	6/30/2025
2	Credit Card B	2,000	33	18.0	300	6/30/2025
3	Car Loan	7,000	307	12.0	36	6/30/2003
4	Parent's Loan	3,000	50	0.0	60	6/30/2005
5						
6						
7						
8						
9						
10						
11						
12						
13						
14						
15						
TOTAL:		$16,000	$457			

NOTE ON USING DEBT REPAYMENT SCHEDULE:
This form should include all debts with the exception of a primary home mortgage. The mortgage obligation is a debt and must be included as a liability when you complete the ***List Your Liabilities*** form. However, the mortgage payment is not included on this form because it will be included in the monthly housing expense category when you complete the ***Estimated Monthly Living Expenses*** form.

Bob and Mary have four separate debts, not including their home mortgage. The schedule shows a current balance of $4,000 for Credit Card A, with minimum monthly payments of $67 and an interest rate of 18%. There are 300 monthly payments left (25 years), if they make only the minimum payment (assuming no new charges are incurred).

Credit Card B has a $2,000 balance, monthly payments of $33 and an interest rate of 18%. This card will also be paid off in 300 payments if no additional charges are incurred.

The Jones' also have a car loan for $7,000 at 12%, and there are 36 remaining monthly payments of $307 each.

Their parents loaned them $3,000 at zero percent interest. There are 60 payments left at $50 per month.

At the bottom of their ***Debt Repayment Schedule***, our fictional couple did the math. It indicated a total consumer debt of $16,000 with total monthly payments of $457. The blacked-out areas indicate spaces where columns are not to be totaled.

Your homework exercise will involve the completion of your own ***Debt Repayment Schedule***. Now you know how it is done, so let's move on and find out how to activate a debt repayment plan.

III. KEY ELEMENTS FOR A DEBT REPAYMENT PLAN TO WORK

Once the ***Debt Repayment Schedule*** is completed, you have a picture of: what is owed, to whom, at what interest rate, and for how long... assuming there are no new charges and assuming there is no extra or accelerated payments. Let's explore the elements necessary for a debt repayment plan to work.

- **UNDERSTANDING THE POSITIVE CASH FLOW MARGIN CONCEPT.** A positive cash flow situation exists when money is left over at the end of the month (after tithing, giving offerings and sowing alms, paying taxes, paying debt payments and accounting for all expense items). Workable repayment strategies are based on having enough money to meet the minimum obligations in your spending plan and using surplus money to attack debts. *(If there is no extra money, the spending plan must be carefully re-worked.)*

- **BOB AND MARY – EXAMPLE #1 MONTHLY CASH FLOW ANALYSIS.** Because the concept of a monthly cash flow margin is so vital to your debt repayment strategy, let us examine Bob and Mary's situation in example # 1. You will be working with these forms in Chapters five and six, so this review will be brief.

MONTHLY CASH FLOW ANALYSIS

Name(s): Bob & Mary Jones (Example #1)	**Date: June 30, 2000**	
Gross Income:		**$4,000**
Less Priority Expenses:		
A. Giving (tithes, offerings & alms)	$415	
B. Taxes (Payroll Records)	$750	
C. Debt (Total Repayments)	$457	
Total Priority Expenses: (-).		**($1,622)**
NET SPENDABLE INCOME: (Gross income less A, B, & C =)		**$2,378**
Monthly Living Expenses:		
A. Housing	$1,072	
B. Food	$500	
C. Clothing	$110	
D. Transportation	$286	
E. Entertainment/recreation	$308	
F. Medical	$120	
G. Insurance	$135	
H. Children	$90	
I. Gifts	$80	
J. Miscellaneous	$175	
TOTAL MONTHLY LIVING EXPENSES:		**$2,876**
Monthly Cash Flow Margin: (Net Spendable Income Minus Total (A-J) Living Expenses)		**($498)**
Your Commitments for Monthly Positive Cash Flow Margin:		
A. Savings	$	
B. Retirement	$	
C. Extra Debt Payment	$	
D. Additional Giving	$	
Total Commitments for + Cash Flow:		**$**
Uncommitted Monthly Cash Flow Margin:		**$**
Comments: There is a serious negative monthly cash flow margin. Immediate corrective action is needed to avoid further debt, and to reduce expenses.		

The top of the form is used to show the family's income less their priority expenses (giving, payroll taxes and debt repayments). The result is a *net spendable income* of $2,378 ($4,000 less $1,622).

The middle section of the form is used to recap the couple's *monthly living expenses*. There are ten categories labeled A through J. You will work with these in Chapter 5, so for now just note that the expenses total $2,876 per month.

Cash flow margin is determined by subtracting the total monthly living expenses of $2,876 from the couple's net spendable income of $2,378. Unfortunately, Bob and Mary quickly see that they have a negative cash flow of $498 each month. This is not good news, and it is impossible to execute a rapid debt repayment strategy when there is more month left at the end of the money.

➢ **GOOD NEWS – EXAMPLE #2 MONTHLY CASH FLOW ANALYSIS.** We do not want to get ahead of Chapters 5 and 6. However, we do need to take a peek at the Jones' situation (about one year after they completed the Financial Freedom in 7 Weeks Plus book and focus group).

MONTHLY CASH FLOW ANALYSIS		
Name(s): Bob & Mary Jones (Example #2)	**Date: August 31, 2001**	
Gross Income:		**$4,000**
Less Priority Expenses:		
A. Giving (Tithes & Offerings)	$415	
B. Taxes (Payroll Records)	$750	
C. Debt (Repayments)	$0	
Total Priority Expenses: (-)		**($1,165)**
NET SPENDABLE INCOME: (Gross income less A, B, & C =)		**$2,835**
Monthly Living Expenses:		
A. Housing	$1,052	
B. Food	$425	
C. Clothing	$95	
D. Transportation	$174	
E. Entertainment/recreation	$110	
F. Medical	$120	
G. Insurance	$35	
H. Children	$90	
I. Gifts	$46	
J. Miscellaneous	$110	
TOTAL MONTHLY LIVING EXPENSES:		**$2,257**
MONTHLY Cash Flow Margin: (Net Spendable Income Minus Total A-J Living Expenses)		**$578**
Your Commitments for Monthly Positive Cash Flow Margin:		
A. Savings	$100	
B. Retirement	$100	
C. Extra Debt Payment - on mortgage	$100	
D. Additional Giving	$50	
Total Commitments for + Cash Flow:		**$350**
Uncommitted Monthly Cash Flow Margin:		**$228**
Comments: Now that high interest debt has been eliminated, this family has a balanced spending plan and is en route to paying off the mortgage. They have $228 per month in uncommitted cash flow and have the freedom to re-work their spending plan as needed.		

The Jones had no change in income, giving or taxes. However, they sold assets and made other sacrifices to eliminate all consumer debt. As a result, their *net spendable income* is now $2,835.

They took separate actions, as a family, to reduce certain *monthly living expenses* and their A-J total is now $2,257. Therefore, it is no surprise that their *monthly cash flow margin* has gone from a negative $498 to a positive $578. Now, they are ideally positioned to make a number of excellent financial decisions, to include extra principal payments on their home mortgage.

Now let's return to the key elements needed for an effective debt repayment plan.

- **USE MONTHLY SURPLUS MONEY TO ATTACK DEBT.** A portion of the positive cash flow, or monthly surplus, should be prayerfully committed to paying down outstanding debt balances. Of course, the first extra monies should be used to bring any past due loans to current status.

- **COMMIT EXTRA INCOME TO DEBT REPAYMENT.** If a believer is sincere about his or her commitment to break out of the debt cycle, he or she should prayerfully consider committing a significant portion of any extra income to paying off loans early. This extra income includes raises, bonuses, inheritances and cash gifts.

DEBT REPAYMENT TIPS

1) Using some of your monthly surplus to attack the highest interest rate loans will have the biggest impact. By paying off an 18% interest-bearing credit card loan, you are making an 18% investment in your future.
2) Some financial advisors favor paying off loans with the smallest balance first. Apparently there is a sense of satisfaction in any debt paid in full. You decide.
3) Of course, while you are making extra payments on the targeted debts, it is essential that you make at least the minimum payments for all other debts on time.

- **AS YOU PAY OFF ONE DEBT, COMMIT MORE MONEY TO ANOTHER.** A key to rapid debt repayment is to agree that as one debt is paid off, the amount of that monthly payment is committed to paying off the next debt. When debt number two is paid in full, the amount you applied to debt # 1 and # 2 is applied totally against debt # 3, and so on until all debts are paid.

  If you have ever played with dominos, envision your credit cards tumbling over, one at a time, until they are all gone. Envision your paid-off credit cards tumbling over, as they are paid-off, cut-up, and the accounts are closed.

- **PRAY ABOUT CUTTING UP CARDS AS THEY ARE PAID-OFF.** If your household has been burdened with high interest credit card debt, we recommend that you pray about cutting up the cards as they are paid-off... or even before they are paid-off. Then, get a *paid in full* statement for your records. Rejoice and give thanks to the Lord for each small victory.

➢ **PRAY DAILY.** Reinforce your covenant with God and daily commit yourself to your debt repayment plan. Be prepared to do spiritual warfare by putting on the whole armor of God *(Ephesians 6:10-18).* Clearly, Ephesians tells us that our struggle is not against flesh and blood, but against the devil, who wants us in all types of bondage. *(If married, pray together.)*

> **Commit Your Plan To The Lord**
> As we see in *Psalm 103:4,* it is the Lord *"who redeems your life from destruction and crowns you with loving kindness and tender mercies, who satisfies your mouth with good things, so that your youth is renewed like the eagle's." (NKJ)*

IV. GO INTO ACTION

The debt repayment process allows you to start kicking the devil out of your finances!

➢ **CHANGE SPENDING HABITS IF NEEDED.** For some people, significant changes in spending habits must take place. In *Proverbs 25:28,* we see how God encourages self-control: *"Like a city whose walls are broken down is a man who lacks self control." (NIV)*

➢ **SELL-OFF NON-ESSENTIAL ASSETS.** Selling non-essential assets (such as a boat, extra vehicle, antique) may be an option. Ask the Holy Spirit for wisdom. *(If you are married, reach an agreement. Then turn any extra cash into accelerated debt payments.)* Once you escape debt bondage, you can agree to treat yourselves to certain nice items. *(In example # 2, Bob and Mary sold assets to drastically reduce debt.)*

➢ **BE WARY OF DEBT CONSOLIDATION LOANS AND HOME EQUITY LOANS.** These are actually second mortgages on your home! You will generally do better with your own debt repayment plan. Unfortunately, these consolidation loans or home equity loans often become new debt and they do not help address core problems.

Wives tend to be more security conscious than husbands. Men are generally more willing to take risk. Any loan that jeopardizes the equity in a home can be a serious cause of concern to a wife, and it should concern all homeowners.

➢ **ATTACK ROOT CAUSES OF DEBT.** It is paramount that you attack the root cause of the debt and/or overspending problem. If the root cause is not corrected, and serious behavior changes are not implemented, any "bailout loan" plan will just allow the problem to get worse.

➢ **COMMUNICATE WITH CREDITORS.** Communication with creditors is essential regarding all past due debts. *Proverbs 15:1* provides wisdom regarding our communications with creditors: *"A gentle answer turns away wrath, but a harsh word stirs up anger." (NIV)*

FOR MARRIED COUPLES

The husband has responsibilities as the head of the household and he should generally be the one to speak with creditors. It is unfair to dump this responsibility on the wife just because she may be the one at home when the creditor calls. *Ephesians 5:23* is one of many scriptures defining the husband's role as head of the family: *"For the husband is the head of the wife, even as Christ is the head of the church, and He is the savior of the body." (KJV)*

V. BANKRUPTCY

The legal system in America provides for several types of personal and business bankruptcies. What does bankruptcy mean for covenant Christians?

- **LEGAL PROTECTION.** In many cases, declaring bankruptcy may provide legal protection from creditors, temporarily or permanently.

- **GOD EXPECTS US TO REPAY.** If we owe money to someone (including a company or the government) for an unpaid bill, then God expects us to repay the debt (regardless of all the bankruptcy laws that exist). *Psalm 37:21 —"The wicked borrows and does not pay back…"* (NAS)

- **DECLARING BANKRUPTCY IS NOT A SIN.** However, we should purpose in our hearts to repay every debt. The only exception would be if the creditor actually releases you from the debt.

VI. SUMMARY

In chapter 3, you learned that God does not want His people in bondage to debt. The combination of high compound interest rates and credit card abuse is drowning many Christians and keeping them from achieving the destiny God has planned.

In this chapter, you studied the concept of developing a positive monthly cash flow margin and learned how to utilize this monthly cash surplus for rapid debt repayment.

In chapters 5 and 6, you will see how easy it is to develop your own flexible *spending plan*, so your situation will resemble Bob and Mary's, as reflected in example # 2.

- **FAITH & TRUST ARE REQUIRED.** Committing to your new debt repayment plan, and making sacrifices, requires faith and trust in God. If you have reached this point in the course prayerfully and in agreement, then you are definitely ready to use the powerful faith spoken in *Hebrews 11:1 "Now faith is the assurance (the confirmation; the title deed) of the things (we) hope for, being the proof of things (we) do not see and the conviction of their reality — faith perceiving as real fact what is not revealed to the senses." (Amplified)*

- **PUT YOUR PLAN INTO ACTION!** Go for it! And may God take you out of debt's bondage and bring you into financial freedom. By God's grace, smash the debt cycle. Commit to breaking the pattern of buying on easy payment terms. Show the world you have the discipline to pay for what you need, to tithe the first fruits of your increase, to give freewill offerings, to sow alms biblically, and to save for emergencies and for the future.

> **LEADERS' NOTE –** Now is the time to preview this week's homework. Close this session with a strong prayer asking the Holy Spirit to grant grace to each participant in changing their bad habit patterns. Get the group to join in this act of spiritual warfare.

CHAPTER 4 (WEEK 4) HOMEWORK

FREEDOM FROM DEBT ACTION PLAN

1. **Pray Hard.** You are about to experience a huge breakthrough as you move toward financial victory. Satan wants you in debt bondage because it leads to strife and bitterness. So, start this homework session by praying hard to reinforce your covenant with God. Remember to do spiritual warfare before going forward. *(Note: You will want to do this on a daily basis, not just at this homework session.)*

2. **Record any special information** you gained from your prayer and warfare session... include revelations or new directions.

   ____

   ____

   ____

3. **Complete the debt repayment schedule form** from this week's teaching. Use a Full Size Form (chapter 15), like the miniature version shown below.

DEBT REPAYMENT SCHEDULE

NAME(S): ______________________________

DATE: ______________________________

	LENDER	$ BALANCE	$ MONTHLY PAYMENT	INT. %	REMAINING PAYMENTS	PAY-OFF DATE
1						
2						
3						
4						
5						
6						
7						
8						
9						
10						
11						
12						
13						
14						
15						
TOTAL:						

NOTE ON USING DEBT REPAYMENT SCHEDULE:
This form should include all debts with the exception of a primary home mortgage. The mortgage obligation is a debt and must be included as a liability when you complete the ***List Your Liabilities*** form. However, the mortgage payment is not included on this form because it will be included in the monthly housing expense category when you complete the ***Estimated Monthly Living Expenses*** form. **If your list of debts exceeds the 15 spaces given, make extra pages. Do not despair, you are on the road to Financial Freedom.**

a. Make six extra copies of the form for future use. The blank forms are located in chapter 15.

b. List each debt you owe using the spaces provided. If you need more space, use two or more forms. We recommend you list the loans, from top to bottom, with the highest interest rate at the top and the rest of the debts in descending order. If you do not have all the information needed, call each lender, as they are obligated to inform you of this information. *(Pray before calling to cut through phone delays. Be persistent. Do not wait to start making these calls!)*

c. Remember not to include a primary home mortgage payment on the ***Debt Repayment Schedule***. It is a debt and our long-range goal should be to pay it off! However, the mortgage payment will be included as one of the monthly housing expense items on the ***Living Expenses*** form you will complete in the *Spending Plan* section of this course.

d. For couples with serious debt challenges, a good short-term goal strategy should be to keep car and mortgage payments current while focusing attention on reducing and eliminating all higher interest debt.

e. Do the math to total the appropriate columns for balances and monthly payments.

f. Complete the name and date blanks and keep this form as a key-working document.

g. Be prepared to discuss your progress during next week's homework sharing time (no specifics need to be discussed).

4. **Take a few minutes to celebrate!** Just by completing this debt repayment schedule you have leaped ahead of the majority of people with debt problems because most of them do not have an accurate picture of their debt status. Now you do, and you have a powerful tool to use in your debt repayment strategy.

5. **Commit prayerfully to a rapid debt repayment plan.** *(For couples who want to achieve success, both spouses must be in complete agreement. Take time to discuss what it will take to be free from debt.)*

a. All loan payments must be kept current.

b. No new debt is to be incurred.

c. The Spending Plan must be worked and/or re-worked to ensure that there is some positive cash flow at the end of the month. You will develop these forms in the coming weeks.

d. Commit to using a set minimum portion of your positive cash flow to make extra payments against the principal balance on your highest interest loan.

e. Commit to using a portion of unexpected increases in income (raises, tax refunds, gifts) to make extra loan principal payments.

f. Once a targeted loan is paid in full, document your records and close that account. If it is a credit card account, we recommend you destroy the card.

g. Commit to using the extra money that was used to make the previous (now paid-off) loan, or loans, to pay down the principal of the next highest interest loan. Then retire that loan and close that account.

h. Commit to repeating this process until all loans are paid off. This strategy takes discipline and sacrifice, but the outcome of true financial freedom is well worth the effort.

6. **Write a commitment statement.** A successful debt repayment plan takes time. In this homework session, you may only be able to establish what your present situation is, then agree on an action plan for the future. We encourage you to write out a statement about your commitment to avoid new debt and to pay-off existing debt. You are encouraged to sign and date your statement to reinforce your commitment to (future) debt free living.

____

____

____

____

Signed: ________________ & ________________ Date: ________________

7. **Record Your Breakthroughs for this week and share them during homework sharing time.**

BREAKTHROUGHS!

FINANCIAL FREEDOM COURSE - RECORD YOUR WEEKLY TESTIMONIES

NAME: ________________________ & ________________________

DATE:	MONEY, CAREER, GIFTS/INHERITANCE, & OTHER

CHAPTER 5

(WEEK 5)

"For which of you, intending to build a tower, does not sit down first and count the cost, whether he has enough to finish it— lest, after he has laid the foundation, and is not able to finish, all who see it begin to mock him, saying, 'This man began to build and was not able to finish'."
Luke 14:28-30 (NKJ)

Developing A Flexible Spending Plan: Part 1

LEADER'S NOTES – WEEKLY PROTOCOL

- Praise Song – A great way to start!
  Suggest Typed Lyrics and Upbeat Music

- Prayer – Led by a Leader or LIT
  Recommend Group Holding Hands

- Spiritual Warfare – in Jesus' mighty name

- Homework Sharing – Normally led by LITs
  Led by Leaders if LITs are Teaching this Week
  Time Control and Equal Sharing are Keys

- Sharing of Weekly Breakthroughs
  Brief but Builds Hope – Celebrate!

- Weekly Offering Time – Opportunity to Sow
  Have a Focus Group Member Pray First
  Put Faith into Action!

- 10 Minute Break
  Beverages & Restroom

- Call Group Together

- Weekly Lesson
  Taught by Leaders or LITs

- Homework Preview

- Dismiss in Prayer – Holding Hands
  Entire Session Should Average 2 to 2 ½ Hours

- Leaders and LITs Complete Weekly Report

CHAPTER 5 (WEEK 5)
DEVELOPING A FLEXIBLE SPENDING PLAN: PART 1

SPENDING PLAN OVERVIEW

By developing and using a *spending plan*, you will take a bite out of stress. Instead of feeling out of control, you will gain tremendous freedom as you use the Biblical principles and easy-to-use forms provided in this section.

This week, we will study example # 1 *(Bob and Mary's finances before they completed this course).* Next week, we will look at example # 2 and observe the positive changes made by Bob, Mary and their family. Example # 2 forms were completed approximately one full year after Bob and Mary faithfully completed the course. *Proverbs 16:3 tells us "Commit to the Lord whatever you do and your plans will succeed." (NIV)*

Your homework for this week will be to start filling out your own set of *spending plan* forms. Good news: the homework assignment will be spread over a two-week period and you have two examples to guide you. So let's get started on the exciting road to financial freedom.

I. WHAT IS A SPENDING PLAN?

- **IT IS NOT A BUDGET** imposed by others. It is developed with the help of wise counsel *(and for couples, with the input of both husband and wife).* The *spending plan* includes the establishment of goals and priorities (with the freedom to make adjustments). Essentially, it puts you in control.

- **IT IS FLEXIBLE.** Because the plan is developed by you, there is room for reasonable flexibility as conditions change.

- **IT REFLECTS YOUR PRIORITIES.** Imagine standing at heaven's gates being asked to toss your checkbook through the door of heaven for thorough examination, what would your check stubs show? Good stewardship of the resources that God had given you? In addition, would your stubs reflect godly priorities? The *spending plan* can help you answer these key questions with a big YES!

- **IT IS COMPREHENSIVE.** The *spending plan* will include your: income, biblical giving, all spending categories, and savings. In addition, it will provide a true picture of your assets, liabilities, net worth, and monthly cash flow. It sounds complex, but in actuality it is a real simple process.

FOR MARRIED COUPLES

As you develop and use this planning process, you <u>will</u> gain control over the very area that plagues so many marriages...finances. Control over your finances will eliminate stress and the tendency to argue or worry about finances. *Philippians 4:6* warns us "to be anxious for nothing."

II. SPENDING PLAN SCRIPTURES

Do Christians even need to set goals, control spending, and save money? Or can we just live for today and trust God for what we need?

- **PROVERBS 21:5** — *"The plans of the diligent lead to profit as surely as haste leads to poverty." (NIV)*
- **PROVERBS 27:23** — *"Be sure you know the condition of your flocks, give careful attention to your herds..." (NIV)* This scripture alerts us to always know the financial, physical and spiritual condition of our family.
- **MATTHEW 25:21** (*the parable of the talents*) — the Lord commended the servant for his faithfulness over little and rewarded him greatly by putting him in charge of much more.
- **PROVERBS 13:18** — *"He who ignores discipline comes to poverty and shame, but whoever heeds correction is honored." (NIV)* Yes the process will take discipline and commitment, but that is clearly God's will.
- **PROVERBS 6:6-8** — We are clearly instructed to gain wisdom about <u>saving</u>, through observing the ant that plans for the winter by storing extra food from the harvest.

GOOD NEWS!

You have already completed your written goals forms!
Now, the development of a complete and flexible *spending plan* will get you on the road to achieving those goals.

III. A LOOK AT EXAMPLE #1

For many of you, this may be the very first time you have developed a comprehensive financial plan. Therefore, we will look at two examples utilizing Bob and Mary Jones. The Jones have two children. In addition, they are buying a home. Unfortunately, they incurred unplanned debt as a result of buying things on credit. Bob is the sole income earner. This week we will study example # 1. Next week, we will look carefully at the corrective measures taken in example # 2 by Bob and Mary.

Example # 1 is dated June 30, 2000 and it reflects Bob & Mary's financial status before they completed the Financial Freedom in 7 Weeks Plus *focus group*. Prior to filling out these forms, they really did not know their financial status. They did not know why there was never enough money left at the end of the month to meet all obligations, or why they always needed to increase debt just to keep running the household.

Now, please look at the seven different forms labeled example # 1. Your course leaders will answer questions. Please try to understand all the numbers. *(If you are married, do not just defer the number crunching to the one who keeps the family's books. For this plan to work, both spouses need to understand and agree on how God's resources will be managed.)*

- **PROJECTED INCOME AND BIBLICAL GIVING FORM** – Bob earns a salary of $4,000 per month or $48,000 per year. Bob and Mary have projected (planned) to give $365 per month ($350 to their church, $10 to missions and $5 to United Way) on a regular basis, plus some non-monthly charitable giving which amounts to an additional $600 during the year. On an average monthly basis they plan to give a total of $415 per month.

  Note: They had not yet learned about tithing. So, their church-related giving falls short of the ten percent first fruit tithe.

LEADERS' NOTE – Walk the group through the process of how Bob and Mary completed the 5 columns. At the bottom, there is a "note on using this form" that should be read. It states: *"This form will help you arrive at an average monthly amount which is crucial for your* **spending plan** *and cash flow management. Record the monthly amount in the first column and then multiply it by 12 months for a yearly subtotal. In the third column, record amounts that do not occur every month. Add columns 2 and 3 together to get the total annual amount for column 4. Finally, divide the total annual amount by 12 to get the average monthly amount. Do this for each line item."*

Encourage participants to get in the habit of completing all appropriate columns. It may help to put a dash in the columns that do not apply.

PROJECTED INCOME AND BIBLICAL GIVING

(Example #1 - Before Course)

NAME(S): Bob and Mary Jones

Date: June 30, 2000

Projected Income

	Amount Paid Monthly	Mo. x 12 =Subtotal for Yr.	Amount Paid Other Than Monthly	Total Annual Amount	Total Annual Amt. Div. by 12 = Avg. Mo. Amt.
Sources:					
Gross wages: husband	$4,000	$48,000		$48,000	$4,000
Gross wages: wife					
Dividends					
Interest					
Rents (cash flow)					
Business Income/"Increase"					
Pensions & annuities					
Other					
TOTAL GROSS INCOME:	**$4,000**	**$48,000**		**$48,000**	**$4,000**

Projected Giving

	Organization	Amount Paid Monthly	Mo. x 12 =Subtotal for Yr.	Amount Paid Other than Monthly	Total Annual Amount	Total Annual Amt. Div. by 12 = Avg. Mo. Amt.
10% Tithe	Church	$350	$4,200		$4,200	$350
Freewill Offerings	Missions	$10	$120		$120	$10
Alms						
Other	Misc. Charities			$600	$600	$50
Other	United Way	$5	$60		$60	$5
Other						
TOTAL GIVING:		**$365**	**$4,380**	**$600**	**$4,980**	**$415**

Once the income is determined, the next step is to determine where it goes. Begin with giving. Project your giving for the year by considering each organization you support. This can be from pledges, percentages of income, past giving, or specific giving goals. You may want to check your actual giving to date and then project what you plan to give for the rest of the year.

NOTE ON USING THIS FORM: This form will help you arrive at an average monthly amount which is crucial for your spending plan and cash flow management. Record the monthly amount in the first column and then multiply by 12 months for a yearly subtotal. In the third column, record amounts that do not occur every month. Add columns 2 and 3 together to get the total annual amount for column 4. Finally, divide the total annual amount by 12 to get the average monthly amount. Do this for each line item.

➢ **LIST YOUR ASSETS FORM** – Bob and Mary's total assets of $173,500 include liquid assets of $10,500 plus $163,000 in non-liquid assets.

LIST YOUR ASSETS		
TYPES OF ASSETS (Example #1)		
1 . Liquid Assets (Easily Converted to Cash)		
Cash on Hand	$200	
Checking Account Balance	$1,800	
Money market funds		
CDs (% interest rate)		
Savings (% interest rate)	$5,000	
Stocks & Bonds		
Life insurance cash values	$3,500	
Other (Describe)		
TOTAL Liquid Assets:		**$10,500**
2. Non-liquid Assets		
Home (market value)	$75,000	
Land (market value)	$25,000	
Net Worth (Value) of Business		
Real Estate investments (Not Home)		
Jet Ski, Camper, RV, Boats, etc.	$10,000	
Automobiles at market value	$20,000	
Furniture & personal property (conservative market value)	$10,000	
Valuable Collections (stamps, coins,etc.)	$3,000	
Retirement Funds Balance	$20,000	
Funds due from others (Receivables)		
Other (Describe)		
Other (Describe)		
TOTAL Non-liquid Assets		**$163,000**
3. Total Assets (1 & 2)		**$173,500**
Name(s): Bob & Mary Jones (Example #1)		
Date of Completion: June 30, 2000		

➤ **DEBT REPAYMENT SCHEDULE** – Bob and Mary's ***Debt Repayment Schedule*** includes four loans with their respective monthly payments. Note that their home mortgage payment is not included on the form because it is included as a monthly housing expense item. Their monthly debt payments amount to $457.

DEBT REPAYMENT SCHEDULE

NAME(S): Bob and Mary Jones (Example #1)

DATE: June 30, 2000

	LENDER	$ BALANCE	$ MONTHLY PAYMENT	INT. %	REMAINING PAYMENTS	PAY-OFF DATE
1	Credit Card A	4,000	67	18.0	300	6/30/2025
2	Credit Card B	2,000	33	18.0	300	6/30/2025
3	Car Loan	7,000	307	12.0	36	6/30/2003
4	Parent's Loan	3,000	50	0.0	60	6/30/2005
5						
6						
7						
8						
9						
10						
11						
12						
13						
14						
15						
TOTAL:		$16,000	$457			

NOTE ON USING DEBT REPAYMENT SCHEDULE:
This form should include all debts with the exception of a primary home mortgage. The mortgage obligation is a debt and must be included as a liability when you complete the ***List Your Liabilities*** form. However, the mortgage payment is not included on this form because it will be included in the monthly housing expense category when you complete the ***Estimated Monthly Living Expenses*** form.

➢ **LIST YOUR LIABILITIES FORM** — The form below shows a total of five debts (two high-interest credit card debts and a sizable car loan). Four of these debts were recorded directly from their ***Debt Repayment Schedule***, and their mortgage was added so that all indebtedness was included. The monthly drain of loan payments totals $1,132 (much too high based on the family income).

LIST YOUR LIABILITIES
(Example #1)

LENDER (CREDITOR):	BALANCE DUE:	INTEREST RATE %	PAYMENT SCHEDULE	
			PER MONTH:	UNTIL (MO./YR.):
1. Credit Card A	$4,000	18.00%	$67	6/30/2025
2. Credit Card B	$2,000	18.00%	$33	6/30/2025
3. Car Loan	$7,000	12.00%	$307	6/30/2003
4. Mortgage	$80,000	9.00%	$675	6/30/2025
5. Parent's Loan	$3,000	0.00%	$50	6/30/2005
6.				
7.				
8.				
9.				
10.				
11.				
12.				
13.				
14.				
15.				
16.				
17.				
18.				
19.				
20.				
21.				
22.				
23.				
TOTALS:	$96,000		$1,132.00	

NAME(S): Bob & Mary Jones (Example #1)

DATE COMPLETED: June 30, 2000

Note: This form should include all debts previously listed on the "*Debt Repayment Schedule*", and should also include the home mortgage.

➢ **BALANCE SHEET & NET WORTH STATEMENT** – The form below actually made Bob and Mary feel pretty good because they have a positive net worth of $77,500. This is good news because a great many American families have a negative net worth (which means they owe more than they own). Sadly, as we will soon see, the Jones family is not financially strong despite their positive net worth.

BALANCE SHEET AND NET WORTH STATEMENT (Example #1)

A. Assets

Liquid Assets:	$10,500	
Non-liquid Assets:	$163,000	
Total Assets:		**$173,500**

B. Less: Total Liabilities: (-) **(96,000)**

C. Net Worth: (Total Assets - Total Liabilities) **$77,500**

Name(s): Bob & Mary Jones (Example #1)

Date Completed: June 30, 2000

Comments:

Note on using this form: *Complete this form using data from your, recently completed,* ***List Your Assets*** *and* ***List Your Liabilities*** *forms. Then, subtract* ***total liabilities*** *from* ***total assets*** *, and record your NET WORTH.*

➤ **ESTIMATED MONTHLY LIVING EXPENSES FORM** – Filling out this form took Bob and Mary a significant amount of time to complete because they had to search for check records and credit card receipts. The results are projected on this 3-page form with the average monthly amounts for each of the ten expense categories. ***(Note: please start pulling your records together so you can complete your living expense estimates.)***

Since some expense items may not occur monthly (like insurance or property tax payments), you will need to arrive at an average for those monthly expenses. Two forms (***Projected Income and Biblical Giving*** and ***Living Expenses***) have been developed to assist you in this process. Both of the forms include a "note on using this form" to walk you through the five-column calculation process.

You will want to take a few minutes to see how this couple was spending their money. This is just an example, but it is fairly representative of how easy it is to overspend in each of the ten major categories. These situations typically get even worse where record keeping is very lax.

Look at Bob & Mary's housing expenses (category A). They have regular monthly expenses which add up to $905. They also have a total of $2,000 in non-monthly expenses per year. So, they multiplied $905 by 12 to get a subtotal of $10,860 for column two. Then they added the $2,000 to the subtotal, for a yearly total housing estimate of $12,860. By dividing the $12,860 by 12 months, they arrived at $1,072 as an average monthly total of all projected housing expenses in column five (far right).

ESTIMATED MONTHLY LIVING EXPENSES

(3 Page Form - Example #1)

EXAMPLE #1 (Page 1 of 3)	**Amount Paid Monthly**	**Mo. x 12 = Subtotal for Yr.**	**Amount Paid Other Than Monthly**	**Total Annual Amount**	**Total Annual Amt. Div. by 12 = Avg. Mo. Amt.**
A. Housing					
Mortgage or Rent Payment	$675	$8,100		$8,100	$675
Insurance for Home			$500	$500	$42
Property taxes (not in House Pmt.)			$1,500	$1,500	$125
Electricity	$60	$720		$720	$60
Heating	$50	$600		$600	$50
Water	$25	$300		$300	$25
Garbage Collection					
Telephone	$50	$600		$600	$50
Cleaning Services					
Repairs/maintenance	$35	$420		$420	$35
Improvements & Furnishings					
Supplies for Home	$10	$120		$120	$10
Other					
TOTAL HOUSING EXPENSES	**$905**	**$10,860**	**$2,000**	**$12,860**	**$1,072**
B. Food	**$500**	**$6,000**		**$6,000**	**$500**
C. Clothing					
Husband	$25	$300		$300	$25
Wife	$35	$420		$420	$35
Children	$50	$600		$600	$50
TOTAL CLOTHING	**$110**	**$1,320**		**$1,320**	**$110**
D. Transportation					
Auto Insurance			$600	$600	$50
Gas & Oil & Filters	$200	$2,400		$2,400	$200
Repairs/Maintenance	$24	$288		$288	$24
Parking	$12	$144		$144	$12
Bus/Train/Subway					
Other					
TOTAL TRANSPORTATION	**$236**	**$2,832**	**$600**	**$3,432**	**$286**

Living Expenses Form (Pg. 2 of 3) Example #1	Amount Paid Monthly	Mo. x 12 = Subtotal for Yr.	Amount Paid Other Than Monthly	Total Annual Amount	Total Annual Amt. Div. by 12 = Avg. Mo. Amt.
E. Entertainment/Recreation:					
Dining Out	$50	$600		$600	$50
Childcare	$15	$180		$180	$15
Newspapers/cable/magazines	$20	$240		$240	$20
Vacation			$2,500	$2,500	$208
Club Dues/Fees					
Classes/Courses/Activities					
Other	$15	$180		$180	$15
TOTAL ENTERTAINMENT:	**$100**	**$1,200**	**$2,500**	**$3,700**	**$308**
F. Medical Expenses					
Medical/Health Insurance	$50	$600		$600	$50
Doctors	$50	$600		$600	$50
Dentists	$10	$120		$120	$10
Drugs	$10	$120		$120	$10
TOTAL MEDICAL:	**$120**	**$1,440**		**$1,440**	**$120**
G. Insurance					
Life (All Family Members)	$135	$1,620		$1,620	$135
Disability					
Other					
TOTAL INSURANCE:	**$135**	**$1,620**		**$1,620**	**$135**
H. Children:					
School lunches	$35	$420		$420	$35
Allowances	$30	$360		$360	$30
School Tuition					
Lessons/Special Fees/Dues	$25	$300		$300	$25
Other					
TOTAL CHILDREN:	**$90**	**$1,080**		**$1,080**	**$90**
I. Gifts/Occasions:					
Christmas			$650	$650	$54
Birthdays			$200	$200	$17
Anniversary			$50	$50	$4
Holidays other than Christmas					
Other			$50	$50	$5
TOTAL GIFTS:			**$950**	**$950**	**$80**

Living Expenses Form (Pg. 3 of 3) Example #1	Amount Paid Monthly	Mo. x 12 = Subtotal for Yr.	Amount Paid Other Than Monthly	Total Annual Amount	Total Annual Amt. Div. by 12 = Avg. Mo. Amt.
J. Miscellaneous					
Toiletries	$20	$240		$240	$20
Husband: lunches, etc.	$55	$660		$660	$55
Wife: lunches, etc.	$35	$420		$420	$35
Dry cleaning/laundry	$35	$420		$420	$35
Pet care (medical/tags/food)					
Beauty/barber	$30	$360		$360	$30
Other					
Other					
TOTAL MISCELLANEOUS:	**$175**	**$2,100**		**$2,100**	**$175**
TOTAL LIVING EXPENSES	**$2,371**	**$28,452**	**$6,050**	**$34,502**	**$2,876**

Name(s): Bob & Mary Jones (Example #1)

Date Completed: June 30, 2000

Conclusions or Comments: This was Bob & Mary's first time to estimate monthly living expenses. They were surprised at some categories and will adjust in Example #2.

NOTE ON USING THIS FORM: This form will help you arrive at an average monthly amount which is crucial for your spending plan and cash flow management. Record the monthly amount in the first column and then multiply by 12 months for a yearly subtotal. In the third column, record amounts that do not occur every month. Add columns 2 and 3 together to get the total annual amount for column 4. Finally, divide the total annual amount by 12 to get the average monthly amount. Do this for each line item (A-J). Add the ten monthly average expense categories (A-J) to arrive at your estimated monthly total living expenses.

Several expenses do not occur monthly, but must be planned for, such as: auto insurance, most gift categories, and home or auto repairs. It is important that these items be placed in the column labeled "Amount Paid Other Than Monthly". In Chapter 7, you will learn how to reserve for these in a "Freedom Account".

Please use pencil and no decimal points. Remember, these are your **best estimates** for an average month. You will learn to adjust and correct, as you use this form several times.

LEADERS' NOTE – For many people, using the ***Living Expenses*** form may be a new experience. Take time to allow class members to study the form. Be willing to take a few clarification-type questions. The goal is: by the end of week six, all group members should have a good grasp of the *spending plan* process and how the numbers flow. (It will make sense, as the group works with their own numbers. The examples will help.)

MONTHLY CASH FLOW ANALYSIS — Here we see a projection of Bob and Mary's monthly cash flow. Since bills need to be handled at least monthly, it is essential that people project cash flow on a monthly basis, not annually.

MONTHLY CASH FLOW ANALYSIS

Name(s): Bob & Mary Jones (Example #1)	**Date: June 30, 2000**	
Gross Income:		**$4,000**
Less Priority Expenses:		
A. Giving (tithes, offerings & alms)	$415	
B. Taxes (Payroll Records)	$750	
C. Debt (Total Repayments)	$457	
Total Priority Expenses: (-)		**($1,622)**
NET SPENDABLE INCOME: (Gross income less A, B, & C =)		**$2,378**
Monthly Living Expenses:		
A. Housing	$1,072	
B. Food	$500	
C. Clothing	$110	
D. Transportation	$286	
E. Entertainment/recreation	$308	
F. Medical	$120	
G. Insurance	$135	
H. Children	$90	
I. Gifts	$80	
J. Miscellaneous	$175	
TOTAL MONTHLY LIVING EXPENSES:		**$2,876**
Monthly Cash Flow Margin: (Net Spendable Income Minus Total (A-J) Living Expenses)		**($498)**
Your Commitments for Monthly Positive Cash Flow Margin:		
A. Savings	$	
B. Retirement	$	
C. Extra Debt Payment	$	
D. Additional Giving	$	
Total Commitments for + Cash Flow:		$
Uncommitted Monthly Cash Flow Margin:		$

Comments: THERE IS A SERIOUS NEGATIVE MONTHLY CASH FLOW MARGIN PROBLEM. IMMEDIATE CORRECTIVE ACTION IS NEEDED TO AVOID FURTHER DEBT AND TO REDUCE EXPENSES.

The *Monthly Cash Flow Analysis* form draws information from the previous forms. Bob's monthly income is at the top. Priority expenses are those that must be deducted before income is spent. These three categories are giving (tithes, offerings and alms), income taxes, and debt repayment.

In reality, the biblical tithe, or ten percent first fruits giving must be priority number one. If you prefer, your *giving beyond the tithe* and *sowing of alms* could be included in a special expense category (below the net spendable income line). However, experience has taught us that without a commitment to a full *biblical giving plan*, most people do not follow through.

For this couple, priority expenses total $1,622. We observe that nearly one third of this is for debt repayment, and we also see that **this couple is not tithing.**

Their expenses on the *Monthly Cash Flow Analysis* form are simply a recap of the ten major subtotals (A-J) from their *Living Expenses* form. The total is $2,876.

Bob and Mary's monthly cash flow margin is a negative $498 per month. This is a very serious problem. They are now faced with borrowing $498 each month (not counting the extra interest on any new debt) just to "balance" their cash flow. If this continues for a full year, they will be worse off by $5,976 ($498 x 12) plus the interest cost on that additional debt. Also, if they do not make major changes, this trend will continue.

GOOD NEWS!

In chapter 6 (week 6), we will see how Bob and Mary corrected this dangerous problem.

SUMMARY

God cares very much about our planning, spending, saving and overall stewardship of His resources. That is evident by the 1,000 plus scriptures. Relating to how we are to use His resources.

So far, the course has provided a set of eight user-friendly forms. You have completed three forms, and you are now learning how to complete the next five forms.

Example # 1 showed Bob and Mary's situation before they took this course. Even though their cash flow was negative, they had hope that God would reveal a better way. Hope is a central key to this course. Combine hope with wisdom, action and discipline, and you will break free and pass on a legacy of financial freedom to future generations.

Remember what you learned in the first four chapters! If the attitude of your heart is right, God wants to bless you and your family. He definitely wants His covenant people to have all the resources needed to accomplish what He has called them to do. This means — all the time, talent, skills, health, and yes...all the money needed to fulfill His will.

You have two weeks to complete the remaining forms, but a lot of effort is required, so pray, do spiritual warfare, and get started now with the knowledge of *Jeremiah 29: 11-13 (NAS).*

> "For I know the plans that I have for you, declares the Lord, plans for welfare and not for calamity to give you a future and a hope. Then you will call upon Me and come and pray to Me, and I will listen to you. And you will seek me and find me, when you search for Me with all your heart."

LEADERS' NOTE – Review chapter five's (week 5) homework. Then, pray and release everyone with a blessing.

EVERYONE, We Encourage you to Contact Your Focus Group Leaders if you Encounter Difficulties During the Week. They are Praying for your Financial Freedom.

CHAPTER 5 & 6 (WEEKS 5 & 6) HOMEWORK

COMPLETING YOUR FAMILY SPENDING PLAN: (PART 1 & 2)

The homework for weeks five and six is to prepare and complete the *spending plan* forms. It takes two full weeks to do this properly, and we urge you to start now.

1. **Form Review –** In these first six chapters, there are a total of eight (8) forms (you have already completed the first three):

    a. You completed the ***Projected Income and Biblical Giving*** form.

    b. You already established measurable, written goals with time targets, using the ***Financial Vision and Faith Goals*** form.

    c. You previously completed your ***Debt Repayment Schedule***.

2. **Important Guidelines.** Now, we will be focusing on five additional forms. These forms are: ***List Your Assets, List Your Liabilities, Balance Sheet & Net Worth Statement, Estimated Monthly Living Expenses*, and *Monthly Cash Flow Analysis.***

    These are user-friendly forms and you already have examples to guide you. Let's establish some important guidelines before we go forward.

    a. Use a sharp **pencil** and have an eraser and a calculator handy.

    b. Fill in all possible blanks; use the examples as a guide.

    c. When you first attempt to complete most forms, **strive for 90 to 95 percent accuracy** — not 100 percent!

    d. Use whole dollar amounts and round up - no decimal points.

    e. Expenses will be estimates, so at first it is best to estimate them slightly higher.

    f. Income projections should be realistic, probably estimated on the conservative side, especially where commissions and bonuses are involved.

    g. **Make a minimum of six extra copies of blank forms, for future use (chapter 15).**

h. Put your **names and the date on all forms** for your records.

i. **Couples must complete forms together,** because **both spouses must understand and accept all numerical values** for the plan to succeed.

3. **Pray hard before starting to develop your financial plan.** Your focus group leaders will provide prayer support. You must avoid guilt, blame and shame from the process. Remember, conviction to change for good comes from God, by His Holy Spirit. Condemnation comes from the devil. Record any special prayer thoughts:

____

____

____

4. Your first form is your *Projected Income and Biblical Giving* form (blank forms – chapter 15).

PROJECTED INCOME AND BIBLICAL GIVING

NAME(S):______________________ Date: ______________

Projected Income

INCOME SOURCES:	Amount Paid Monthly	Mo. x 12 =Subtotal for Yr.	Amount Paid Other Than Monthly	Total Annual Amount	Total Annual Amt. Div. by 12 = Avg. Mo. Amt.
Gross wages: husband					
Gross wages: wife					
Dividends					
Interest					
Rents (Income Less Expenses)					
Business Income/"Increase"					
Retirement Funds					
Other					
TOTAL GROSS INCOME:	$	$	$	$	$

Projected Giving

	Organization	Amount Paid Monthly	Mo. x 12 =Subtotal for Yr.	Amount Paid Other than Monthly	Total Annual Amount	Total Annual Amt. Div. by 12 = Avg. Mo. Amt.
10% Tithe						
Freewill Offerings						
Alms (Poor)						
Other Charities						
Other Charities						
Other Giving						
TOTAL GIVING:		$	$	$	$	$

Once the income is determined, the next step is to determine where it goes. Begin with giving. Project your giving for the year by considering each organization you support. This can be from specific giving goals, percentages of income, or past giving records. You may want to check your actual giving to date and then project what you plan to give for the rest of the year.

NOTE ON USING THIS FORM: This form will help you arrive at an average monthly amount which is crucial for your spending plan and cash flow management. Record the monthly amount in the first column and then multiply by 12 months for a yearly subtotal. In the third column, record amounts that do not occur every month. Add columns 2 and 3 together to get the total annual amount for column 4. Finally, divide the total annual amount by 12 to get the average monthly amount. Do this for each line item.

a. Good news: previously you completed this form, so now is a good time for a quick review. If your situation has changed, then do a new form.

b. Your projected income should be estimated and totaled, using the top portion of this form.

c. Your biblical giving plan *(paying tithes, giving freewill offerings, and sowing alms)* plus other planned charitable giving should be estimated and totaled using the bottom portion of this form. *(Please read the special note on how to use the five columns for calculations.)*

5. Previously you listed your goals on the form entitled ***Financial Vision and Faith Goals.*** Unless you need to revise those goals, progress to the next forms (blank forms – chapter 15).

FINANCIAL VISION AND FAITH GOALS

This Form may be used for 1 yr. up to 5 yr. Goals (Page 1 of 4)

Name(s):______________________ Date Goal Form Completed: ____________

By(month & year): ______________________ we see the following faith goals being accomplished.

BIBLICAL GIVING GOALS:

We will pay our 10% tithe plus give & sow ____________% of our increase for offerings & alms.

We will be making additional gifts each year of ____________ to ____________

First Action Step:

First Action Step By (Month & Year):

SAVING GOALS:

Type of Savings Account (Do Not Include Investments)	*Amount*	*Annual Return*
	$	%
	$	%
TOTAL AMOUNT	$	

First Action Step:

First Action Step By (Month & Year):

EDUCATION FUND GOALS:

A college or special education fund will exist for each of our children/grandchildren:

Child	*Type of College*	*Approximate Annual Cost*	*Approximate Total Cost*	*Goal Amount*
		$	$	$
		$	$	$
		$	$	$
		$	$	$

First Action Step:

First Action Step By (Month & Year):

FINANCIAL VISION AND FAITH GOALS

(Page 2 of 4)

DEBT REPAYMENT GOALS:

We will have paid off the following debts:

Creditors	*Total Owed*
______________	$ ______________
______________	$ ______________
______________	$ ______________
______________	$ ______________
______________	$ ______________
______________	$ ______________
______________	$ ______________

First Action Step:

First Action Step By (Month & Year):

MAJOR PURCHASES:

We will have made the following major purchases/expenditures: (new home, car, vacations, etc.)

Purchase/Expenditure	*Goal Amount*
______________	$ ______________
______________	$ ______________
______________	$ ______________
______________	$ ______________
______________	$ ______________
______________	$ ______________

First Action Step:

First Action Step By (Month & Year):

LIFESTYLE GOALS:

For the Next ______ Years, My (Our) intention(s) is (are) to achieve one of the following lifestyles:

Check One:

________ Maintain Present Level (Giving, Saving & Spending).

________ Enlarge Spending Plan (Giving, Saving & Spending).

________ Cut Back on Lifestyle and Spending Plan.

Following is a brief explanation of the strategy to achieve the Lifestyle selection checked above: ______________________________

First Action Step:

First Action Step By (Month & Year):

FINANCIAL VISION AND FAITH GOALS

(Page 3 of 4)

START A BUSINESS:

I (We) will have started our own business which will require an approximate investment of: $ ______

Describe Your Business: ______

______

______

First Action Step:

First Action Step By (Month & Year):

INVESTMENT GOALS:

I (We) will have the following investments (Stocks, Bonds, Mutual Funds, Real Estate, Savings, Etc.):

Type of Investment	***Amount Invested***	***Annual Return***
	$	$
	$	$
	$	$
	$	$
	$	$
	$	$
Total Goal:	$	

First Action Step:

First Action Step By (Month & Year):

OTHER GOALS: (list, explain & estimate values if applicable)

______

______

______

______

First Action Step:

First Action Step By (Month & Year):

FINANCIAL VISION AND FAITH GOALS

(Page 4 of 4)

ESTATE PLANNING:

I (We) would like to pass on to my spouse (children) the following estate (describe basics):

First Action Step:

First Action Step By (Month & Year):

CONGRATULATIONS:

Once Godly goals are established, you are ahead of 95% of the people in the world.

The very next step is to begin taking your First Action Steps to accomplish the goals that God has given you. These may be very small steps. For example, a savings plan goal may start by your opening a savings account with a $5 deposit. It may seem small, but in reality it is a huge action step.....so don't delay.

MOVE IN FAITH:

You need to move in faith. You prayed and set these goals knowing that God has a wonderful plan for you (see Jeremiah 29:11). God has the resources. You need to supply the faith and the diligence to be a good and faithful steward. Then let God be God, He is your pilot and your provider.

REVIEW/REVISE ANNUALLY:

Make a commitment to review your goals at least once a year; maybe at the start of the New Year. Thank God for progress and for Breakthrough! Set new goals, or revise; these are your goals.

Married Couples: Be sure to do your goal setting, and goals review, as a one flesh couple.

6. Previously, you also completed your ***Debt Repayment Schedule.*** No new work is required on this form, unless your status has recently changed. Remember, addressing a list of debts could be a stressful and difficult experience. Do not give the devil an opening. Be patient and keep your heavenly armor in place in accordance with *Ephesians 6:10-18*. Absolutely do not allow condemnation to creep into these activities. Conviction and correction, however, are acceptable. If you are experiencing strife, stop and pray. (Reminder — full-sized blank forms are in chapter 15.)

Debt Repayment Schedule

NAME(S): ______________________________

DATE: ______________________________

	LENDER	$ BALANCE	$ MONTHLY PAYMENT	INT. %	REMAINING PAYMENTS	PAY-OFF DATE
1						
2						
3						
4						
5						
6						
7						
8						
9						
10						
11						
12						
13						
14						
15						
TOTAL:						

NOTE ON USING DEBT REPAYMENT SCHEDULE:
This form should include all debts with the exception of a primary home mortgage. The mortgage obligation is a debt and must be included as a liability when you complete the ***List Your Liabilities*** form. However, the mortgage payment is not included on this form because it will be included in the monthly housing expense category when you complete the ***Estimated Monthly Living Expenses*** form. **If your list of debts exceeds the 15 spaces given, make extra pages. Do not despair, you are on the road to Financial Freedom.**

7. **List Your Assets Form** – This is simply a one-page form where you list your family assets, or what you own. (Copy your sets of blank forms from chapter 15.) Use the spaces for various asset categories. Ninety to ninety-five percent accuracy is fine for now. Refer to example # 1 if you need a guide.

LIST YOUR ASSETS	
TYPES OF ASSETS	
1. Liquid Assets (Easily Converted to Cash)	
Cash on Hand	
Checking Account Balance	
Money market funds	
CDs (% interest rate)	
Savings (% interest rate)	
Stocks & Bonds	
Life insurance cash values	
Other (Describe)	
TOTAL Liquid Assets:	$
2. Non-liquid Assets	
Home (market value)	
Land (market value)	
Net Worth (Value) of Business	
Real Estate investments (Not Home)	
Jet Ski, Camper, RV, Boats, etc.	
Automobiles at market value	
Furniture & personal property (conservative market value)	
Valuable Collections (stamps, coins,etc.)	
Retirement Funds Balance	
Funds due from others (Receivables)	
Other (Describe)	
Other (Describe)	
TOTAL Non-liquid Assets	$
3. Total Assets (1 & 2)	$
Name(s):	
Date of Completion:	

a. **Liquid assets are easily converted to cash** if needed for emergencies.

b. **Non-liquid assets have real value but could not be converted to cash rapidly.**

c. <u>Cars and home values should be realistic market resale values.</u>

d. All assets should be realistically and conservatively valued. For example, think of what you would pay for someone else's used television, freezer, sofa or clothing.

e. Subtotal both the liquid and non-liquid asset categories, and then arrive at a grand total.

f. Bob and Mary's assets, before taking this course, are shown in example # 1.

8. **List Your Liabilities Form** – This form is used to determine what you owe. (Use a copy of full-sized form from chapter 15.)

LIST YOUR LIABILITIES

LENDER (CREDITOR):	BALANCE DUE:	INTEREST RATE %	PAYMENT SCHEDULE	
			PER MONTH:	UNTIL (MO./YR.):
1.	$		$	
2.				
3.				
4.				
5.				
6.				
7.				
8.				
9.				
10.				
11.				
12.				
13.				
14.				
15.				
16.				
17.				
18.				
19.				
20.				
21.				
22.				
23.				
TOTALS:	$		$	

NAME(S):

DATE COMPLETED:

Note: This form should include all debts previously listed on the "Debt Repayment Schedule", and should also include the home mortgage.

a. You can easily complete this form by using your ***Debt Repayment Schedule*** from the homework you completed in chapter four (week 4).

b. Refer to example # 1, to see Bob and Mary's Debt Repayment Schedule.

c. Now, look at their ***List Your Liabilities*** form in example # 1.

d. Since we omitted the primary home mortgage payment from the ***Debt Repayment Schedule***, please be sure to add that information now to the ***List Your Liabilities*** form. *(You will observe in example # 1 that the Jones family added their $80,000 mortgage to their list of liabilities.)* If you have a mortgage, add it to your form and fill out all the appropriate information for each column.

e. Total the two columns labeled "balance due" and "per month." These totals will show your total liabilities, or what your family owes, and the total of your monthly debt payments.

9. **Balance Sheet and Net Worth Statement –** Do not be intimidated. This is a very simple form to complete. You need to use the information from the two previous forms to complete this form. (Again, you are reminded to copy and use forms from chapter 15.)

BALANCE SHEET AND NET WORTH STATEMENT

A. Assets

Liquid Assets: $ ________

Non-liquid Assets: $ ________

Total Assets: $ ________

B. Less: Total Liabilities: (-) $ ________

C. Net Worth: (Total Assets - Total Liabilities) $ ________

Name(s):

Date Completed:

Comments:

Note on Using this Form: *Complete this form using data from your, recently completed* ***List Your Assets*** *&* ***List Your Liabilities*** *Forms. Then, subtract* ***total liabilities*** *from* ***total assets*** *& Record your NET WORTH.*

a. Enter your family's assets from the ***List Your Assets*** form: liquid, non-liquid, and total assets. *(Check example # 1 for help.)*

b. Enter your total liabilities from the ***List Your Liabilities*** form.

c. Calculate your household's net worth by subtracting total liabilities from total assets. *(In example # 1, Bob and Mary's net worth is $77,500.)*

d. Congratulations! Now you are starting to get an understanding of the financial status of your household. You are closing in on the process of developing a financial plan. This is a big deal... a huge step... way to go!

10. **Estimated Monthly Living Expenses Form** – Living expenses can now be estimated using the three-page form. It will be very important that you do not get bogged down in the number crunching process by trying to arrive at a perfect number. Strive for 90 to 95 percent accuracy, not perfection. (Blank forms are in chapter 15.)

ESTIMATED MONTHLY LIVING EXPENSES (3 Page Form)					
Living Expenses Form (Page 1 of 3)	**Amount Paid Monthly**	**Mo. x 12 = Subtotal for Yr.**	**Amount Paid Other Than Monthly**	**Total Annual Amount**	**Total Annual Amt. Div. by 12 = Avg. Mo. Amt.**
A. Housing					
Mortgage or Rent Payment					
Insurance for Home					
Property taxes (not in House Pmt.)					
Electricity					
Heating					
Water					
Garbage Collection					
Telephone					
Cleaning Services					
Repairs/maintenance					
Improvements & Furnishings					
Supplies for Home					
Other					
TOTAL HOUSING EXPENSES	$	$	$	$	$
B. Food	$	$	$	$	$
C. Clothing					
Husband					
Wife					
Children					
TOTAL CLOTHING	$	$	$	$	$
D. Transportation					
Auto Insurance					
Gas & Oil & Filters					
Repairs/Maintenance					
Parking					
Bus/Train/Subway					
Other					
TOTAL TRANSPORTATION	$	$	$	$	$

Living Expenses Form (Pg. 2 of 3)	Amount Paid Monthly	Mo. x 12 = Subtotal for Yr.	Amount Paid Other Than Monthly	Total Annual Amount	Total Annual Amt. Div. by 12 = Avg. Mo. Amt.
E. Entertainment/Recreation:					
Dining Out					
Childcare					
Newspapers/cable/magazines					
Vacation					
Club Dues/Fees					
Classes/Courses/Activities					
Other					
TOTAL ENTERTAINMENT:	$	$	$	$	$
F. Medical Expenses					
Medical/Health Insurance					
Doctors					
Dentists					
Drugs					
TOTAL MEDICAL:	$	$	$	$	$
G. Insurance					
Life (All Family Members)					
Disability					
Other					
TOTAL INSURANCE:	$	$	$	$	$
H. Children:					
School lunches					
Allowances					
School Tuition					
Lessons/Special Fees/Dues					
Other					
TOTAL CHILDREN:	$	$	$	$	$
I. Gifts/Occasions:					
Christmas					
Birthdays					
Anniversary					
Holidays other than Christmas					
Other					
TOTAL GIFTS:	$	$	$	$	$

Living Expenses Form (Pg. 3 of 3)	Amount Paid Monthly	Mo. x 12 = Subtotal for Yr.	Amount Paid Other Than Monthly	Total Annual Amount	Total Annual Amt. Div. by 12 = Avg. Mo. Amt.
J. Miscellaneous					
Toiletries					
Husband: lunches, etc.					
Wife: lunches, etc.					
Dry cleaning/laundry					
Pet care (medical/tags/food)					
Beauty/barber					
Other					
Other					
TOTAL MISCELLANEOUS:	$	$	$	$	$
TOTAL LIVING EXPENSES	$	$	$	$	$

Name(s): ______________________

Date Completed: ______________________

Conclusions or Comments:

NOTES ON USING THIS FORM: This form will help you arrive at an average monthly amount which is crucial for your spending plan and cash flow management. Record the monthly amount in the first column and then multiply by 12 months for a yearly subtotal. In the third column, record amounts that do not occur every month. Add columns 2 and 3 together to get the total annual amount for column 4. Finally, divide the total annual amount by 12 to get the average monthly amount. Do this for each line item (A-J). Add the ten monthly average expense categories (A-J) to arrive at your estimated monthly total living expenses.

Several expenses do not occur monthly, but must be planned for, such as: auto insurance, most gift categories, and home or auto repairs. It is important that these items be placed in the column labeled "Amount Paid Other Than Monthly". In Chapter 7, you will learn how to reserve for these in a "Freedom Account".

Please use pencil and no decimal points. Remember, these are your **best estimates** for an average month. You will learn to adjust and correct, as you use this form several times.

a. Use records, files, your checkbook register or your best estimate for each category. You will be adjusting this form in future *spending plans*. This is your first start.

b. Carefully consider each of the ten expense categories labeled A through J. Enter your estimates in pencil and subtotal each category. Use only whole dollars, no decimals.

c. Some expenses are not regular monthly items. Enter these non-monthly expenses in the column labeled "amount paid other than monthly."

d. Total each column and then add the ten section (A-J) subtotals on page three (on the line labeled ***Total Living Expenses***). (*Please read the note on page three for instructions on how to use the five columns for calculations.*)

e. Date and add your names to the form, and add any additional thoughts in the *conclusions or comments section* of the form.

f. (Optional: review Bob and Mary's three-page ***Living Expenses*** forms, example # 1 and # 2.)

11. **Your Monthly Cash Flow Analysis Form –** This next form is basically a compilation of your prior work. It is an essential tool in your financial planning process. *(Therefore, if you skipped completing any previous forms, please go back and complete them before proceeding; shortcuts will not work!)*

MONTHLY CASH FLOW ANALYSIS

Name(s): **Date:**

Gross Income: . . . . **$** ______

Less Priority Expenses:

A. Giving (Tithes & Offerings) $ ____________________

B. Taxes (Payroll Records) $ ____________________

C. Debt (Total Repayments) $ ____________________

Total Priority Expenses: (-) . . . . **$ (** ______ **)**

NET SPENDABLE INCOME:
(Gross income less A, B, & C =) **$** ______

Monthly Living Expenses:

A. Housing ______
B. Food ______
C. Clothing ______
D. Transportation ______
E. Entertainment/recreation ______
F. Medical ______
G. Insurance ______
H. Children ______
I. Gifts ______
J. Miscellaneous ______

TOTAL MONTHLY LIVING EXPENSES: **$** ______

Monthly Cash Flow Margin: **$** ______
(Net Spendable Income Minus Total A-J Living Expenses)

Your Commitments For Monthly Positive Cash Flow Margin:

A. Savings $ ______
B. Retirement $ ______
C. Extra Debt Payments $ ______
D. Additional Giving $ ______

Total Commitments for + Cash Flow: **$** ______

Uncommitted Monthly Cash Flow Margin: **$** ______

Comments: (What will you change?):

a. Refer to Bob and Mary's example # 1 or # 2 cash-flow form, if you need a guide.

b. Start by putting combined gross income on the top line.

c. Priority expenses are those that take precedence over your controllable living expenses.

   1) First, on line A, you list your biblical giving (tithes, freewill offerings, and alms).

   2) On line B, put an estimate of your federal and (any) state income taxes (your payroll records will be helpful).

   3) On line C, add the total of your monthly payments from your ***Debt Repayment Schedule.*** Remember, this includes all your debts with the exception of a home mortgage payment or a rent payment (which is to be included as a monthly housing expense item on the ***Estimated Monthly Living Expenses*** form).

d. Your family's net spendable income is calculated by deducting priority expenses (giving, taxes and debt repayments) from your gross income. (*Net Spendable Income* is really the amount you have to work with in the short term.) In other words, you need to manage your current spending plan within the limits of your *net spendable income.*

e. The living expense data should be copied directly from the three-page ***Estimated Monthly Living Expenses*** form. Items A through J are the same on the *cash flow* form as on the *living expenses* form.

f. Your cash flow margin is the amount of surplus (positive margin) or deficit (negative margin) that remains at the end of the month.

g. If you have planned for a positive cash flow margin, there is a place to commit portions of this surplus to savings, retirement, accelerated debt repayments (extra principal payments) or other categories you care to name.

h. The bottom of this form provides a place for you to record additional but uncommitted positive cash flow. You can decide how to commit this extra money in the future but, you should plan and not just spend it.

i. Since flow of cash is crucial in a family *spending plan*, we recommend that the cash flow analysis form be calculated on a monthly basis. If you would like to add a set of columns for annual cash flow calculations, do so without excluding the family's monthly calculations.

j. As we observe in example # 1, Bob and Mary have a ($498) negative monthly cash flow. In example # 2 we see how Bob and Mary corrected the negative cash flow with God's help and with God's principles of finance.

12. **Congratulations for completing all eight forms!** Even if the forms are looking rough and you are dissatisfied with the monthly cash flow results, you have taken a huge step toward financial freedom and God is pleased. Pat yourself (and your mate, if married) on the back, and give thanks to God Almighty for His grace and wisdom.

13. In the homework sharing time (weeks six and seven), be prepared to discuss the process, the trials and the successes you experienced as you completed your *spending plan.*

14. **REMEMBER...** approximately 30 to 45 days after week seven, you will meet with your focus group leaders. This private review session will allow about an hour and a half review, plus discussion and assistance to ensure your plan is on a successful and Godly track. Start planning now to get the most of your review sessions. <u>Be prepared to demonstrate your diligence and good stewardship to God, and to be accountable to the leaders who have sown their time, prayer and spiritual warfare into you and your family</u>.

15. **Closing thoughts on weeks five and six homework:**

    a. It might take several attempts to complete a comprehensive financial plan. Don't worry, your leaders will assist you in this matter.

    b. It is vital that you ignore worldly counsel that conflicts with God's Word.

> **Married Couples Absolutely Must** work together to develop and complete the family *spending plan.* The two halves of the "one flesh" must understand all forms and be able to discuss them thoroughly. Further, we recommend that children be involved in some parts of this process.

    c. As time permits, complete additional revisions of all these forms. Date and discuss each version until you have a plan (with a balanced or positive monthly cash flow) that works. **This will be an ongoing process <u>necessary for a life of true financial freedom</u>.**

    d. Brief all family members on your plan and put the plan into action.

    e. In the first year, at a minimum, you will want to check your actual results monthly and make reasonable adjustments. Remember, this is your family's *spending plan* and you are in control.

    f. Once you have developed a well-balanced *spending plan*, it is important to revise it annually.

    g. **When you schedule your 30-45 day post-course review with your leaders, be prepared to bring <u>all</u> forms (the most current) completed in <u>pencil</u>.**

16. **Record Your Breakthroughs for the week and share them during homework sharing time.**

BREAKTHROUGHS!

FINANCIAL FREEDOM COURSE - RECORD YOUR WEEKLY TESTIMONIES

NAME: ______________________ & ______________________

DATE: MONEY, CAREER, GIFTS/INHERITANCE, & OTHER

_____ ____

_____ ____

_____ ____

_____ ____

_____ ____

_____ ____

CHAPTER 6

(WEEK 6)

"Commit to the Lord whatever you do, and your plans will succeed."
Proverbs 16:3 (NIV)

"The plans of the diligent lead to profit as surely as haste leads to poverty."
Proverbs 21:5 (NIV)

Completing Your Family Spending Plan: Part II

LEADER'S NOTES – WEEKLY PROTOCOL

- Praise Song – A great way to start!
  Suggest Typed Lyrics and Upbeat Music

- Prayer – Led by a Leader or LIT
  Recommend Group Holding Hands

- Spiritual Warfare – in Jesus' mighty name

- Homework Sharing – Normally led by LITs
  Led by Leaders if LITs are Teaching this Week
  Time Control and Equal Sharing are Keys

- Sharing of Weekly Breakthroughs
  Brief but Builds Hope – Celebrate!

- Weekly Offering Time – Opportunity to Sow
  Have a Focus Group Member Pray First
  Put Faith into Action!

- 10 Minute Break
  Beverages & Restroom

- Call Group Together

- Weekly Lesson
  Taught by Leaders or LITs

- Homework Preview

- Dismiss in Prayer – Holding Hands
  Entire Session Should Average 2 to 2 ½ Hours

- Leaders and LITs Complete Weekly Report

CHAPTER 6 (WEEK 6)

COMPLETING YOUR FAMILY SPENDING PLAN: PART II

LEADERS' NOTE – Based on the homework discussion, you will get a feel for how comfortable the group is with the *spending plan* concept. This observation will help guide you in setting the pace for discussion of example # 2. Remember, the group has one more week to complete the *spending plan* forms. Also, everyone will have an individual review session with the leaders approximately 30 to 45 days after completing the course.

REVIEW

Last week, we introduced you to several new forms, as part of your journey toward a financial freedom plan. For some, this process may have been like drinking water from a fire hydrant. So this week we will again focus on Bob and Mary's Spending Plan.

I. A LOOK AT EXAMPLE #2

Example # 2 dated August 30, 2001 reflects Bob and Mary's financial plan one year after they completed the Financial Freedom in 7 Weeks Plus course. Again, we emphasize this is an example. However, you will see how the Jones' were able to make major changes once they learned what God's Word had to say about finances and after they sought and heeded wise Christian counsel. Let us review their forms one at a time.

- **THE PROJECTED INCOME AND BIBLICAL GIVING FORM** reflects no change in family income. This couple might have considered having Mary work outside the home, but when they considered the costs of childcare, transportation, additional clothing and extra taxes, they opted for her to be a full-time mother and homemaker.

PROJECTED INCOME AND BIBLICAL GIVING

(Example #2 - After Course)

NAME(S): Bob and Mary Jones Date: August 31, 2001

Projected Income

	Amount Paid Monthly	Mo. x 12 =Subtotal for Yr.	Amount Paid Other Than Monthly	Total Annual Amount	Total Annual Amt. Div. by 12 = Avg. Mo. Amt.
Sources:					
Gross wages: husband	$4,000	$48,000		$48,000	$4,000
Gross wages: wife					
Dividends					
Interest					
Rents (cash flow)					
Business Income/"Increase"					
Pensions & annuities					
Other					
TOTAL GROSS INCOME:	**$4,000**	**$48,000**		**$48,000**	**$4,000**

Projected Giving

	Organization	Amount Paid Monthly	Mo. x 12 =Subtotal for Yr.	Amount Paid Other than Monthly	Total Annual Amount	Total Annual Amt. Div. by 12 = Avg. Mo. Amt.
10% Tithe	Church	$400	$4,800		$4,800	$400
Freewill Offerings	Missions	$5	$60		$60	$5
Alms	Benevolence	$5	$60		$60	$5
Other	United Way	$5	$60		$60	$5
Other						
Other						
TOTAL GIVING:		**$415**	**$4,980**		**$4,980**	**$415**

Once the income is determined, the next step is to determine where it goes. Begin with giving. Project your giving for the year by considering each organization you support. This can be from pledges, percentages of income, past giving, or specific giving goals. You may want to check your actual giving to date and then project what you plan to give for the rest of the year.

NOTE ON USING THIS FORM: This form will help you arrive at an average monthly amount which is crucial for your spending plan and cash flow management. Record the monthly amount in the first column and then multiply by 12 months for a yearly subtotal. In the third column, record amounts that do not occur every month. Add columns 2 and 3 together to get the total annual amount for column 4. Finally, divide the total annual amount by 12 to get the average monthly amount. Do this for each line item.

Bob and Mary's giving plan includes an important shift. Now, they are committed to paying a full 10 percent tithe on Bob's monthly gross pay. They understand this needs to be the first 10 percent and before all other spending. Once they learned what God's Word had to say about giving freewill offerings and sowing alms, they decided to rearrange their Giving Plan. They now give a $5 monthly offering to an evangelistic missionary ministry and they sow $5 a month into their church's benevolence fund for the needy (widows, orphans and poor). They are now in order with God's instructions to tithe freely and cheerfully, give additional freewill offerings, and to sow alms. This Biblical giving commitment pleases God and puts the couple in position to receive a Malachi 3 blessing. Finally, Bob and Mary will receive wisdom and grace to make major lifestyle changes if they simply ask God. *(See James 1:5)*

➢ **LIST YOUR ASSETS.** There are significant changes here. Bob and Mary were saddled with high interest debt payments that put them under tremendous monthly pressure. Therefore, they prayed, agreed and decided to liquidate several non-essential assets in order to pay-off considerable debt.

LIST YOUR ASSETS		
TYPES OF ASSETS (Example #2)		
1 . Liquid Assets (Easily Converted to Cash)		
Cash on Hand	$200	
Checking Account Balance	$1,800	
Money market funds		
CDs (% interest rate)		
Savings (% interest rate)	$5,500	
Stocks & Bonds		
Life insurance cash values	$0	
Other (Describe)		
TOTAL Liquid Assets:		**$7,500**
2. Non-liquid Assets		
Home (market value)	$75,000	
Land (market value)	$25,000	
Net Worth (Value) of Business		
Real Estate investments (Not Home)		
Jet Ski, Camper, RV, Boats, etc. (Sold)	$0	
Automobiles at market value	$20,000	
Furniture & personal property (conservative market value)	$10,000	
Valuable Collections (stamps, coins,etc.) (Sold)	$0	
Retirement Funds Balance	$20,000	
Funds due from others (Receivables)		
Other (Describe)		
Other (Describe)		
TOTAL Non-liquid Assets		**$150,000**
3. Total Assets (1 & 2)		**$157,500**
Name(s): Bob & Mary Jones (Example #2)		
Date of Completion: August 31, 2001		

Their first plan (example # 1) included whole life insurance with a cash value of $3,500. By shopping for a competitive term life policy, they were able to cut life insurance premiums by $100 a month without lowering Bob's coverage. They applied the cash value of the whole life policy toward immediate debt reduction. (Since they used the $3,500, they now have zero for the cash value of their insurance policy.)

In addition, they used an extra $500 from their sale of assets to actually increase their savings account balance from $5,000 to $5,500. Total liquid assets are now $7,500.

In the non-liquid asset section, we see that they sold their $10,000 boat and their $3,000 coin collection. Total non-liquid assets are now $150,000 and their Total Assets are now $157,500 which is $16,500 less than example # 1.

➢ **DEBT REPAYMENT SCHEDULE.** Bob & Mary were able to sell off assets and actually pay off their four debts from example # 1. This took sacrifice and dedication, but they not only got free of consumer debt, they committed to operating free of consumer debt in the future.

DEBT REPAYMENT SCHEDULE

NAME(S): Bob and Mary Jones (Example #2)
DATE: August 31, 2001

	LENDER	$ BALANCE	$ MONTHLY PAYMENT	INT. %	REMAINING PAYMENTS	PAY-OFF DATE
1	Credit Card A	$0				
2	Credit Card B	$0				
3	Car Loan	$0				
4	Parent's Loan	$0				
5						
6						
7						
8						
9						
10						
11						
12						
13						
14						
15						
TOTAL:		$0	$0			

NOTE ON USING DEBT REPAYMENT SCHEDULE:
This form should include all debts with the exception of a primary home mortgage. The mortgage obligation is a debt and must be included as a liability when you complete the ***List Your Liabilities*** form. However, the mortgage payment is not included on this form because it will be included in the monthly housing expense category when you complete the ***Estimated Monthly Living Expenses*** form.

➢ **LIST YOUR LIABILITIES FORM** – This reflects the wise use of the money from their asset sales to completely pay-off two credit cards, the car loan, and the loan to parents. They agreed to cut up one credit card and to use the other card with very strict guidelines, including paying off the balance in full every month. As a result, they have only one monthly debt and that is their $675 home mortgage payment at 9% interest.

LIST YOUR LIABILITIES (Example #2)				
LENDER (CREDITOR):	BALANCE DUE:	INTEREST RATE %	PAYMENT SCHEDULE PER MONTH:	UNTIL (MO./YR.):
1. Credit Card A	$0			
2. Credit Card B	$0			
3. Car Loan	$0			
4. Mortgage **	$80,000	9.00%	$675	6/30/2025
5. Parent's Loan	$0			
6.				
7.				
8.				
9.				
10.				
11.				
12.				
13.				
14.				
15.				
16.				
17.				
18.				
19.				
20.				
21.				
22.				
23.				
TOTALS:	$80,000		$675	

NAME(S): Bob & Mary Jones (Example #2)

DATE COMPLETED: August 31, 2001

****Note: For Simplicity, we left the mortgage balance at $80,000. In reality, the balance would be slightly lower, due to one year of principal payments.**

Note: This form should include all debts previously listed on the "Debt Repayment Schedule", and should also include the home mortgage.

➢ **BALANCE SHEET & NET WORTH STATEMENT** — This statement now reflects different values for both assets and for liabilities, but the net worth remains unchanged at $77,500.

BALANCE SHEET AND NET WORTH STATEMENT (Example #2)

A. Assets

Liquid Assets:	$7,500	
Non-liquid Assets:	$150,000	
Total Assets:		**$157,500**
B. Less: Total Liabilities: (-)		**(80,000)**
C. Net Worth: (Total Assets - Total Liabilities)		**$77,500**

Name(s): Bob & Mary Jones (Example #2)

Date Completed: August 31, 2001

Comments:

Note on Using this Form: *Complete this form using data from your, recently completed, **List Your Assets** & **List Your Liabilities** Forms. Then, subtract **total liabilities** from **total assets** & Record your NET WORTH.*

The reason there is no immediate change in net worth is because this couple sold some assets and paid off an equal amount of debt. So, for now, the assets were reduced by the same amount as liabilities (debts).

We will soon see that the Jones Family is now much stronger financially as a result of these prudent changes. In example # 1, Bob and Mary were running a large monthly negative cash flow. The only way they could continue with that plan was to increase their debts every month. However, as debts grow, interest costs grow, and liabilities grow larger and larger each month. This means their net worth would actually get lower and lower every month. **In example # 2, with zero consumer debt payments and a positive monthly cash flow, their net worth will increase steadily if they do not waste their surplus.**

- **ESTIMATED MONTHLY LIVING EXPENSES FORM** — Living expense reductions require significant lifestyle changes. Bob and Mary included their young children in their financial plans. As they prayed, they received grace and wisdom on how to revise their plan.

ESTIMATED MONTHLY LIVING EXPENSES

(3 Page Form - Example #2)

EXAMPLE #2 (Page 1 of 3)	Amount Paid Monthly	Mo. x 12 = Subtotal for Yr.	Amount Paid Other Than Monthly	Total Annual Amount	Total Annual Amt. Div. by 12 = Avg. Mo. Amt.
A. Housing					
Mortgage or Rent Payment	$675	$8,100		$8,100	$675
Insurance for Home			$500	$500	$42
Property taxes (not in House Pmt.)			$1,500	$1,500	$125
Electricity	$60	$720		$720	$60
Heating	$50	$600		$600	$50
Water	$25	$300		$300	$25
Garbage Collection					
Telephone	$40	$480		$480	$40
Cleaning Services					
Repairs/maintenance	$25	$300		$300	$25
Improvements & Furnishings					
Supplies for Home	$10	$120		$120	$10
Other					
TOTAL HOUSING EXPENSES	**$885**	**$10,620**	**$2,000**	**$12,620**	**$1,052**
B. Food	**$425**	**$5,100**	**$**	**$5,100**	**$425**
C. Clothing					
Husband	$20	$240		$240	$20
Wife	$30	$360		$360	$30
Children	$45	$540		$540	$45
TOTAL CLOTHING	**$95**	**$1,140**	**$**	**$1,140**	**$95**
D. Transportation					
Auto Insurance			$600	$600	$50
Gas & Oil & Filters	$100	$1,200		$1,200	$100
Repairs/Maintenance	$12	$144		$144	$12
Parking	$12	$144		$144	$12
Bus/Train/Subway					
Other					
TOTAL TRANSPORTATION	**$124**	**$1,488**	**$600**	**$2,088**	**$174**

Living Expenses Form (Pg. 2 of 3) Example #2	Amount Paid Monthly	Mo. x 12 = Subtotal for Yr.	Amount Paid Other Than Monthly	Total Annual Amount	Total Annual Amt. Div. by 12 = Avg. Mo. Amt.
E. Entertainment/Recreation:					
Dining Out	$25	$300		$300	$25
Childcare	$5	$60		$60	$5
Newspapers/cable/magazines	$10	$120		$120	$10
Vacation			$720	$720	$60
Club Dues/Fees					
Classes/Courses/Activities					
Other	$10	$120		$120	$10
TOTAL ENTERTAINMENT:	**$50**	**$600**	**$720**	**$1,320**	**$110**
F. Medical Expenses					
Medical/Health Insurance	$50	$600		$600	$50
Doctors	$50	$600		$600	$50
Dentists	$10	$120		$120	$10
Drugs	$10	$120		$120	$10
TOTAL MEDICAL:	**$120**	**$1,440**	**$**	**$1,440**	**$120**
G. Insurance					
Life (All Family Members)	$35	$420		$420	$35
Disability					
Other					
TOTAL INSURANCE:	**$35**	**$420**	**$**	**$420**	**$35**
H. Children:					
School lunches	$35	$420		$420	$35
Allowances	$30	$360		$360	$30
School Tuition					
Lessons/Special Fees/Dues	$25	$300		$300	$25
Other					
TOTAL CHILDREN:	**$90**	**$1,080**	**$**	**$1,080**	**$90**
I. Gifts/Occasions:					
Christmas			$360	$360	$30
Birthdays			$120	$120	$10
Anniversary			$50	$50	$4
Holidays other than Christmas					
Other			$24	$24	$2
TOTAL GIFTS:	**$**	**$**	**$554**	**$554**	**$46**

Living Expenses Form (Pg. 3 of 3) Example #2	Amount Paid Monthly	Mo. x 12 = Subtotal for Yr.	Amount Paid Other Than Monthly	Total Annual Amount	Total Annual Amt. Div. by 12 = Avg. Mo. Amt.
J. Miscellaneous					
Toiletries	$15	$180		$180	$15
Husband: lunches, etc.	$35	$420		$420	$35
Wife: lunches, etc.	$20	$240		$240	$20
Dry cleaning/laundry	$20	$240		$240	$20
Pet care (medical/tags/food)					
Beauty/barber	$20	$240		$240	$20
Other					
Other					
TOTAL MISCELLANEOUS:	**$110**	**$1,320**	**$**	**$1,320**	**$110**
TOTAL LIVING EXPENSES	**$1,934**	**$23,208**	**$3,874**	**$27,082**	**$2,257**

Name(s): Bob & Mary Jones (Example #2)
Date Completed: August 31, 2001
Conclusions or Comments:

NOTE ON USING THIS FORM: This form will help you arrive at an average monthly amount which is crucial for your spending plan and cash flow management. Record the monthly amount in the first column and then multiply by 12 months for a yearly subtotal. In the third column, record amounts that do not occur every month. Add columns 2 and 3 together to get the total annual amount for column 4. Finally, divide the total annual amount by 12 to get the average monthly amount. Do this for each line item (A-J). Add the ten monthly average expense categories (A-J) to arrive at your estimated monthly total living expenses.

Several expenses do not occur monthly, but must be planned for, such as: auto insurance, most gift categories, and home or auto repairs. It is important that these items be placed in the column labeled "Amount Paid Other Than Monthly". In Chapter 7, you will learn how to reserve for these in a "Freedom Account".

Please use pencil and no decimal points. Remember, these are your **best estimates** for an average month. You will learn to adjust and correct, as you use this form several times.

For Married Couples: Living expense adjustments must be agreed to by both halves of the One Flesh couple. You are also encouraged to include the children. Results are better when all family members buy-in to the *spending plan.* Pray & Do Warfare First!

The following is a recap of expense reductions Bob and Mary made in their new Spending Plan.

1. Housing expense was lowered by $20 by minimizing long distance calls and having Bob do some of the minor maintenance work.

2. Food expense was trimmed to $425 by using planned menus, coupons, and by taking advantage of selected bulk quantity purchases. Expensive junk food and costly convenience food items were dramatically cut. (Nutrition actually improved.)

3. Clothing was reduced by just $15 a month, but it all adds up. Mary reactivated her sewing machine and they agreed to shop harder for good buys.

4. Transportation was cut from $236 to $124 per month. Bob embarked in a carpool to his job and they agreed to consider the cost of unnecessary driving trips. Also by doing their own oil and filter changes, vehicle maintenance was cut in half.

5. Entertainment and recreation was cut by over 50%. They decided to eat out less and at lower priced restaurants. Likewise, each category was scrutinized. The family agreed to vacation at a lake cabin closer to home, at least for this year.

6. No cuts were possible in the medical area. However, the family agreed to pray for excellent health and to be good stewards of their bodies through exercise and proper eating habits.

7. Life insurance was cut by $100 a month by shopping for a good term life policy with the same death benefit.

8. After studying the children's expenses no changes were made. However, the two young children will be accountable for more household jobs and this will benefit the entire family's quality of life. The children are also learning Godly principles about stewardship, work, tithing, giving offerings, sowing alms, and saving (from their allowances).

9. By pre-planning for gift situations and making some gifts, this monthly expense was cut from $80 to $46.

10. Miscellaneous expenses can often get out of hand. Bob and Mary looked for creative ways to save. Bob agreed to take his lunch more often or to eat in the company cafeteria. Mary will look for quantity dry cleaning specials, etc. The net result is a monthly savings of $65.

MONTHLY CASH FLOW ANALYSIS		
Name(s): Bob & Mary Jones (Example #2)	**Date: August 31, 2001**	
Gross Income:		**$4,000**
Less Priority Expenses:		
A. Giving (Tithes & Offerings)	$415	
B. Taxes (Payroll Records)	$750	
C. Debt (Repayments)	$0	
Total Priority Expenses: (-)		**($1,165)**
NET SPENDABLE INCOME: (Gross income less A, B, & C =)		**$2,835**
Monthly Living Expenses:		
A. Housing	$1,052	
B. Food	$425	
C. Clothing	$95	
D. Transportation	$174	
E. Entertainment/recreation	$110	
F. Medical	$120	
G. Insurance	$35	
H. Children	$90	
I. Gifts	$46	
J. Miscellaneous	$110	
TOTAL MONTHLY LIVING EXPENSES:		**$2,257**
MONTHLY Cash Flow Margin: (Net Spendable Income Minus Total A-J Living Expenses)		**$578**
Your Commitments for Monthly Positive Cash Flow Margin:		
A. Savings	$100	
B. Retirement	$100	
C. Extra Debt Payment - on mortgage	$100	
D. Additional Giving	$50	
Total Commitments for + Cash Flow:		**$350**
Uncommitted Monthly Cash Flow Margin:		**$228**
Comments: Now that high interest debt has been eliminated, this family has a balanced spending plan and is en route to paying off the mortgage. They have $228 per month in uncommitted cash flow and have the freedom to re-work their spending plan as needed.		

The Form above provides the opportunity to study Bob and Mary's *Monthly Cash Flow Analysis Form* (example # 2). This is a composite of the financial data you just observed.

1. Gross Income remains at $4,000 per month.

2. Priority Expenses include $415 from the ***Projected Income and Biblical Giving Form***; and $750 in (monthly payroll deduction) income tax. Debt repayments are now zero, as you observed in their restructured ***Debt Repayment Form***.

3. Net Spendable Income is now $2,835. This is much better than example # 1 because their consumer debt payments are now zero.

4. The Estimated Monthly Living Expenses Form projects a new total of $2,257 for the ten categories (A-J).

5. Good news! The cash flow margin is now a positive $578 each month. What a change from a negative $498 per month in example # 1.

6. Because they have planned to have money left over each month, they can also plan to commit some of this positive cash flow margin as follows: $100 to Savings; an extra $100 to a Retirement Fund; an extra $100 payment against the principal on their home mortgage; and $50 in additional giving.

7. Their good stewardship practices produced $228 in uncommitted monthly cash flow. Their flexible Spending Plan allows the freedom to rework their living expenses, especially if some expense categories were squeezed too tightly. They can also begin using this uncommitted monthly cash flow to build a reserve for: major purchases, a dream vacation, or a fund to start a business on a debt free basis.

CELEBRATE!

Going from a negative to a positive monthly cash flow is definitely cause for a, modest but sincere, family celebration. Bob and Mary took the family to an ice cream parlor so all could feel good about their breakthroughs and their progress toward true family financial freedom.

EXAMPLE #2 REVIEW

In example # 2, the Jones family made two major moves to get their *spending plan* in balance. First, they sold non-essential assets to pay-off consumer debts, which increased their net spendable income significantly. Second, they combined planning and sacrifice to make cuts in many living expense categories. They kept looking for savings, re-worked their numbers, and were amazed to see a plan with a positive monthly cash flow of $578. This is a major improvement in comparison with example # 1, in which they were headed for disaster. This positive monthly cash flow also allowed Bob and Mary to make five positive moves: start a long-term savings plan, add to a retirement fund, make extra principal payments on their mortgage, increase their giving, and have additional uncommitted monthly surplus.

We realize that example # 2 versus # 1 shows Bob and Mary turning their situation around in just over one year. This is just an example. Your situation may take considerably longer and could require even more drastic actions, but the point is to understand how plans can be changed (with dedication), and how to include God in the whole process. There is definitely hope and God has a "plan A" for you!

LEADERS' NOTE – Ask the group if they have any questions concerning example # 2. Please be sure all participants are really comfortable with the development of the numbers and the use of the forms before moving on.

TIPS ON REDUCING LIVING EXPENSES, LOWERING DEBT PAYMENTS, AND/OR INCREASING INCOME can be found in a variety of excellent Christian resource materials.

See chapter 11 "Additional References" for a list of several excellent resources. These resources can only benefit you if you go get them and use them. Action is the key!

II. SAVINGS – IS IT A BIBLICAL CONCEPT?

After six weeks of dealing with debt and spending plans, and with a new grasp of cash flow, you can certainly see that it would be great to have the security of a sizeable savings account. Let's explore what the Bible says about saving regularly.

➢ BIBLICAL REFERENCES

1. In Proverbs 6:6-8, we are instructed, *"Go to the ant you sluggard; consider its ways and be wise! It has no commander, no overseer, or ruler, yet it stores its provisions in summer and gathers its food at harvest." (NIV)*

2. Proverbs 21:20 says, *"In the house of the wise are stores of choice food and oil, but a foolish man devours all he has." (NIV)*

3. Relating to providing for one's family now and via an inheritance, we refer to *1 Timothy 5:8 — "If anyone does not provide for his relatives, and especially for his immediate family, he has denied the faith and is worse than an unbeliever." (NIV)*

WHAT ABOUT RETIREMENT?

Retirement, especially as we know the concept in North America, is not based on biblical wisdom. However, we recommend that you use retirement and savings plans to prepare for the future, to include uncertainties and/or to position you and your family financially to do whatever God calls you to do. This could involve launching a new career or accepting a full or part-time ministry call. Regardless of the option, you will be better prepared for the future if you have developed and implemented a savings plan.

III. SEQUENTIAL STRATEGIES FOR SAVING AND INVESTING

While we will not make specific recommendations, we will provide a logical sequence of events to help guide you as you use your positive cash flow to save and invest. Remember, these important steps all require that you start with a positive monthly cash flow.

"Though skillful and Godly Wisdom is a house (a life, a home, a family) built, and by understanding it is established (on a sound and good foundation). And by knowledge shall the chambers (of its every area) be filled with all precious and pleasant riches."
Proverbs 24:3-4 (Amplified)

- **STEP ONE:** Pay off high interest debt as quickly as possible and commit to no new debt. Get a Will ASAP if you don't already have one. This is an absolute must for good stewardship.

- **STEP TWO:** Build a small reserve for emergencies — At least a few hundred dollars in your joint checking account.

- **STEP THREE:** Add to an interest-bearing savings account until you have at least enough reserve to cover all family expenses for a full month. Limit access only to emergency situations and by mutual agreement.

  *Stay within your **spending plan** guidelines as you complete steps 1, 2 and 3.*

- **STEP FOUR:** If you really need to increase some living expense categories, do so, but with caution. *(If you are married, do so by mutual agreement only.)*

- **STEP FIVE:** Build up a three-to-six-month living expense reserve in an interest-bearing money market or savings account. Shop for the best deal that is secure. Start or add to college funds now.

- **STEP SIX:** Don't miss out on company-provided retirement funds, such as 401K plans, especially if there are company matching fund provisions. These deals are just too good to miss.

- **STEP SEVEN:** Look for the best interest returns for certificates of deposit (CDs) or a money market account to build up a reserve so you can pay cash for major purchases, such as furniture, a car, or home improvements.

- **STEP EIGHT:** This is a very good time to make extra principal payments on your home mortgage.

  You can also save huge amounts of interest by paying twice a month. (Note: This does not mean making two full mortgage payments a month, but it means dividing your one monthly payment into two half payments made at the beginning and the middle of the month.) Ask your mortgage provider. You could easily take this twice-a-month-step in conjunction with steps 1, 2 and 3.

- **STEP NINE:** Seek excellent investment counsel as you grow a diversified investment portfolio. Avoid high-risk investments until you have a solid base that will provide for future needs, such as retirement or major lifestyle changes.

> **For Married Couples:** Husbands and wives should openly discuss anything that involves risk. Seek one flesh agreement and do not proceed without agreement. If you both do not understand the investment, we recommend that you pass.

- **STEP TEN:** Revise your giving plans continually as God blesses you. You should be able to give a much larger percentage of your total income as your lifestyle changes and as your savings and investments grow. Consider special gifts to your church, your favorite ministries, and to your family.

Keep God in your plan always, and remember that prosperity is not being rich in the world's view. It is having all the resources needed to do what God has called you to do.

> **MORE ABOUT INVESTING,**
> **ESTATE PLANNING & INSURANCE**
>
> This course will not attempt to dive deeply into these subjects. We do encourage you to seek wise Christian counsel regarding each of these important elements of your financial plan.
>
> Never invest in ventures you do not fully understand. All investments have risk and God expects you to be wise and faithful stewards of His resources.
>
> **Remember all financial decisions are spiritual decisions.**

LOOKING AHEAD

The *spending plan* homework for week six is to revise and/or complete all forms that were started in week 5. Bring your completed *spending plan* forms to next week's session to discuss.

Please remember to:

- Pray and do spiritual warfare before starting homework.
- Make six extra copies of all blank forms (see chapter 15).
- Use pencil and shoot for 90 to 95 percent accuracy.
- Get your paying of tithes, giving of freewill offerings, and sowing of alms in biblical order so God can lead you out of the wilderness.

Next week is your final full focus group session. Your Leaders will introduce you to various **Cash Control Systems** to enable you to keep track of God's money. Then you will be equipped with the tools which will help you stick to your *spending plan*. **Cash Control is the final link in your chain to Family Financial Freedom. Come excited and expecting!**

Please remember to call your focus group leaders if you get bogged down during the homework.

LEADERS' NOTE – Congratulate the group for getting this far!

- In the closing prayer, pray hard for each group member — for unity and hope.
- Encourage everyone to press forward for the prize of true Financial Freedom.
- The Prayer of Jabez is always appropriate, and so is spiritual warfare!

CHAPTER 6 (WEEK 6) HOMEWORK

COMPLETING YOUR OWN FLEXIBLE SPENDING PLAN

1. The homework for weeks five and six is for you to complete your flexible family *spending plan.*
2. The homework was previously explained in detail, following chapter five (week five). Please refer there, and/or to Bob and Mary's example # 1 and example # 2, if you desire further clarification.
3. Reminder – married couples must complete these forms together.
4. Be prepared to discuss your progress during the homework sharing time for week six.
5. Celebrate as you progress through this process. This is "A Big Deal"!!!
6. **Record Your Breakthroughs for the week and share them during homework sharing time.**

BREAKTHROUGHS!

FINANCIAL FREEDOM COURSE – RECORD YOUR WEEKLY TESTIMONIES

NAME: ______________________________ & ______________________________

DATE:	MONEY, CAREER, GIFTS/INHERITANCE, & OTHER
______	______________________________
______	______________________________
______	______________________________
______	______________________________
______	______________________________
______	______________________________

CHAPTER 7

(WEEK 7)

"And so he that had received five talents came and brought other five talents, saying, Lord, thou deliveredst unto me five talents: behold, I have gained beside them five talents more.

His Lord said unto him, Well done, thou good and faithful servant: thou hast been faithful over a few things, I will make thee ruler over many things: enter thou into the joy of thy Lord."
Matthew 25:20-21 (KJV)

CASH FLOW CONTROL: Keeping Track of God's Money

LEADER'S NOTES – WEEKLY PROTOCOL

- Praise Song – A great way to start!
  Suggest Typed Lyrics and Upbeat Music

- Prayer – Led by a Leader or LIT
  Recommend Group Holding Hands

- Spiritual Warfare – in Jesus' mighty name

- Homework Sharing – Normally led by LITs
  Led by Leaders if LITs are Teaching this Week
  Time Control and Equal Sharing are Keys

- Sharing of Weekly Breakthroughs
  Brief but Builds Hope – Celebrate!

- Weekly Offering Time – Opportunity to Sow
  Have a Focus Group Member Pray First
  Put Faith into Action!

- 10 Minute Break
  Beverages & Restroom

- Call Group Together

- Weekly Lesson
  Taught by Leaders or LITs

- Homework Preview

- Dismiss in Prayer – Holding Hands
  Entire Session Should Average 2 to 2 ½ Hours

- Leaders and LITs Complete Weekly Report

CHAPTER 7 (WEEK 7)
CASH FLOW CONTROL: KEEPING TRACK OF GOD'S MONEY

OVERVIEW

In chapters five and six, you developed a godly *spending plan* that launched you on the path to freedom from debt and to a positive monthly cash flow. Celebrate (Hooray!) as you see that true financial freedom can be a reality, for you and your family!

This is an exciting chapter because you will learn how to use some basic cash flow techniques that will enable you to keep track of God's money on a daily, weekly, monthly and a yearly basis.

This lesson involves basic number crunching and three more user-friendly forms. Our goal is to teach you how to be good and faithful stewards.

This may also be a good time to re-examine your heart attitude about money.

If you need to stop and pray or even do spiritual warfare, then please obey the Holy Spirit. If married, please remember to do your warfare as a one-flesh couple.

I. STEWARDSHIP PRINCIPLES REVISITED

- **GOD OWNS EVERYTHING** and it is God who gives us the power and ability to get wealth. He requires His people to be good stewards of what He has given them.

- **WE MUST BE FAITHFUL FIRST WITH LITTLE**. In the *parable of the talents* (*Matthew 25)*, Jesus reminds us that it is the good and faithful servants who are faithful first in little that are given much more to steward or manage.

- **GOD WANTS US TO PLAN WISELY** *(Proverbs 21:5).*

- **GOD WANTS US TO BE AWARE OF THE CONDITION OF OUR RESOURCES.** In *Proverbs 27: 23-27* we are instructed to know the condition of our "flocks." Today, most of us are responsible for resources other than livestock. We look after our spouse, children, cars, income producing assets, and maybe a business but the advice still remains the same: *"Be sure you know the condition of your flocks, give careful attention to your herds; for riches do not endure forever, and a crown is not secure for all generations... the lambs will provide you with clothing and goats with plenty of goat's milk to feed you and your family and to nourish your servant girls." (NIV)*

➢ **GOD WANTS OUR HEARTS TO BE RIGHT**. He does not need our money, but He calls us to treat all financial decisions as spiritual decisions. In other words, he wants us to be faithful stewards.

II. CASH FLOW CONTROL – WHAT AND WHY

➢ **WHAT IS CASH FLOW CONTROL?** Cash flow control is simply keeping track of where your money goes – how it is spent, saved or wasted. This chapter will deal with three basic systems of keeping track of money:

1. ENVELOPE SYSTEM
2. COMPUTERIZED SYSTEMS *(brief reference)*
3. USER-FRIENDLY MANUAL SYSTEM *(our main focus)*

➢ **WHY DO YOU NEED A SYSTEM TO CONTROL CASH FLOW?** Experience has shown that an old-fashioned "budget" or even a more flexible *spending plan* can look good on paper but might not work out at the end of a month. The reason is — without a good cash tracking system, small and large amounts of money can slip right out of our wallets or purses without us being aware of it. If this happens on a regular basis, we will experience the ugly pattern of having *"too much month left at the end of the money."* In other words, we end up with a negative cash flow and don't know why.

III. HOW TO IMPROVE EFFECTIVENESS OF CASH FLOW CONTROL

➢ **KEEP GOOD RECORDS**. Accurate checkbook balances and properly rectified monthly checking statement balances are necessary.

➢ **CARRY A SMALL POCKET LOGBOOK** in which you can record daily uses of cash. Perfection is not expected, but you need to know where cash is spent.

➢ **CONSIDER GETTING MULTIPLE CHECKING ACCOUNTS.** For married couples, we are not talking about "his money" or "her money." Here is a situation where four separate checking accounts might actually benefit a married couple. (Seek-out checking accounts with no service charges.)

1. One main joint checking account used for most family expenses. Income from all sources should be deposited first into this main checking account. One designated spouse, who is also accountable to his or her one-flesh partner, should maintain this checkbook.

2. A second joint checking account, called a *freedom account*, is used primarily for those planned expenses which do not occur monthly. For example, quarterly or semi-annual insurance or home repair bills which are planned for in the ***Estimated Monthly Living Expenses*** form. Each month, a planned amount is deposited into the *freedom account* from the main family checking account. Then, when these irregular (non-monthly) expenses occur, you have the freedom of knowing you have one account just for these expenses.

3. Each spouse may also choose, by mutual agreement, to carry his/her own separate checking account. This account is used only for weekly or monthly "spending money" as allocated in the

spending plan. For example, if both spouses work outside the home they may have a plan that provides $30 per week for meals for each spouse. In this example, a $30 check would be written on the main family checking account and deposited at the beginning of each week in the wife's individual "spending money" checking account. Another $30 check would be deposited into the husband's "spending money" checking account. This may seem like a lot of check writing, but if a lack of discipline exists, this approach will definitely help you control and track your spending.

- **USE CHECKS WHENEVER POSSIBLE.** Checks allow for an accurate record of spending.
- **TRACK & RECORD ALL NON-CHECKBOOK TRANSACTIONS.** ATM withdrawals, automatic bank drafts, and direct bank deposits must all be recorded or your checkbook balances will be distorted. Failure to account for ATM cash withdrawals has derailed many *spending plans* for families.
- **DO NOT WRITE BAD CHECKS.** Writing a bad check is absolutely not acceptable! It is illegal and a terrible witness. Therefore, you must know your balance prior to writing a check!
- **NEVER WRITE POSTDATED CHECKS.** Regardless of the date, the check can be cashed once you sign it, and you are liable if there are insufficient funds.

IV. THE ENVELOPE SYSTEM – SIMPLE AND EFFECTIVE

It's simple, but it works! You just need to create an envelope for each major *spending plan* category.

LEADERS' NOTE – Make a simple visual by labeling envelopes for each category (A-J) shown on the ***Estimated Monthly Living Expenses*** form. Use a shoebox as a file holder.

- **LABEL ENVELOPES**. For example: food, transportation, medical, clothing, and housing.
- **PLACE THE DESIGNATED MONIES IN THE APPROPRIATE ENVELOPE WHEN YOU CASH YOUR PAYCHECK.** (This should coincide with your *spending plan*.)
- **WRITE OUT CHECKS FOR FIXED EXPENSES** and place them in the envelope for safekeeping until it's time to mail them. Fixed expenses include rent or mortgage payment.
- **USE SPECIFIED MONIES AS NEEDED.** Assuming the *spending plan* is balanced (or has a positive monthly cash flow), there should be sufficient money to fully fund each envelope. Once the funds from an envelope are used, spending from that specific category must stop for the month.

Married Couples Must Absolutely work together on this envelope system. Surprises must be avoided — trust and discipline are essential.

- **TRANSFER FUNDS FROM ANOTHER ENVELOPE** only if you must spend more than the available amount from a particular envelope. Hopefully, new debt is not an easy option. If money is used from one envelope to compensate for another, then spending on that category must be curtailed accordingly.

- **IF ONE ENVELOPE IS OVERDRAWN, TIGHTEN UP.** If you operate the envelope system properly, you will not run short of funds during the month. However, if one envelope is overdrawn, you need to take immediate "belt-tightening" measures to cut equal amounts of spending from one or more other envelopes.

- **RESTRAINT AND DISCIPLINE ARE ABSOLUTELY REQUIRED** for the envelope system (or any cash flow control system) to work! You only have so much money to support your group of envelopes. The amounts for each category has been set by your *spending plan* and are reflected on your *Monthly Cash Flow Analysis* form.

- **FLEXIBILITY EXISTS.** If you need to adjust the categories, then do so in your *spending plan* and reflect the changes on your *Monthly Cash Flow Analysis* form. Finally, change the values on selected envelopes.

- **PROPERLY MAINTAIN CHECKBOOKS AND BANK STATEMENTS.** Checkbooks and bank statements must be accurately maintained for any system to work... no exceptions!

- **DEVELOP A SIMPLE LOG SHEET.** To go one step further with the envelope control system, you may wish to also develop a simple log sheet to track activity for each envelope category. This can be used to log cash in and out, in the same manner you use a checkbook register. However, we recommend that you use a separate page to log, or keep track of, each category. Some people actually obtain several blank checkbook registers and label one for each envelope category (these extra check registers serve as the log sheet, or log book, for each designated category).

➤ **SAMPLE ENVELOPE LOG SHEET.** Below you see an example of how Bob and Mary Jones prepared a log sheet for the category "food." This log sheet allows them to record and track the cash (or check) activity going into and out of that envelope.

ENVELOPE SYSTEM LOG SHEET

Name(s): Bob and Mary Jones | Year: 2001

For Category: Food

Monthly Allocation for This Category: $ 425.00

Or Twice a Month Allocation: $ N/A

Or Weekly Allocation: $ N/A

Date	Transaction	Deposit	Withdraw	Balance
08/30/2001	Cash to envelope from pay check	$425	$0	$425
09/04/2001	HEB Grocery Cash Purchases	$0	($125)	$300
09/13/2001	Albertson's Grocery Cash Purchases	$0	($105)	$195
09/27/2001	ABC Grocery Cash Purchases	$0	($165)	$30
09/30/2001	Cash to envelope from pay check	$425	$0	$455

➤ **KEEP A SAVINGS ENVELOPE.** Hopefully the savings envelope grows steadily. We recommend depositing most surplus funds, beyond a small emergency cushion, into an actual interest-earning savings account. Develop a saving habit. By transferring extra (savings) money out of your checking account, and into a separate savings account, you will reduce the temptation to spend your savings.

A REAL LIFE EXAMPLE

When Bill and Maureen were a young married couple, in the Army with two babies, a basic envelope cash control system was used. As the monthly paycheck was cashed, all envelopes received their cash or checks and the "surplus funds" envelope received $30 or one dollar per day. The plan was simple and it worked! If used correctly, it is not possible to "overdraw" the envelope system.

➤ **BLANK ENVELOPE SYSTEM LOG SHEET FORM.** The following blank form is available (with author's permission) for owners of this book (only) to copy and use, as part of the envelope system of cash flow control. If you photocopy it in full size, it can be stapled or taped to the front of a large (recycled) 9-inch by 12-inch envelope.

ENVELOPE SYSTEM LOG SHEET

Name(s): ______________________ Year: __________

For Category: ______________________

Monthly Allocation for This Category: ______________________

Or Twice a Month Allocation: ______________________

Or Weekly Allocation: ______________________

Date	Transaction	Deposit	Withdraw	Balance

V. COMPUTERIZED CASH FLOW CONTROL

If you are comfortable with computer basics, you may want to consider using one of several commercially available and reasonably priced finance tracking or budgeting software packages. There are several good ones and they will work, but only if used with discipline.

- **DISCIPLINE AND ACCURACY ARE VITAL.** There is a very old saying about computers: "garbage in and garbage out." Very simply, this means that the fancy printed financial status reports will be only as good as the data that is regularly provided as input. If this scares you, then skip to the manual system of cash control.

- **FAITHFULLY INPUT ALL TRANSACTIONS** and you will reap easy-to-read reports that can be customized for various uses. At tax time, or when doing an annual plan, it is a wonderful benefit to have detailed summaries of your income and expenses that are broken out by the major categories you pre-select. For example, you can customize most reports to match your *spending plan* and *biblical giving plan* categories.

- **A FEW PC-BASED SOFTWARE PACKAGES** – There are many more that you will discover as you visit computer software stores and read more about this subject. If you have friends who are both PC users and are financially savvy, ask them for recommendations for user-friendly systems.

  1. Quicken and Quick Books Pro are two very popular software packages offered by Intuit. These are available in most computer stores. They are reasonable, have good training packages available, and allow you to reasonably customize reports. *(Note: Maureen and Bill use Quicken for their small business accounting and for their personal records. Actually they have an excellent employee who maintains the records and their tax accountant loves the reports produced.)* Visit: www.quickbooks.com/2001 or call 1-800-624-1735.
  2. Money Matters Basic and Money Matters Deluxe are two software packages available from Crown Financial Ministries. Larry Burkett's team developed these software packages and they sell for less than $40. Phone 1-866-424-4000 or visit: www.crown.org.
  3. Microsoft offers finance software called Microsoft Money, which is generally included in some of Microsoft's suites of programs, such as Microsoft Office.

UNDERSTANDING IS A MUST!

Even if you decide to use a PC-based cash flow control plan, you absolutely must understand the mechanics of how a manual system works. If you don't feel that a software approach is for you, then you definitely need to understand the manual system. So let us go forward and really learn how to keep track of God's money... daily, weekly, monthly and annually.

VI. A MANUAL CASH FLOW CONTROL SYSTEM

This user-friendly manual cash flow control system is built around the use of three forms which will be introduced in this chapter. During this session, you will study all three forms. The sample forms labeled example A, B and C present Bob and Mary Jones' results approximately one full year after they completed this course. The numbers used in these three cash flow forms were taken from their various *spending plan* forms as shown in example # 2. The easiest way to explain the use of these forms is for you to study the three example forms provided.

LEADERS' NOTE – It is definitely recommended that you become very comfortable with the three forms *(example A, example B, and example C)* before reviewing the examples with the class. However, do not be intimidated; you do not need to be an expert. The forms will always work if blanks are filled in properly and the math is done correctly.

At first glance, the *cash flow control* forms may appear to be complicated. They are primarily a recap of data already gathered, coupled with simple boxes to record daily activity. Leaders should be sensitive to "walk" the group through each form.

➢ EXAMPLE A: MONTHLY CASH FLOW CONTROL FORM (CF-1).

MONTHLY CASH FLOW CONTROL FORM (CF-1)

Financial Freedom Plan: "Keeping Track of God's Money"

EXAMPLE A: One Year After Course Completion
Based on Data From Prior Example #2 Spending Plan.

Name(s): Bob & Mary Jones **Date Completed:** 8/31/01 **For Month:** August **Year:** 2001

Projected/Plan			Actual This Month							Comparison		
			Week 1	Week 2	Week 3	Week 4	Week 5	Monthly Total		Mo Plan	Mo Actual	Plus/ Minus ( )
Monthly Gross Inc.-Cash Flow Form	4,000	---	1,000	1,000	1,000	1,000	0	4,000		4,000	4,000	0
Less Total Giving-Cash Flow Form	-415	---	-115	-100	-100	-100	0	-415		-415	-415	0
Less Taxes-Cash Flow Form	-750	---	-188	-187	-188	-187	0	-750		-750	-750	0
Less Debt Repayment-Cash Flow Form	0	---	0	0	0	0	0	0		0	0	0
Net Spendable Inc.-Cash Flow Form	2,835	Total	697	713	712	713	0	2,835	Total:	2,835	2,835	0

LIV. EXP:	1	2	3	4	5	6	7	8	9	10	11	12	13	14	15	16	17	18	19	20	21	22	23	24	25	26	27	28	29	30	31	Actual Total	Month Plan	Diff.
A-J: (See Living Expenses Form)																																		
A-Housing					735					50					25					40			25					10				885	1,052	167
B-Food	100						125											100								100						425	425	0
C-Clothing			20					30								40																90	95	5
D-Trans.		12					25							25							25				40			25		32		184	174	-10
E-Ent./Rec.	10				10						5				15				48											10		98	110	12
F-Med.Ex.									30								50								50							130	120	-10
G-Insurance							35																									35	35	0
H-Children	5		8				5			8				5			8	25			7			8				5			8	92	90	-2
I-Gifts/Spec. Occ.				20								15																				35	46	11
J-Misc.		18						20					5				25					21				11			6			106	110	4
Total (A-J):	115	30	28	20	745	0	190	50	30	58	5	15	5	30	40	40	83	125	48	40	32	21	25	8	90	111	0	40	6	42	8	2,080	2,257	177

RECAP MONTHLY DATA

Actual Net Spendable Income:	$ 2,835
Less Actual (A-J) Living Expenses:	(2,080)
Actual Cash Flow Margin this Month:	$ 755
Planned CF From Monthly CF Analysis Form:	$ 578
Temporary Surplus or Deficit ( ) this Month:	$ 177

After completing this form, proceed to form CF-2 to display & track your uses of positive cash flow.

Note: If CF is Negative or Zero, then the Form CF-2 will **not Yet** apply; proceed to annual summary form (CF-3).

Comments/Action Needed: Bob & Mary actually have $177 more cash flow than an average month per their plan. This $177 temporary surplus will be depositied into their special "Freedom Account" checking account, which will be used when they need to pay bills for planned expenses, like insurance, that do not occur every month.

Advice on Using Form: *Only use a very sharp pencil; no decimals, round-up to nearest dollar; use a minus sign or brackets ( ) to indicate minus numbers; fill in all possible blanks; recheck math, and if possible use a calculator with adding machine tape.*

1. **The box at the top left** of this form is just a recap of Bob and Mary's data from the form labeled ***Monthly Cash Flow Analysis***, which you studied as example # 2 in week six. You will see that their *net spendable income* was projected to be $2,835.

2. The **Actual This Month** box at the top center provides a place to enter actual transactions for this month, which is August 2001 in this case.

   - Bob earns $4,000 gross each month. However, for example purposes, we show that he actually gets a weekly check of $1,000 gross, which amounts to $4,000 as shown in the monthly total column.

   - Biblical giving is $415 a month. For this example, $115 is given in week one and $100 per week is given in weeks two, three and four. The total column shows $415.

   - Income taxes are deducted from Bob's weekly paychecks. For this example, we show a deduction of $188 in weeks one and three, and $187 in weeks two and four. The total tax for the month is shown as $750.

   - Since the Jones' have no consumer debt payment, per example # 2, the *debt repayment* value is shown as zero. (It is best to fill in each blank space or box to avoid errors.)

   - Finally, the monthly *net spendable income* value is obtained by subtracting the priority expenses, giving, taxes and debt repayment, from actual gross income. In this example, the result is $2,835.

3. The **Comparison** box at the top right of form CF-1 provides a place for Bob and Mary to compare their planned *net spendable income* to what actually took place. In this example, the plan and actual numbers matched. However, this will not always be the case. Just record what happened, compare it to your plan, and move forward. If you find a major discrepancy, then recheck your calculations.

4. The **Living Expenses** section of form CF-1 may look more difficult than it really is. The ten expense categories (A-J) are actually the same categories used in the *spending plan.*

   - Bob and Mary used this form to record how much money (in whole dollar amounts) they actually spent, on each category, on a daily basis. For example, on August 5, they made a $735 mortgage payment and also spent $10 on entertainment or recreation.

   - They recorded their spending on a daily basis, using their checkbook or a handy pocket logbook. Then they recorded the information on form CF-1. The numbers are probably not 100% perfect, but they are good estimates of their spending.

   - At the bottom of the daily columns there is space for a total of the day's spending on each of the ten categories (A-J).

   - At the right of the 31 daily spaces, there is a place to display the total of all monthly spending on each of the ten (A-J) categories. For example, the clothing total (across) is $90.

   - Just to the right of the "Actual Total" column is a column for displaying the monthly values planned for each category. For example, in Bob and Mary's projected living expenses, in example # 2, they planned $95 for clothing in an "average" month.

- The column to the far right is (column labeled "Diff.") for recording the difference between the actual and planned values. We can see that Bob and Mary actually spent $5 less on clothing than projected. The value is displayed as $5 because it was less than projected. If they spent more than planned, there would be a minus sign, or parenthesis ( ), in front of the dollar amount.

- Spreadsheets like this form allow you to record values and add columns both down and across, to verify accuracy. The daily totals are added across to arrive at a 31-day actual total of $2,080. Fortunately, when the actual values for each category are added vertically, the total also checks-out at $2,080.

- The vertical totals from the monthly plan amounted to $2,257.

- The difference (actual minus planned) was a positive $177. This means that, at least for this one month, there is a <u>temporary surplus</u> of $177.

- In this example, the $177 was deposited into a separate "freedom account" checking account for use when planned, non-monthly expenses occur: such as, insurance payments, gifts, and for a planned vacation. (Remember, these are non-monthly expenses that were planned for in the ***Estimated Monthly Living Expenses*** form.)

5. Recap of Actual Month's Data

   - The box near the bottom left of the form provides a place to recap the data just developed. We see that Bob and Mary started with *net spendable income* of $2,835 and deducted actual monthly expenses of $2,080 to arrive at a positive cash flow margin for the month of $755.

   - Since there is a positive cash flow value, this example continues on form CF-2. If there is no positive cash flow, they would not use CF-2 (not needing to use CF-2 is not a good thing, because it means there is no positive cash to track).

➢ EXAMPLE B: USING FORM CF-2 TO TRACK THE DAILY AND MONTHLY USE OF POSITIVE CASH FLOW MARGIN.

Bob and Mary had a positive cash flow for the month of August 2001, as shown on form CF-1 in example A. Now on form CF-2, in example B, Bob and Mary use this form to track their actual daily use of this positive cash flow money.

TRACKING USE OF MONTHLY POSITIVE CASH FLOW MARGIN (FORM CF-2)

"Keeping Track of God's Cash Flow"

Name(s): Bob & Mary Jones Date Completed: 8/31/01 For Month: August Year: 2001

EXAMPLE B: One Year After Completion Based on Data From Bob & Mary's CF-1 Form.

Actual Net Spendable Income:	$2,835
Less Actual (A-J) Living Expenses:	($2,080)
Actual Cash Flow Margin this Month:	$755
Planned CF From Monthly CF Analysis Form:	$578
Temporary Surplus or Deficit ( ) this Month:	$177

Below, Record Daily Transactions & Totals:

Uses For Positive Cash Flow Margin	1	2	3	4	5	6	7	8	9	10	11	12	13	14	15	16	17	18	19	20	21	22	23	24	25	26	27	28	29	30	31	Actual Tot.
"Freedom Acct."																														177		177
Ex. Debt Repay.					100																											100
Savings																														100		100
Extra Giving															50																	50
Retirement																														100		100
Money Market																														228		228
Other (Explain):																																
TOTALS:	0	0	0	0	100	0	0	0	0	0	0	0	0	0	50	0	0	0	0	0	0	0	0	0	0	0	0	0	0	605	0	755

Step 1:	Add each daily column to get a daily total.	Step 4:	Add the monthly totals down. The total must equal step 2 total.
Step 2:	When the month is complete add the daily (1-31) totals across & record in actual total space.	Step 5:	To check your calculations, the actual total monthly cash flow must equal the Actual Cash Flow Margin value in the box at the top of this form.
Step 3:	Also, when month is complete, add across for each category (example "Freedom Account") and record total in appropriate total space for that category.	Step 6:	Now proceed to Form CF-3: Yearly Cash Flow Summary.

Comments/Action Needed: Bob & Mary waited until near the end of the month to use most of their positive cash flow, this gave them some extra reserve funds during the month. The $177 temporary surplus was deposited into their special "Freedom Account" checking account for non-monthly, but planned, expenses.

1. **At the top of the CF-2 form,** there is another place to recap actual cash flow for the month. We show a value of $755 that came directly from the previous form CF-1. (Recap of Monthly Data.)

2. **In the same box (at the top**) we can now compare the planned "average" monthly cash flow of $578 to the actual value of $755. By doing the subtraction, we verify a temporary monthly cash flow surplus of $177. In the **Comments/Action Needed** box at the bottom of form CF-2, we see that this $177 was deposited in a "freedom account" checking account, for use to pay future (other than monthly) planned expenses.

3. **The main part of form CF-2** is provided to record actual daily uses of cash flow dollars. For example, $100 was used to make an extra payment on their home mortgage, on the 5th of the month. And $50 of extra giving was recorded on the 15th.

4. As in form CF-1, daily values are totaled down each column. Category totals are also added across the spreadsheet.

5. An actual total for each category, and for the month, is recorded. Here, we see verification that the total use of all cash flow dollars is $755 for the month. This is good, because all cash flow money should be accounted for.

6. We see in the comments section that Bob and Mary were pretty conservative. They did not commit most of their positive cash flow dollars until near the end of the month. This delay gave them a little extra reserve in their regular checking account.

7. Now we are ready to proceed to the annual summary form CF-3.

➤ **EXAMPLE C: YEARLY CASH FLOW SUMMARY FORM (CF-3).** The *Yearly Cash Flow Summary Form (CF-3)* is very easy to complete. It provides a place to quickly record the monthly data from forms CF-1 and CF-2. In this example, we will only look at Bob and Mary's data for the month of August 2001.

YEARLY CASH FLOW SUMMARY (FORM CF-3)

"Keeping Track of God's Money Annually"

Actual Summary by Month (From Monthly Cash Flow Control Forms: CF-1 & CF-2)

EXAMPLE C: One Year After Course Completion Based on Date From Bob & Mary's CF-1 & CF-2 Forms.

Name(s): Bob & Mary Jones **Date Completed:** 8/31/01 **Year:** 2001

		Jan.	Feb.	Mar.	April	May	June	July	Aug.	Sept.	Oct.	Nov.	Dec.	Year Total	Year Plan	Diff.
	Monthly Income								4,000							
	Less Giving								-415							
	Less Taxes								-750							
	Less Debt Repay.								0							
1	*Equals-Net Spend.*								2,835							
	Living Exps. (A-J)															
	A-Housing								885							
	B-Food								425							
	C-Clothing								90							
	D-Transportation								184							
	E-Ent./Rec.								98							
	F-Med. Expenses								130							
	G-Insurance								35							
	H-Children								92							
	I-Gifts/Spec. Occ.								35							
	J-Miscellaneous								106							
2	***Sub Total (A-J):***								2,080							
	Cash Flow Uses:															
	"Freedom Account"								177							
	Ex. Debt Repayment								100							
	Savings								100							
	Extra Giving								50							
	Retirement								100							
	Money Market								228							
	Other (Explain):								0							
3	**Sub Tot. C.F. Uses:**								755							
4	**TOTAL: 2 + 3 =4**								2,835							
	4 Should = 1															

Comments/Action Needed: This is just an example. A family can start their plan in any month. Do not put off starting; any month is a great time to begin!

Advice on using this Form: Use a very sharp pencil & have a calculator & eraser handy. Round all values to nearest whole dollar; no decimals.

1. As you look at example C, you see that all the data came from their two previous forms. Therefore, it is no surprise that *net spendable income* is $2,835, the sub total for *living expenses* (A-J) is $2,080, and the month's total positive cash flow uses amounts to $755.

2. At the bottom of the spreadsheet there is a place (box #4) to add (item #2) *living expenses* A-J to (item #3) cash flow uses. The total of $2,835 should equal the (item #1) value for *net spendable income*, and it does.

3. This form is used monthly and kept as part of an annual financial freedom plan, along with all the other forms used in this course.

ADVICE ON USING CASH FLOW CONTROL FORMS (CF-1, CF-2 and CF-3)

1. START YOUR PLAN NOW! Although the annual form (CF-3) starts with January, you are encouraged to start your plan now, regardless of the month. Do not delay until January.

2. These three forms probably look more complex than they are. That is why we started by looking at Bob and Mary's example forms: example A, B and C.

3. We realize that the spaces provided in the spreadsheets are pretty small. Please use a sharp pencil and remember to use only whole dollar values. Have an eraser handy and make your entries very clear.

4. A calculator or adding machine is a must. We recommend a calculator with an adding machine tape so you can check your math.

5. Remember, perfection is not necessary. The goal is to put a system in place that will help you keep track of God's money. If you use these forms on a disciplined basis, you will achieve good results!

➢ BLANK FORMS: CF-1, CF-2 & CF-3

1. Now, please locate the three blank forms located in chapter 15.

2. We asked you to make six copies of all the previous blank forms in this course. For this manual cash flow system, you will actually need:

   - 12 copies of forms CF-1 and CF-2, as you will use one each month during a year.

   - Six copies of the annual summary form CF-3.

3. For this week's homework, you will see that using these three forms will be part of your preparation for your private, scheduled, follow-up session with your leader couples.

- **ACCOUNTABILITY PARTNERS.** If you are married, you already know that this course requires mutual involvement and accountability. Non-married focus group members may need to find a suitable accountability partner. We typically recommend wise Christians of the same sex as the group member.

VII. CASH FLOW CONTROL SUMMARY

We trust that you now understand that accountability and good stewardship go hand-in-hand.

- **A CASH FLOW CONTROL SYSTEM HELPS YOU KEEP TRACK OF GOD'S MONEY ON A DAILY, MONTHLY AND A YEARLY BASIS.** In *Luke 16: 1-3*, Jesus gave us a parable about a shrewd manager whose superior called him to: "*give an account of your management.*" (NIV) This manager was in charge of certain resources, just as we are responsible for God-given resources.

- **WE HAVE EXAMINED 3 CASH FLOW CONTROL SYSTEMS:**

  1. Envelopes with supporting log sheets or log books for tracking daily envelope transactions.
  2. Computerized PC-based software packages.
  3. A manual cash flow control system with three forms provided.

Pick the system that works best for you. Then, use your preferred system and you will have no trouble giving God a very good "account of your management" of His resources.

VIII. CONCLUSION TO 7-WEEK COURSE

This has been a very busy and mind-stretching seven weeks for many of you. The road to true Financial Freedom requires commitment, discipline and ample doses of God's grace.

- ***CELEBRATE!*** We congratulate you on staying the course to complete this class. You have already positioned your family far ahead of the average.

- Now you have a basic understanding of several financial planning tools that you need to use on a regular basis. You probably learned some terms that previously seemed complex. Now you know that you can understand and use these user-friendly forms to develop a plan that will eventually point you to freedom from debt and on to Financial Freedom.

- Your leaders and LITs have sown a great deal of effort and prayer into you. You are encouraged to sow these principles into your family members, your loved ones and associates.

- Let's all be part of God's plan to give His people a new paradigm free from the crushing cycle of debt.

- **Let us commit to passing on a legacy of Godly prosperity — having all the resources we need *(time, talent, health and money)* to accomplish what God has called us to do.**

LEADERS' NOTE – Before closing in prayer, it is very important that you look at this week's homework and discuss the scheduled 30-45 day follow-up review sessions.

CLOSE IN PRAYER

- *Prayer of Thanksgiving*
- *Prayer of Jabez*
  (1 Chronicles 4: 9-10)
- *Spiritual Warfare*

May God Richly Bless You!

CHAPTER 7 (WEEK 7) HOMEWORK

CASH FLOW CONTROL:

KEEPING TRACK OF GOD'S MONEY

1. **Open in prayer and include spiritual warfare.** By now, we hope you have made this a standard part of homework sessions. Use these same techniques when you sit down to work on or discuss future financial issues and/or to revise forms. Involve your family when possible.

2. **Take a few minutes to thank God for helping you complete the course.** Ask the Holy Spirit for help with the homework. Consider taking communion, first repent of sin and prepare your heart to remember Jesus' precious sacrifice and all of God's promises.

3. **Congratulate yourself and if married, each other!** You have just taken a big step.

4. **The homework for Week Seven is to complete these manual Cash Flow Control Forms (CF-1, CF-2 & CF-3).** Also, you will probably need to review and revise all of your (previously completed) *spending plan* forms. The good news is that you have about one month to prepare for your individual review session.

   a. Manual Cash Flow Control Forms (CF-1, CF-2 and CF-3)

      1) Even if you decided to use the envelope system or a computerized system of cash-flow control as your personal system, you need to be able to use and understand the three-manual system forms used in week seven. Therefore, it is essential that you complete these three forms!

      2) Make 12 photocopies of forms CF-1 and CF-2 and make six copies of form CF-3.

      3) In pencil (only) use forms CF-1 and CF-2 to record your daily use of cash. Fill in all spaces and do the math. CF-2 is used for positive monthly cash-flow situations. If you are temporarily cash flow negative or neutral, proceed from CF-1 to CF-3.

      4) At the end of the month, record the data from forms CF-1 and CF-2 onto the ***Yearly Cash-Flow Summary*** form CF-3.

      5) Refer to the examples provided, as needed.

Couples need to be sure that both spouses understand the forms and can explain (account for) the numbers recorded on your forms. This is very important!

b. **Spending Plan — Review Forms and Revise as Needed**

1) In weeks five and six you completed a series of *spending plan* forms. In earlier weeks you also completed forms relating to: *goal setting, income and biblical giving, debt repayment, assets, liabilities, balance sheet and net worth, living expenses, and a recap of monthly cash flow.*

2) This is a good time to review all of those forms and make changes as needed.

REMINDER:
Always keep a supply of blank forms. Always use pencil and round off to whole dollar amounts.

5. Approximately two weeks after week seven, call your focus group leaders and schedule a private 90-minute session to meet with the leaders and LITs. This review session should take place approximately 30 to 45 days after week seven.

a. The purpose of the private follow-up session is to review and assess your progress.

b. Bring all completed forms from this course. NO EXCEPTIONS:

- *Projected Income and Biblical Giving*
- *Financial Vision and Faith Goals*
- *Debt Repayment Schedule*
- *List Your Assets*
- *List Your Liabilities*
- *Balance Sheet and Net Worth Statement*
- *Estimated Monthly Living Expenses (3 page form)*
- *Monthly Cash Flow Analysis*
- *Monthly Cash Flow Control Form (CF-1)*
- *Tracking Use of Monthly Positive Cash Flow Margin (CF-2)*
- *Yearly Cash Flow Summary (CF-3)*

c. Plan on a full 90 minutes for the session. Be well organized and be prompt! Your leaders are reserving their valuable time just for you.

d. Bring extra blank forms, a calculator, pencils and erasers. This is not your leaders responsibility.

e. Be prepared to give an account of your stewardship.

LEADERS' NOTE – You are advised to establish a one-week period (specific dates) during which all group members are responsible to call the focus group leaders to establish a 90-minute appointment.

6. **Call your leaders in advance of the follow-up appointment if you get bogged down.** However, this is a big and very vital assignment, so do not delay getting started.

7. **Please pray about the possibility of leading a future Financial Freedom in 7 Weeks Plus focus group.** Talk to your leaders if you feel God may be calling you to leadership. (You will probably start as a leader-in-training, so don't be nervous.)

8. **Record Your Breakthroughs for the week and share them during homework sharing with your leaders, at the review session.**

BREAKTHROUGHS!

FINANCIAL FREEDOM COURSE – RECORD YOUR WEEKLY TESTIMONIES

NAME: ______________________________ & ______________________________

DATE:	MONEY, CAREER, GIFTS/INHERITANCE, & OTHER
______	____
______	____
______	____
______	____
______	____
______	____

CHAPTER 8

"…give an account of your management,…." From Luke 16:2 (NIV)

ACCOUNTABILITY: Your Private 30 to 45 Day Review Session

CHAPTER 8
ACCOUNTABILITY:
Your Private 30 to 45 Day Review Session

- **JESUS EMPHASIZED ACCOUNTABILITY...PARABLE OF THE TALENTS.** In Matthew 25:14-30, Jesus taught very clearly on the subjects of accountability and stewardship. You are encouraged to re-read this powerful scripture, which is printed in red in many Bible translations; meaning these are Jesus' own words. Three servants were entrusted with sizable amounts of money. Those given five and two talents invested diligently and doubled their master's resources. To both, the master's words were exactly the same: "*Well done good and faithful servant. You have been faithful with a few things; I will put you in charge of many things. Come and share your master's happiness.*" (NIV) As you read further, you will see the severe consequences for the servant who was unfaithful with his one talent.

- **JESUS STRESSED TRUST...REGARDLESS OF THE AMOUNT.** In Luke 16:1-15, Jesus taught *the parable of the shrewd manager*. He again stressed accountability for resources. In verses 10 and 11, He said, "*Whoever can be trusted with very little can also be trusted with much, and whoever is dishonest with very little will also be dishonest with much. So if you have not been trustworthy in handling worldly wealth, who will trust you with true riches?*" (NIV)

- **OKAY, YOU GET THE POINT. NOW, LET'S DISCUSS YOUR VITAL 30 TO 45 DAY PRIVATE REVIEW SESSION.**

I. SCHEDULING YOUR PRIVATE REVIEW SESSION.

1. You are responsible to call your focus group leaders to schedule a 90-minute private session.

2. Remember, your leaders are busy and will be scheduling sessions for other group members. Therefore, you need to be flexible and provide ample scheduling lead-time.

II. PREPARING FOR YOUR REVIEW

1. Refer to the homework for week seven for a checklist of everything you need to complete and take to your private review session.

2. Every form used during the seven weeks must be completely filled out in pencil and brought to the meeting.

Married Couples Reminder:
It is essential that both spouses understand and are prepared to discuss all forms and numbers!

3. Do not waste your leader's time by showing-up unprepared. Results do not need to be perfect, but there is no excuse for not completing all forms.

PRAYER & SPIRITUAL WARFARE

By now you should be in the habit of praying and doing spiritual warfare before tackling your forms. Do not let your guard down!

III. CONFIDENTIALITY

1. Focus group leaders, and their leaders-in-training, are committed to keep your information strictly confidential. They do need to see your numbers in order to verify that you understand how to develop a complete financial freedom plan.

2. These sessions are private and no children, including babies, or guests should be included. Give this review session your full attention.

3. Leaders will review your forms and comment as appropriate. Typically, there is no reason for them to retain a copy of your data.

4. If your leaders point out areas that need attention, you should commit to making appropriate changes and/or revisions. Hopefully, you will not need an additional follow-up session, but this can be arranged by mutual agreement.

IV. CONCLUSION OF THE REVIEW SESSION

1. Your leaders will close the session with final comments and recommendations.

2. We suggest your leaders join you in prayer, then release you from the group.

3. We hope that all focus group participants are under the covering of a local church or ministry. If you are, your focus group leaders will report back to your church or ministry coordinator that you have fully completed the course.

4. Local churches and ministries are encouraged to award course graduates with a certificate of completion.

5. Pass the good word. If this course blessed you, then pass your recommendations on to your covering church or ministry and to friends and family.

V. CALL FOR NEW FOCUS GROUP LEADERS

1. If you feel called to lead future Financial Freedom in 7 Weeks Plus focus groups, then consult your leaders who will advise your church or ministry coordinator.

2. Remember, you will most likely start by serving as a leader-in-training. This will give you extra time to be discipled by your assigned focus group leaders.

3. God may lead you to serve under leaders you do not know well. Be open to new relationships and let the Holy Spirit build a strong leadership team. You will probably make excellent new friends for life.

4. Please pray for past, present and future focus group leaders and for all members of your focus group. There is incredible power in mass prayer.

➢ **CONGRATULATIONS...***"well done good and faithful stewards."*

➢ **PASS ON THE LEGACY OF FINANCIAL FREEDOM.** Psalm 26:12 and 13 explains the legacy God intends for those who respect (fear) and obey Him. *"Who, then is the man that fears the Lord? He will instruct him in the way chosen for him. He will spend his days in prosperity, and his descendents will inherit the land." (NIV)*

➢ **WWW.DEBTFREELEGACY.COM** is the website we have reserved to provide fresh information in the future. Please pray for the successful development of this website and that God will use it, and Bill and Maureen Sitter, to further His Kingdom principles. Thank You!

➢ **BREAKTHROUGHS...ONE MORE FORM TO CELEBRATE WHAT GOD HAS DONE.** Now is a great time to reflect on breakthroughs, large and small, that you have experienced since your last focus group session, week seven. Write them down and share with your leaders at the review session. Give God the glory.

BREAKTHROUGHS!

FINANCIAL FREEDOM COURSE – RECORD YOUR WEEKLY TESTIMONIES

NAME: ______________________________ & ______________________________

DATE: MONEY, CAREER, GIFTS/INHERITANCE, & OTHER

______ ____

______ ____

______ ____

______ ____

______ ____

CHAPTER 9

"For we wrestle not against flesh and blood, but against principalities, against powers, against the rulers of the darkness of this world, against spiritual wickedness in high places."
Ephesians 6:12 (KJV)

Breaking Curses, Blockages & Strongholds That Control Our Finances

CHAPTER 9
BREAKING CURSES, BLOCKAGES & STRONGHOLDS THAT CONTROL OUR FINANCES

I. INTRODUCTION

For many people, this chapter contains the instructions needed to finally achieve true freedom; not only financial freedom, but true freedom to live, breathe, work, play, love and be loved as our Lord and Savior intended.

We (Bill and Maureen) met Rick Faulk through Marriage Ministries International, while Rick and Becky served as regional directors over several Southern States. We are deeply indebted to Rick for granting us full permission to edit and use the following "dynamite" material on how to identify and destroy curses, blockages and strongholds.

For some readers this may seem a bit "far out" or spooky. In fact, we believe that a key ingredient of this course is the instruction from God's Word on: prayer, spiritual warfare, and "Breaking Curses, Blockages and Strongholds." Before you skip past these important pages, please ask the Holy Spirit to show you how to grasp and apply this information.

Let us proceed directly to Rick Faulk's information, much of which is provided in outline format. We encourage you to dig deep into the powerful scriptural references, then pray and meditate over areas of special need.

This topic will discuss how sins, curses, and strongholds may affect your finances and hinder your ability to earn a living. Our purpose is to provide you with biblical strategies that will remove any of the hindrances and strongholds that limit your walk and destiny in God. Jeremiah reminds us that the Lord has plans and a good future for each of us: "*For I know the plans I have for you, says the Lord, Plans for welfare and not for evil, to give you a future and a hope. Then you will call upon me and come and pray to me, and I will hear you. You will seek me and find me; when you seek me with ALL your heart, I will be found by you, says the Lord, and I will restore your fortunes*" Jer. 29:11-13 (RSV).

You may not have heard much about this topic, but that does not make it any less real. We know that "*My people are destroyed for lack of knowledge*;" Hosea 4:6 (RSV), so we intend to shed light on this subject. It may be review for some, but there may be some areas that have not been examined, and it is important to cover them to ensure that we are free from areas where the "enemy of our soul" can rob and steal from us.

In this chapter, we will cover:

- What are curses, hexes and vexes?

- Sources of curses:
    a. Believing in false gods

b. Involvement in idolatry, witchcraft and the occult
c. Not tithing and giving offerings
d. Sin (general sin, sexual sin & unfaithfulness to spouse)
e. Not honoring father & mother
f. Generational curses

- Sources of blockages to God's blessings and abundance:
  a. Not being sensitive to our spouse
  b. Not forgiving
  c. From strongholds

- Five steps for breaking curses and strongholds:
  a. Renounce involvement
  b. Repent and confess your sin
  c. Ask the Lord to take back all ground that was given over to the enemy
  d. Bind and loose
  e. Walk as a child of the light

II. WHAT ARE CURSES, HEXES AND VEXES?

For the sake of clarity, we will define a curse as "calling upon divine or supernatural power to send injury upon another. A prayer or invocation for harm or injury to come upon one."

Curses, hexes and vexes are all very similar. Some dictionaries do not separate their meanings, but there are subtle differences. Hexes are curses that come from those who practice witchcraft. Vexes are curses that come from those not involved in witchcraft. Vexes are usually not as powerful as witchcraft or Satanic coven curses and hexes. They can cause distress and/or agitation, which can negatively affect one's productivity or income. For example, a curse or hex could bring about loss of job, home, health and family. A vex could come from a co-worker "jinxing" a presentation, project, or relationships which affect an employee's ability to earn income. A vexing headache could also cripple a person's ability to earn an income when the headache interferes with his/her ability to perform a job. Likewise, a person could be vexed through kids who have such bad behavioral problems that the parents are consumed with their care and with bailing them out of trouble.

- **LIFE AND DEATH ARE IN THE POWER OF THE TONGUE.** Curses, hexes and vexes can come through others, as well as ourselves. Just as others may speak ill over us, we may speak evil over ourselves. The Book of James reminds us that life and death are in the power of the tongue: "*From the same mouth came blessing and cursing. My brethren this ought not be so*" James 3:10 (RSV). The Old Testament has an illustration of this when Balak, the King of Moab, asked Balaam (a false prophet) to curse Israel. "*Come now, curse this people for me, since they are too mighty for me; perhaps I shall be able to defeat them and drive them from the land; for I know that he whom you bless is blessed, and he whom you curse is cursed.*" Numbers 22:6 (RSV). Religious curses can come also from witches, warlocks, voodoo witch doctors, etc.

  We recommend you read and meditate on the entire third chapter of James.

  James reminds us that the tongue is unrighteous, a restless evil, full of deadly poison, and with it we bless God and curse men. The Word tells us man alone is incapable of taming the tongue. However, God will give us the wonderful grace and wisdom to use our tongue to bless others.

- **EXAMPLE:** *While Rick Faulk was doing missionary work in Haiti, he witnessed a man in his 60's being brought to him on a stretcher for prayer. The interpreter said that his body was filled with cancer, and the doctor said that he would die very shortly. The Lord showed Rick that he had been cursed by a voodoo witch doctor, so Rick broke the curse over him. The minute he broke the curse, the gentleman leapt to his feet, grabbed hold of Rick's hands, started jumping up and down with excitement, and then danced across the front of the church. God is so good! He was able to return to his family and work, relieving his two daughters of caring for him and paying for his past medical bills.*

- **OUR WORDS ARE EXTREMELY POWERFUL...THIS IS NO JOKING MATTER.** Our words are powerful and can hold blessings or curses. Proverbs 12:13-14 reminds us that, "*An evil man is ensnared by the transgression of his lips, but the righteous escapes from trouble. From the fruit of his words a man is satisfied with good, and the work of a man's hands comes back to him*". (RSV) Consequently, it is important to guard the words we speak over others, ourselves, and especially our family (e.g., "You are such a klutz, a jerk, a wimp, etc." Likewise, you may have also heard words like, "you will never amount to anything.").

- **JESUS ASSURES US HIS WORD IS TRUTH, AND TRUTH HAS THE POWER TO SET US FREE...IF WE ACT ON IT**. Jesus exhorts us to pray for those who persecute and abuse us (Luke 6:28, Matthew 5:44), while Paul reminds us to bless those who persecute you and do not curse them (Romans 12:14). Jesus wants us to experience His total freedom. In the Gospel of John 8:36, we are reminded: "... *if the Son makes you free, you will be free indeed!" (RSV)*

  Later in this chapter we will discuss a method for breaking hexes, vexes or curses.

III. SOURCES OF CURSES

Besides those curses that are directly spoken over us by others or by ourselves, there are several other ways that we can pick up curses. By definition, when we are cursed, we are injured by a supernatural power. We are less able to build the kingdom of God, fulfill our destiny, and raise a Godly family. One of the easiest ways for the Enemy of our souls to derail us from our calling is to attack our finances, our health and our relationships. Although you may be personally aware of many of the following ways that people can pick up curses, it is important to revisit these (and some for the first time) to ensure that we close all doors to these attacks.

- **WE MAY RECEIVE A CURSE:**

  1. **Curses From Believing in Wrong Gods**
     The Word is consistent from Genesis through Revelation that if we are faithful to God we are blessed, if we are not— we are cursed.

     - Paul states in Galatians 3:10 that all who are under the Law are under a curse (i.e., those who have not made Jesus Lord and Redeemer of their lives). Paul goes on to say: "*If any one has no love for the Lord, let him be accursed. Our Lord Come!*" 1 Corinthians 16:22 (RSV)

     - Jesus said, "*He who is not with Me is against Me; and he who does not gather with Me scatters*" Luke 11:23 (RSV)

SALVATION OR REDICATION IS VITAL:
Consequently, it is essential that if we have not accepted Jesus as Savior and Lord, we do so now. It is also important that if we have fallen away from Him, that we confess our sin and rededicate our life to Him. This is the first step toward living a wise and prosperous life.

2. **Curses From Involvement in Idolatry, Witchcraft and the Occult.**
In Deuteronomy 18:9-13, the Lord commanded His people not to get involved in "*abominable practices.*" (RSV) The Bible defined abominable practices as sacrificing children, fortune telling (divination), soothsaying, sorcery (witchcraft), and hypnotism. He also made it clear not to visit a medium (someone who consults with familiar spirits), a wizard (a clairvoyant or psychic), an augur or a necromancer (a medium who consults with the dead). The Lord hated these practices so much that He instructed Israel (in verse 12) to show no mercy, and to drive them out of the land.

GOD HATES FORTUNE TELLING AND ALL OCCULT ACTIVITIES

SOME EXAMPLES OF INVOLVEMENT IN THE OCCULT:

* fortune telling	* astrology	* free masonry
* ouija board	* speaking in a trance	* palm-reading
* clairvoyance	* mind control	* hypnosis
* tarot cards	* telepathy (mind to mind communication)	

Paul tells us that no idolater "*has any inheritance in the Kingdom of Christ and God*" Ephesians 5:5 (RSV). In 1 Corinthians 6:9 and 10 (RSV), Paul lumps idolaters with the immoral, adulterers, perverts, thieves, greedy, drunkards, revilers, robbers, and states that none of them will inherit the kingdom of God. In Revelation 21:8, we read that those who do these practices "*shall be in the lake that burns with fire and sulfur, which is the second death*". *(RSV)*

John paints another picture in the next chapter of the final book of the Bible; Revelation 22: 14-15: "*Blessed are those who wash their robes that they may have the right to the tree of life and that they may enter the city by the gates. Outside are the dogs and sorcerers and fornicators and murderers and idolaters, and every one who loves and practices falsehood.*" *(RSV)*

Free Masonry may have started as a simple trade association. However, in the book: The Secret Teachings of the Masonic Lodge, John Ankerberg and John Weldon provide a modern day Christian perspective. This book is included in the list of references in chapter 11. Two of Alan Vincent's tape series are also included as additional references and these messages also refer to Free Masonry as an occult activity that often attacks in the area of finances.

In very simple terms, why would any true Christian be interested in a secret society or secret oaths of any kind? In Jesus, we have access to the "real thing" and it is no secret!

3. **Curses From Not Tithing and Giving Offerings**
Malachi 3:7-10 states, "*Return to me and I will return to you, says the Lord of hosts. But you say, How shall we return? Will a man rob God? Yet you are robbing me. But you say, how are we robbing thee? In your tithes and offerings. You are cursed with a curse, for you are robbing me; the whole nation of you. Bring the full tithes into the storehouse, that there may be good in my house; and thereby put me to the test, says the Lord of hosts, if I will not open the windows of heaven for you and pour down for you an overflowing blessing.*" *(RSV)*

Requirements for God to break the curse of poverty from not tithing and from not giving freewill offerings Malachi 3:7-10 (RSV) says:

- Return to God. Give God what His Word tells us to give: tithes and offerings.
- Stop Robbing God, by not paying the tithe and giving offerings.
- Bring the full tithes (10% of your "increase") into the storehouse.

So that God will do what He promises in Malachi 3:10 and 11 (RSV)

- Open the windows of heaven.
- Pour down an overflowing blessing.
- Rebuke the devourer for you to prevent him (Satan) from destroying the fruits of your soil (or labor), and that your vine shall bear fruit.

IF YOU FEEL THE DEVIL IS DEVOURING YOUR RESOURCES... THEN MEDITATE ON WHAT YOU JUST READ. READ MALACHI 3:7-12 AGAIN!

Giving also releases the favor of God. Jesus said, "*give and it shall be given to you, pressed down, shaken together, running over, will be put into your lap. For the measure you give will be the measure you get back.*" Luke 6:38 (RSV). The Lord instructs us to give: willingly in Exodus 25:2 (RSV); ungrudgingly and cheerfully in 2 Corinthians 9:7; liberally in Proverbs 11:25 (RSV), and sacrificially in 2 Corinthians 8:1-4 (RSV) and Mark 12:43-44 (RSV).

4. **Curses From Sin**
When Adam and Eve disobeyed God by eating from the tree of knowledge, they were banished from the garden and received individual curses. Eve suffered the pain of childbirth and pain of having to submit to her husband, while Adam suffered the pain of hard work, frustration, and a cursed ground Genesis 3:16-19 (RSV). <u>Sin causes us to labor hard with little gain</u>.

In 1 John 5:3 (RSV), John the Apostle states that we will know that we are children of God when we love God and keep his commandments. In John 5:3-5 (RSV), He goes on to say that the commandments are not burdensome, and whatever is born of God overcomes the world; and this is the victory that overcomes the world, our faith. Who is it that overcomes the world but he who believes that Jesus is the Son of God?

➢ **READ REVELATION CHAPTER 2 AND 3 (RSV).** Those who remain faithful to the end will receive their inheritance (Revelation 2:11, 17, 26-28, 3:20-21). Those who do not will face ruin (Revelation 2:5, 20-23, 3:3, 3:15-16).

Now we will focus on general sin, sexual sin and unfaithfulness to a spouse.

1. **Curses From General Sin**
Most people have an inward sense that if they do something wrong (i.e., they sin), God is going to punish them. However, we also carry a belief that God is good, and a good God would not do bad things to us. Actually the Word is consistent; there are consequences to a sinful life style. Malachi 3:5, provides a list of several things that will bring God's judgment upon us. "*I will draw near to you for judgment. I will be a swift witness against sorcerers, against adulterers, those who swear falsely (liars), against those who oppress hirelings in his wages (those who do not pay a fair wage), the widow and the orphan, against those who thrust aside the sojourner (traveler) and do not fear me, says the Lord." (RSV)*

   Proverbs 6:16-19, also states that, "*There are six things which the Lord hates, seven which are an abomination to him; haughty eyes, a lying tongue, hands that shed innocent blood, a heart that devises wicked plans, feet that make haste to run to evil, a false witness who breathes out lies, and a man who sows discord among brothers". (RSV)*

2. **Curses From Sexual Sin & Unfaithfulness to Spouse**
Proverbs 5:8-9, warns us to stay away from a harlot or illicit sexual relationships. The Holy Spirit also warns us of the consequences, if we do not: "*Keep your way far from her, (loose women), and do not go near the door of her house; lest you give your honor to others, and your years to the merciless". (RSV)*
Consequently, those who have affairs could suffer from extremely hard work with little recognition and little pay. In addition to this, they may also face loss of possessions (Proverbs 5:10); sickness and poor health (Proverbs 5:11, and suffer from a poor reputation (Proverbs 5:14).

ADULTERY, FORNICATION, AND HARLOTRY RESULT IN LOSS OF SELF WORTH AND IN PUNISHMENT... FOR MEN AND WOMEN

Proverbs 6:26, "*for a harlot may be hired for a loaf of bread, but an adulteress stalks a man's very life. Can a man carry fire in his bosom (temptation) and his clothes not be burned? Or can one walk upon hot coals and his feet not be scorched? So is he who goes in to his neighbor's wife; none who touches her will go unpunished." (RSV)*

Proverbs 6:32, "*He who commits adultery has no sense; he who does it destroys himself.*" (RSV)

➢ **PORNOGRAPHY IS A TERRIBLE CURSE TODAY.** Jesus says that if you lust in your heart after a woman, it is the same as adultery (Matthew 5:28). Consequently, dirty movies and pornography bring the same curse as adultery.

The consequences of unfaithfulness are huge. Besides the warnings and curses listed above for an unfaithful spouse, we may also develop: a hardened heart, a breech of trust in our marriage, defilement of the marriage bed, ungodly soul ties, a devastated family, and sometimes without repentance we can pass on generational sins and curses.

1. **Curses From Not Honoring Father & Mother**
   Paul reminds us "*Children, obey your parents in the Lord, for this is right. Honor your father and mother" (this is the first commandment with a promise), that it may be well with you and that you may live long on the earth*" Ephesians 6:1-3 (RSV). Thus in every way that we honor our father and mother we will prosper with health, wealth, relationships, and long life. And in every way that we do not honor our father and mother, things will not go well with us.

   The 10 Commandments were not created to make us feel bad and frustrate us because we cannot live up to them. They are part of God's blueprint for living a healthy, happy and full life. Spiritual laws work much the same as natural laws. After all, God established both of them. Gravity works whether we can see it or whether we believe in it. For example, if you fell off a roof and did not believe in gravity, it would not stop you from hitting the ground. Likewise, if you do not honor your father and mother there will be negative consequences.

   Many kids muddle through their lives at home, and become frustrated and angry with their parents. They often judge their parents, and make inner vows to not be like their parents. What most often happens is that they reap children just like themselves and become like their parents. In every way that children make judgments, are disobedient or are rebellious they DO NOT honor their mother and father. The spiritual laws of honoring mother and father and sowing and reaping, work hand in hand. There are countless examples, of abusive parents having children who end up abusing their children. Statistically, over 90% of abused kids end up being abusive parents!

2. **Curses Resulting From Generational Curses:**
   Curses can be passed down from one generation to the next and beyond. "*I the Lord your God am a jealous God, visiting the iniquity of the fathers upon the children to the third and fourth generation of those who hate me*" (Exodus 20:5, also see Numbers 14:18, Deuteronomy 23:2).

   We can pass on poverty, sickness and early death... a sin pattern. For example, deceit was passed on from Abraham to Jacob, and on to Jacob's sons, who sold Joseph into slavery.

EXAMPLE: JUKES AND EDWARDS FAMILIES

Two American families have been well documented to show the continuation of a family line of generational curses, and another family line which passed on a legacy of success.

The Jukes family produced generation after generation of criminals. The Edwards family passed on an incredible legacy which produced preachers, educators, doctors, legislators and college presidents.

Look at your life, your parents, your grandparents, and ask them about their ancestors to determine whether you have any generational curses that have been passed on. Do not discount diseases as just biological. Your doctor knows that genetics and psychological factors can be passed on. Does cancer, heart problems, high blood pressure, hearing loss, back problems, etc. run in your family? There are dozens of other physical and psychological problems that can be passed on. Otherwise, you would not be asked about your parents' health history. Look for sin patterns in your family: anger, abuse, fear, lust, divorce, addictions, theft, adultery, etc. Ask the Holy Spirit to identify generational influences in your life. Generational influences can be both good and bad. However, for our purposes, we are concerned only about reversing any negative generational curses.

IV. SOURCES OF BLOCKAGE TO GOD'S BLESSING AND ABUNDANCE

A blockage is something that causes God's hand of blessing to be held back from you. The Bible is clear on two things that will cause blockage to God's blessing, mercy and provision.

1. **Not Being Sensitive to Our Spouse Causes Blockages.**
   We are told that curses can come from not being sensitive and understanding to our wife. "*Likewise, you husbands, live considerately with your wives, bestowing honor on the woman as the weaker sex, since you are joint heirs of the grace of life, in order **that your prayers may not be hindered***" 1 Peter 3:7 (RSV). In this passage we are exhorted to be sensitive to our wife and show her honor. If you have fallen short in this area, then turn over a new leaf!

   Wives also receive instructions to honor their husbands in 1 Peter 3:1-6 (RSV).

2. **Not Forgiving also Causes Blockages**
   Forgiveness is a must for everyone who wants to walk in victory. As we forgive, we are forgiven. Likewise unless we forgive others, we will not be forgiven. Matthew 6:14-15, "*For if you forgive men their trespasses, your Heavenly Father also will forgive you; but if you do not forgive men their trespasses, neither will your Father forgive your trespasses.*" (RSV)

   Our prayers will not be answered if we do not forgive (Mark 11:25).

   Unforgiveness holds us in bondage. Jesus spoke of this bondage in terms of being imprisoned, in Mathew 18:35, "*So also my Heavenly Father will do to every one of you (put in prison), if you do not forgive your brother from your heart.*" (RSV)

   Unforgiveness can affect our finances. For example, in this passage (Mathew 18:34 RSV) the (tormentors) jailers were part of the prison system. Not only did they cause pain and suffering, but they also required forced labor for very low wages until the debt was paid off.

- **A LACK OF FORGIVENESS CAN MANIFEST IN PHYSICAL AND MENTAL ILLNESS:** Ulcers, intestinal and heart problems, migraines, high blood pressure, depression, extreme anger, bitterness, etc.

A lack of forgiveness is often the root of demonic strongholds, e.g., "*do not let the sun go down on your anger, and give not opportunity (or place) to the devil*" Ephesians 4:26-27 (RSV). When we let the sun go down on our anger, we actually give the devil a legal right to control a part of our life. The more we allow anger to fester in our life, the more control we give over to Satan.

- **UNFORGIVENESS BLOCKS THE PROMISE OF GOD AND HINDERS OUR PRAYERS**. In Mark 11:23, Jesus tells us that if we have faith, we can speak to our mountains (problems) and they will be removed, if we believe in our heart. However in verse 11:25, we see that lack of forgiveness is a clear act of disobedience and will block our prayers. "*And whenever you stand praying, forgive, if you have anything against any one; so that your Father also who is in heaven may forgive your trespasses.*" (RSV)

  The solution to unforgiveness is to forgive. It may not be easy, but it is required. For example, God instructs us to forgive our brother **before** we pray. Justification for not forgiving only perpetuates the sin and continues our bondage.

  Even if we do not "**feel**" like forgiving, we must. Forgiveness is not a feeling; it is an act of the will. We must choose to forgive. After we have decided to forgive, our feelings will line up with our will.

  Ask the Lord to release you from the bondage of unforgiveness once you have forgiven others. Remember, whatever we ask in His name will be granted, according to Matthew 7:7, "*And whatever you ask in prayer, you will receive it, if you have faith.*" (RSV)

- **Blockages From Strongholds**
  A stronghold is defined as a way of thinking or system of beliefs that is contrary to the will of God. The main battle takes place in our mind and thoughts. Fear can be a stronghold. Paul described this well when he said, "*for the weapons of our warfare are not worldly but have divine power to destroy strongholds. We destroy arguments and every proud obstacle to the knowledge of God, and take every thought captive to obey Christ*" 2 Corinthians 10:4-5 (RSV). Paul cannot make it more clear that the battle ground is in our minds and that we must take every thought captive. This is also the reason why Paul says that we must renew our mind, in Romans 12:2, "*Do not be conformed to this world but be transformed by the renewal of your mind.*" (RSV)

  When our thoughts become habitual and are contrary to God's word, we have given Satan a place of residence in our mind. By continuing to agree with Satan's way of thinking and acting we have given him legal right to that area of our life by either a persistent thinking and sin pattern and/or generational sin pattern that we have inherited.

  A stronghold affects our actions and relationships. It can create a "leanness" in our hearts and soul. In Psalm 106:15, we read: "*He gave them what they asked for but sent a wasting disease.*" (RSV)

  A stronghold decreases our capacity to respond to God. It is also a place from which the enemy can "torment" or attack us in other aspects of our life, with: bitterness, fear, anger, worry, lust, and all sorts of addictions.

- **THE CENTER OF A STRONGHOLD IS IN THE MIND**. It is the place where we must fight the battle, as we see in Romans 8:5-7, "*For those who live according to the flesh set their minds on the things of the flesh, but those who live according to the Spirit set their minds on the things of the Spirit. To set the mind on the flesh is death, but to set the mind on the Spirit is life and peace.*" (RSV)

  All strongholds harden our heart toward God and each other.

➢ **SPECIAL WARNING-AVOID FILTHY INTERNET SITES.** All strongholds can affect our finances and relationships. For example: pornography, lust, fear, anxiety, alcohol, as well as soap operas and romance novels can rob an individual of his/her ability to earn a living and be productive. A stronghold of lust can dominate a person's thinking and cause him/her to get on the Internet at work and waste time on X-rated sites. This type of wasting time could jeopardize a job and/or render the person less productive and effective. Consequently, a stronghold can negatively impact a marriage and earning power.

Many people wonder why their prayers do not work after they have prayed for a stronghold to be broken. This could be because they have given themselves to Satan to such an extent that they are powerless in this area of their life. For example, if you sold a piece of property to someone and that person took possession of it, could you order him off the land? Of course not! The new owner takes up residence on his/her land. Likewise when someone has a demonic stronghold, Satan acts as if he legally possesses that area of your mind and actions. The only way that Satan will give up a stronghold is for someone else to "pay the price" for the land. Because Jesus paid our debt, only He can take possession of the land for us. Then we can become his "bond servants". Jesus gives us authority to pull down strongholds as part of our weapons of warfare. We studied this previously, in 2 Corinthians 10:4 (RSV). Our weapons can become dull and ineffective when we do not use them in battle against the enemy of our souls. Let us sharpen our swords for the real battle!

V. FIVE STEPS FOR BREAKING CURSES AND STRONGHOLDS

1. **Renounce Involvement**
   Renounce your former sinful ways and renounce any stronghold(s) that have held you captive. Renounce any occult involvement, practices or participation in false religions, however minor or major your participation. There is only "one way" to the Father and that is through Jesus. John 14:6, "*I am the way, the truth and the life; no one comes to the Father, but by me*". (RSV) The early church would have new believers renounce Satan and all his ways and works before they were baptized. Many of the liturgical churches continued this practice of "renunciation" when they made a profession of faith at Confirmation.

2. **Repent and Confess your Sin**
   "*If we confess our sins, he is faithful and just, and will forgive our sins and cleanse us from all unrighteousness. If we say we have not sinned, we make him a liar, and his Word is not in us.*"
   1 John 1:9 (RSV).

   Do not participate in your former sinful life patterns. It may require you not to associate with those who are trapped in darkness [Read Ephesians 5:7-13 (RSV)], until you are strong enough to witness to them and show them a way out of their situation. Walk the walk "as children of the light" (Ephesians 5:8). Learn what is pleasing to the Lord (Ephesians 5:10).

3. **Ask the Lord to Take Back All Ground that was Given Over to the Enemy**
   We surrender "ground" to Satan every time we let the sun go down upon our wrath Ephesians 4:26-27 (RSV) and when we enter into repetitive sin without repentance. Every time we give ground to the enemy of our souls, we should ask God to reclaim this ground. Psalm 23:3 says, "*He restores my soul*" ("restore in Hebrew means to "return to the starting point"); and it goes on to say: "*He leads me in paths of righteousness for His name's sake.*" (RSV)

4. **Bind Curses and Loose Blessings**
Matthew 16:19: "*I will give you the keys of the kingdom of heaven, and whatever you bind on earth shall be bound in heaven, and whatever you loose on earth shall be loosed in heaven.*" (RSV)

Use your God given authority, from this scripture in Jesus' own words, to bind and take authority over the curses that have been holding you captive.

Loose the blessing of God and by faith "prophesy" the opposite of the curse you, your family and marriage have experienced (e.g., just as Ezekiel prophesied over the dry bones). **For example, if you are under a curse of poverty you bind that curse and pray for the Lord to loose a blessing that you may prosper in the Lord in all ways.**

Proclaim out loud who you are in Christ according to 2 Corinthians 5:17-21 (RSV)

"Therefore, if any one is in Christ, he is a new creation; the old has passed away, behold the new has come. All this is from God, who through Christ reconciled us to himself and gave us the ministry of reconciliation, this is, in Christ God was reconciling the world to himself, not counting their trespasses against them, and entrusting to us the message of reconciliation. So we are ambassadors for Christ, God making his appeal through us. We beseech you on behalf of Christ, be reconciled to God. For our sake he made him to be sin who knew no sin, so that in him we might become the righteousness of God."

5. **Walk as a Child of the Light**
Practice Romans 12:9-13: "*Let love be genuine; hate what is evil, hold fast to what is good; love one another with brotherly affection; outdo one another in showing honor. Never flag in zeal, be aglow with the Spirit, and serve the Lord. Rejoice in your hope, be patient in tribulation, be constant in prayer. Contribute to the needs of the saints, practice hospitality.*"

If you fall, stand up and dust yourself off. Remember the law of sowing and reaping is still in effect. Keep sowing good seed and you will see victory!

PRELUDE TO PRACTICAL APPLICATION EXERCISES TO BREAK FINANCIAL CURSES AND STRONGHOLDS

Since there are only seven weeks in this course, there is no mandatory homework assignment for chapter eight. However, our experience has shown that most individuals really need to put Rick Faulk's excellent teaching to work as soon as possible. After all, if the devil has been standing on your neck, don't you want to kick him off?... and right now!

We encourage you to dive into the following practical application exercises for chapter nine.

Before you start:

- Pray.
- Do Spiritual Warfare.
- If married, work as a one Flesh Team.
- Consider taking communion, after repenting of any unconfessed sins.

CHAPTER 9

PRACTICAL APPLICATION EXERCISES

Breaking Financial Curses and Strongholds

Before and during these practical application exercises, ask the Lord to bring to your attention anything that would rob you from your entire inheritance in the Lord.

Step 1: **RENOUNCE INVOLVEMENT**

This exercise is designed to help you identify ungodly involvement that you may have had. This is not a complete list, but it does touch on the major ones.

Ask the Lord to reveal your previous involvement in the occult, false religions, or false teachers you may have read or listened to. You may or may not have known they were false teachers or religions at the time. Some examples are: astral projection, ouija board, speaking in a trance, automatic writing, telepathy, clairvoyance, fortune telling, tarot cards, palm reading, astrology, hypnosis, mind control, divining, human or animal sacrifice, horoscopes, transcendental meditation, and free masonry.

You may use this space to record what God has revealed to you:

____

____

____

____

Circle any involvement you or your ancestors have had in idolatry (this includes but is not limited to:

- **False religions**
- **False gods**
- **Free Masonry**
- **Agnosticism** (believing that nothing is or can be known about the existence of God)
- **Atheism** (belief that there is no God)
- **Voodoo**
- **American Indian Religions/Rituals**
- **Mayan Religion/Rituals**
- **Aztec Religion/Rituals**
- **Inca Religion/Rituals**
- **Gypsy ancestry**
- **Eastern Religions** (Zen, Buddhism, Shintuism, Hinduism, New Age Movement, incantations, etc.)

Ask Him to reveal to you any occult or pagan religious objects, relics or artifacts, psychic healing, esoteric (secret) philosophy, etc. that you have purchased, inherited, or were given. If you have any non-Christian religious art or relics, get rid of them. Israel was sternly warned against possessing such objects [Numbers 33:52], "*destroy all their figured stones, and destroy all their molten images, and demolish all their high places.*" (RSV) In Deuteronomy 29:16-21 (RSV), read where Achan and his family lost their lives for hiding false idols under his tent.

Renounce involvement in each false religion or occult practice that you have ever been involved in.

> ***"Father, I confess that I have participated in ___________.***
> ***I ask you to forgive me for my involvement. I renounce Satan, all his works, and my involvement in a counterfeit to true Christianity."***

Do not be surprised if you encounter demonic resistance as you pray. **If you experience resistance, command evil spirits to leave in the name of Jesus.** If married, make this one flesh confession together and support each other.

Step 2: **REPENT AND CONFESS YOUR SIN**

Ask the Lord to forgive you if you have not tithed (given the first ten percent of your "increase" to the Lord) and not given offerings (above the tithe). Giving the first ten percent to the Lord helps to establish our faith and trust in Him. If you have not begun tithing, ask the Lord to help you get your priorities in line with His, and help you to trust Him in your finances and every aspect of your life. (Review chapter two on biblical giving, as needed.)

Ask the Lord to reveal the ways you judged, were rebellious to, and did not honor your parents, then write them down. Ask the Lord to forgive each offense. Finally, ask the Lord to break any curse or judgment associated with not honoring your father and mother.

Use these spaces to record what the Holy Spirit Reveals:

____

____

____

____

Ask the Lord to forgive un-confessed sexual sin or marital unfaithfulness. If you have not already done so, ask the Lord to sever ungodly soul ties to those you had sexual relations with outside of your marriage. If you or an ancestor were born outside of wedlock, ask the Lord to remove the curse of the sin off of you, your children and future generations. Ask the Lord to forgive you for lusting after others, and to remove any stronghold of lust. Finally, ask the Lord to soften your heart and purify your relationship with your spouse.

(Husbands and Wives): Ask the Lord to show you instances where you were not sensitive to your spouse and where you did not honor her or him. Write them down. After you have genuinely repented, ask your one flesh mate for her or his forgiveness. Ask your spouse to pray with you to soften your heart and make you more sensitive. Ask your mate when he/she feels honored by you and how it makes her/him feel. Ask your spouse for specific ways that you can honor her/him. Ask the Lord to show you how to honor your spouse. Then both of you pray that the Lord will remove any hindrances to your prayers.

____

____

____

____

____

____

Step 3: **ASK THE LORD TO TAKE BACK ALL GROUND THAT WAS GIVEN OVER TO THE ENEMY.** Ask the Lord to forgive you for each time you *"let the sun go down on your anger."* Ask the Lord to take back all ground that was given over to the enemy through anger, lust, sexual sin, unforgiveness, etc. Ask Him to pull down any stronghold that you have in your life.

Step 4: **BIND CURSES AND LOOSE BLESSINGS**

Write down all the curses, hexès, and vexes that you can remember being spoken over you. This may include negative words spoken by parents, siblings, teachers, other relatives or people of importance in your life. Then ask Jesus to break the power of those curses, hexes or vexes over you.

____

____

____

____

____

____

Write down all the curses, hexes and vexes that you spoke over someone, including yourself. Ask the Lord to forgive you and to render your words null and void. Now, pray blessing on all whom you have cursed, hexed and vexed (Romans 12:14).

____

____

____

____

____

____

PRAY

"Lord you promised in Malachi 3, that if we tithed You would open the windows of heaven, pour down an overflowing blessing to me and my family. Lord rebuke the devourer, prevent him (Satan) from destroying the fruits of my labor that I may prosper spiritually, relationally and financially. Lord, I thank you for providing these blessings. In Jesus' Name, Amen."

Step 5: **WALK AS A CHILD OF THE LIGHT**

Deuteronomy 10:12-13, "*what does the Lord your God require of you, but to fear the Lord your God, to walk in all his ways, to love him, to serve the Lord your God with all your heart and with all your soul, and to keep the commandments and statutes of the Lord.*" (RSV)

- **Read the Word on a daily basis.**
- **Establish Godly accountability relationships.**

Special Note: You may have to work through this section several times. Persist until all blockages are gone; then continue spiritual warfare as a permanent life pattern.

CONGRATULATIONS!

By gaining a deeper understanding of "Breaking Curses, Blockages and Strongholds that try to Control your Finances", you now have the weapons and the armor to gain full victory.

Now step out on the water and put into practice what you diligently learned.

CHAPTER 10

"Then Jesus came to them and said, 'All authority in heaven and on earth has been given to me. Therefore go and make disciples of all nations, baptizing them in the name of the Father and of the Son and of the Holy Spirit, and teaching them to obey everything I have commanded you. And surely I am with you always, to the very end of the age'."
Matthew 28: 18-20 (NIV)

"It was He who gave some to be apostles, some to be prophets, some to be evangelists, and some to be pastors and teachers, to prepare God's people for works of service, so that the body of Christ may be built up until we all reach unity in the faith and in the knowledge of the Son of God and become mature, attaining to the whole measure of the fullness of Christ."
Ephesians 4:11-13 (NIV)

Focus Group Leaders' Instructions

CHAPTER 10
FOCUS GROUP LEADERS' INSTRUCTIONS

- **THE FOCUS GROUP CONCEPT**
  Financial Freedom in 7 Weeks Plus is ideally presented in a small focus group setting, such as a home, which is a private, secure and comfortable environment. Ideally, these focus groups will be under the covering of a local church or ministry and will report to a financial freedom coordinator, designated by that church or ministry.

  The focus group approach has been tested and found to produce "good fruit."

- **LEADERS TRAINING AND DISCIPLING FUTURE LEADERS**
  The concept of leaders training or discipling future leaders is centuries old and was most notably used by Our Lord, Jesus Christ.

  This chapter is intended to provide guidelines and advice to the focus group leadership team. Ideally, this team will consist of a designated trained and committed leadership couple, with the support of an assistant leadership couple who are leaders-in-training (LITs). This concept of leaders and LITs has proven to be very successful in the "Married for Life" courses presented by Marriage Ministries International, in over 90 countries. (Qualified single adults may also be selected for leadership roles and this is explained in this chapter.)

  As leaders train LITs they are equipping them to serve as leaders of an upcoming focus group of their own. Leaders and the sponsoring church or ministry should seek LITs who are faithful stewards and committed to serve now and to be trained to lead. If LITs are "good soil" they will normally never repeat as LITs, but will be released and empowered to lead, as the need for this training is so great.

  At the conclusion of the 7-week focus group, and the individual review sessions, the leaders should advise the sponsoring church or ministry coordinator if the LITs are recommended for full focus group leadership.

I. LEADERSHIP CALLING AND COMMITMENT

We trust that you feel a spiritual calling to help people get financially free. For some, this may involve leading just a few focus groups and for others it may be a longer term calling. All leaders have an incredible opportunity to sow the Word of God into their groups and to provide practical application tools to enable true financial freedom.

Leadership is a big commitment, as the team meets twice each week: once for one to two hours to train and pray; and again for the actual focus group session. Additionally, leadership will meet for post-course 90-minute follow-up sessions with each participant or participating couple.

We know God will bless you for your diligence and will equip and guide you, if you humbly seek His wisdom. His Word also promises you a reward. Proverbs 19:17, "*He who is kind to the poor lends to the Lord, and He will reward him for what he has done.*" (NIV)

II. WHO CAN LEAD A FOCUS GROUP?

1. First, we need to clarify that focus group leaders can be single adults. We do suggest that, in this situation, the leader team would be two unmarried adults of the same sex. We definitely do not recommend that only one half of a married couple serve as a full-time leader. The "covering church" authority may wish to deviate from this pattern. However, our experience has shown that group members respond best to a leadership team comprised of two married couples, with each couple showing a "one flesh" commitment to the material. In fact, we strongly urge both spouses to share in the teaching, using their own style and gifts.

2. We encourage the sponsoring local church or ministry to provide Financial Freedom in 7 Weeks Plus training as it is outlined, and to carefully screen, select, and monitor the leadership teams.

3. Following are suggestions which the sponsoring church or ministry may want to use as "minimum qualifications" for the selection of focus group leaders or LITs:

   - Salvation
   - Baptism
   - Faithful tithing (ideally giving beyond the tithe)
   - Committed church or ministry members
   - Committed to learn and to teach this Bible-based course material

III. LEADERS' ROLE

1. The leaders are fully responsible for all aspects of this seven-week group training, to include completing the 30 to 45-day follow-up review sessions (90 minutes each) with individual group members and/or with couples. Please include the LITs whenever possible in these reviews, as part of their training to lead their own focus groups.

2. The selection of the LITs is normally the leader's responsibility, but is to be: discussed with, prayed about, and authorized by the covering local church or ministry. This is a serious decision! (The selection decision may fall to the local Church or Ministry Coordinator.)

3. Leaders select the place and establish the start time for the seven weekly 2 to 2 ½ hour sessions. You need a quiet environment — no phones and no children. Send a letter to each group member ASAP with directions and full details. Focus group members should have received the letter, and at least one call or personal visit from the leaders, ten days prior to the first session. We also recommend that you phone students to confirm all details, a few days before the first meeting. (The devil will attempt to confuse, so be proactive!)

4. Refreshments should be limited to beverages. The leaders may invite the group to share in the cost of soft drinks, coffee, iced tea or lemonade. Please make sure cups and condiments are available and set up the beverages beforehand to minimize delays during the short break. If you want to make an exception for week seven, then plan extra time after the session closes or have a separate "Night Out" or picnic.

5. A weekly report form is provided, along with an example. The leaders and LITs need to complete the report after each class and submit it promptly to the local church or ministry coordinator.

   a. The original of the report and all offering checks should be mailed or hand delivered to the Church or Ministry Coordinator ASAP. *(No exceptions!)*

   b. The leaders and LITs should each keep a copy of the report, which is confidential.

   c. Leaders are responsible to fill out one *Focus Group Registration Form* with all contact information for every group member, including leaders. One copy goes to the local church or ministry coordinator. The leaders and LIT's should each keep a copy. This form provides current contact information that will prove valuable.

6. Course Registration and Fees. This book is the workbook or manual for the course. It will be essential for each focus group member to have his or her own book; married couples should share one manual and must do homework assignments together. The sponsoring church or ministry should control registration and decide what fees to collect. Obviously the fee must include the cost of this book, as a minimum.

   We encourage the use of checks for registration fees and for weekly offerings. Accountability is much easier and all focus group participants then have individual records. The course registration fee is normally not tax deductible. However, weekly offerings will normally be tax deductible (in the US) if checks are payable to a (501c3) registered charity, ministry, or church.

7. Focus Group Size. Although there is no absolute set size for a focus group, we recommend approximately 14 people including the leaders and LITs. Most groups enjoy meeting in homes or other private areas and space is often a constraint. Group homework sharing is a key element of each weekly session and if a group is too large, time and crowd intimidation can be concerns. For couples groups, we like the "Married for Life" group model of seven couples, including one leader couple, one LIT couple plus five student couples.

8. Weekly Offering. We strongly encourage the group's church or ministry covering to authorize a weekly offering. Actually, we suggest that it be in the form of "sowing alms" as taught in chapter two/week 2: Proverbs 19:17 says, "*He who has pity on the poor lends to the Lord, and He will pay back what he has given.*" (NKJ) In some of the early test groups, we have had great success with alms being designated for the "Benevolence Fund" of the sponsoring church or special offerings to an overseas ministry. **Checks should be used so there is no cash to handle, and the weekly report should be signed by one of the leaders and one LIT, to provide a measure of accountability.**

9. Weekly meetings with LITs. The leaders and LITs should agree to meet once a week (separate from the focus group meeting) to pray for the couples and to preview the coming week's lesson. This meeting is important and is reported on the first page of the weekly report.

   a. Ideally, this *leadership session* will be held after the LITs have completed their homework and have read the next week's lesson. Then the leaders can review homework with the LITs and discuss how the LITs will lead the homework sharing time. Leaders should also discuss the upcoming lesson and clarify as needed.

b. Experience indicates that at least one, and ideally two full hours are needed for this leadership session. It is acceptable to add time for a meal or snack, as the leadership team will definitely bond closely during the course.

c. Remember, the leaders are discipling the LITs so they can lead future focus groups.

d. If the LITs teach a specific weekly lesson, then the leaders should lead that week's homework sharing time.

e. By preparing the LIT's to lead, and then letting them present one or two weekly lessons, the leaders are building their confidence to lead a future focus group. Leaders should make certain their LITs are very well prepared!

10. Weekly calls/letters/or e-mails to focus group members. We find it very important to contact each participant during the week. This can be a telephone call, letter, e-mail, or a personal visit. The purpose is to encourage them and pray for them. This is a good opportunity to remind them to complete the weekly homework so they will be ready to share at the coming week's session.

    Leaders and LITs may elect to divide this responsibility, but these weekly contacts are very important. Remember, the devil does not want anyone to get financially free... especially Christians!

11. 30 to 45-Day Follow-Up Sessions. These are private sessions, 90 minutes long, where one focus group member, or couple, at a time meets with the leadership team to review progress. The "students" need to call the leaders to schedule a time. They should bring all completed forms and be ready to discuss them. At the end of the session, the leadership team should pray for and release each student. We suggest the leaders establish a two-week period, after week seven, when "students" are to call the leaders to schedule the 90-minute session. (See chapter eight for details.)

IV. LEADERS IN TRAINING RESPONSIBILITY

As LITs, you will be blessed to be a blessing. Your leaders are going to sow tremendous effort, time and prayer into your future. This is a serious role and you need to be fully committed to assist them in every possible way. **You will be counted on to lead at least one or two future focus groups.**

1. Make firm commitments to the time schedule of the course and arrive early to help the leaders set up for each class. LITs and leaders should pray and do spiritual warfare, prior to each focus group. The devil will try to disrupt with problems involving strife, transportation, childcare, work schedules, etc.

2. Plan on staying after the class, for at least 30 minutes, to pray, recap the focus group session and to complete the weekly report. This is very important and can be a lot of fun, as you bond with your leaders.

3. Make sure you do your homework ASAP and read the next lesson in advance. This will make your weekly leaders' meeting much more valuable and will prepare you, as LITs, to lead the weekly homework sharing time. When you preview the lesson, provide feedback to the leaders as it may help them with the upcoming lesson.

4. Unless the LITs have been through a previous focus group, or are very well prepared, it is normally not expected that they teach weekly lessons. However, the leaders are encouraged to call on LITs for a testimony or for a special example, to get them more involved.

5. If the leaders feel the LITs are capable of teaching a lesson, then the lesson should be presented to the leaders at the weekly leadership meeting. The focus group deserves a very good presentation.

6. LITs should study and take notes in preparation to lead a focus group in the very near future. The need is great!

V. GUARD AGAINST OUTSIDE MATERIAL

1. There are lots of teachings, tapes and books on finance. We urge the leadership team to avoid using outside materials which may conflict with this Bible-based teaching and the processes being taught in this course.

2. If in doubt, please check with your covering church pastor or church/ministry coordinator in advance before using any outside material or other resources beyond the Bible and this course manual.

3. Do not allow group members to inject outside material or take over a session. Leaders must maintain order and control the flow of the teaching and the homework sharing.

4. **Under no circumstances are financial products, services or specific investment-type recommendations to be made or permitted.**

VI. NO TIME FOR MAKE-UP SESSIONS

We encourage leaders to seek a full seven-week commitment from focus group members. These seven weeks will fly by and you will be hard pressed to squeeze in make-up sessions. However, leaders have the option to provide a make-up class for very special situations.

VII. GRADUATION CERTIFICATES

We encourage you to award special certificates for participants who complete the course and the 30-45 day follow-up session. Make this a "big deal" and have fun with it. A sample certificate is provided in this chapter; use it as a guide and be creative.

The first focus group in Fiji planned a major graduation event with certificates presented by the church pastor, in front of the whole congregation.

VIII. VISUAL AIDS & SOUND EFFECTS

We know people learn in different ways — hearing, seeing, touching, words, pictures and sounds. That is why we included this section, which injects fun and joy into the learning process.

How many people do you know that get excited about attending a class on finances? Perhaps they think…BORING! Therefore, we include suggestions for visual aids and sound effects for instruction and to provide comic relief, so people will relax and be more receptive to receiving God's truth about finances.

Basically, we want to build Hope in people that debt freedom is possible. We pray that people will allow God to change their hearts and thus bless their financial situations.

- **HEART VISUAL AIDS.** Throughout this course, we emphasize the point that God wants our hearts, not our money. Therefore, heart visual aids are especially meaningful to focus group members. Valentine's Day is probably the best time of year to acquire heart supplies. Party stores have great sales on heart products after Valentine's Day!

  <u>**SOME EXAMPLES OF HEART SUPPLIES ARE:**</u>

  1. Heart balloons can be tied to chair backs. Mylar balloons may last for weeks! We tie balloons to chairs to present a festive atmosphere. When people come in, their hearts and minds are encouraged.

  2. Heart jewelry. Ladies you can wear this while you teach. People will see the hearts during the entire class.

  3. Clothing with hearts.

  4. Candy with sayings on them like, "Love You", etc. You can put one on each person's chair.

  5. Heart balloons on a stick with "Love" printed on them- they last for years.

  6. Poster board cutout hearts in various sizes are available. (Ask your children to help you by cutting out construction paper hearts.) We tape a paper with "God" written on it to the center of one heart balloon and tape a large dollar bill on the other.

  We talk about who or what has the most influence in their hearts? Where is their treasure? Leave this visual in front of the class; you can use it each week.

  7. Fabric with hearts on it can be draped over a table.

- **PLAY MONEY** is available in packages at discount stores. Use some very large denomination bills, such as one thousand dollar bills. Grocery stores are also a good source for children's party favors and you can normally buy packs of small play money. Remember, be creative and have fun with it.

1. You can tape money to a table so people can see it. This may build hope in them to believe they can be debt free and have extra money.

2. Hang a wreath on the door with play money stuck all over it and a sign pinned to it saying, "Y'all Come In Expecting". (Sorry for the "Ya'll" but the authors live in Texas.) We build hope when we make responsible choices. By being good stewards, repenting for wrong choices and being obedient to God's Word, we have a right to expect God's help and financial breakthroughs. Always give God the glory for every breakthrough, as all good gifts come from Him!

3. Place play money on each chair; it gets the group to "lighten-up".

4. We made a "money tree" by hanging play money, by ribbons, all over an artificial tree. Near it, we made a "credit card tree." We hung (expired) credit cards, by ribbon, onto that tree. We used anything that resembled a credit card for effect. These trees were called the "tree of life" and the "tree of the knowledge of good and evil." They served as weekly reminders to our focus groups.

5. You can use the small play money to throw up in the air while teaching on biblical giving, or when suggesting the use of cash versus credit cards, or to celebrate a breakthrough.

➢ SOUND EFFECTS

We use several "talking magnets" while teaching. People like the comic relief and it seems to relax them. We don't want people to think this is a stodgy, difficult class. Perhaps you can find something like these to use. Kitchen, bath, and grocery stores may be a source for these noisemakers.

1. For "good reports" and "breakthroughs", we sound a cheerful talking magnet with balloons on it that has people yelling, "Ole! Ole!" Find your own "fun" noisemakers.

2. When discussing creditors calling and past due bill notices, we sound a talking magnet that says, "You've got mail," And it plays a little tune.

3. When debt is mentioned, or the overuse of credit cards, we push a "panic button" magnet that is the Danger! Dive! sound on submarines: "Wh-ooga! Wh-ooga!" We hope that sound will stay in their minds if they think about going into new debt. They laugh, but the point is made that debt equals danger.

4. We have a small bag of children's band instruments. When people come into the meeting, we remind them to pick up a noisemaker to use when they tell us about their breakthroughs. It gets them involved and builds hope and excitement in them. We have tambourines, maracas, clackers, drums, and shakers. Look in toy stores for ideas. Be creative.

➢ OTHER VISUAL AIDS

1. In the *biblical giving* chapter, we used a piece of flexible conduit, or pipe, to illustrate how God wants us to be "conduits for giving." He blesses us with finances as we freely give. We don't wait for God to give, we give first. Sometimes, however, our "conduit" is stopped up with problems. Write the following words on folded pieces of paper: "unforgiveness", "curse of poverty", "disobedience", "greed", "not tithing." Stuff those papers in one end of the conduit and drop coins or paper money in the other end. When they do not come out, look in the other end and begin taking out the papers one by one. Finally, unfold and read them. When they are all out,

drop some more money back in and it will flow through the conduit and come out freely. This is a great illustration that depicts how God will bless us when we unplug our own pipelines!

2. For married couples, we use a big sign on brightly colored poster board. On the top half of the paper, we write, "Your spouse is <u>not</u> your enemy!" On the bottom half, write, "Satan Satan Satan is your enemy!" You can bend it in the middle and use the half that applies.

3. We found some Dr. Seuss hats — black-and-white striped — to wear when discussing debt bondage. The stripes resemble convict stripes. Yes, it is corny, but it will bring a laugh and drive home (again) the fact that debt equals bondage.

➢ **ATMOSPHERE**

<u>Music changes the atmosphere</u>. We recommend that you play up-beat Christian music before every focus group session while the group is arriving and again during the break.

Choose music with a message of hope. Look for exciting "get you going" songs! People may arrive with heavy hearts and defeated attitudes about their financial situation. We like to use songs about deliverance, having faith in God to change circumstances, and songs about breakthroughs!

➢ **BREAKTHROUGH REPORTS...HOORAY!**

Before you begin sharing homework, ask the class if they had breakthroughs. Teach them to expect breakthroughs. Have everyone fill out their ***Breakthrough Form*** weekly. (Included with each weekly homework section.) This will encourage them and sharing their breakthrough reports will definitely bless others.

➢ **ENCOURAGE AND BUILD HOPE**

Keep this motivation in your heart and the Lord will show you more creative ideas that will work especially for your groups. Keep your eyes and ears tuned in to the Holy Spirit- great and fun ideas can come from anywhere! Leaders and LIT's are the cheerleaders for their focus groups.

May the Lord Bless you for your diligence and commitment. **Remember, the words of the book of James 1:17 *"Every good and perfect gift is from above..."* *(NIV)***

IX. SEMINARS – FINANCIAL FREEDOM IN 7 WEEKS PLUS

Bill and Maureen have been blessed with the opportunity from their church to present several one half day seminars. These seminars have been free to the community and have included highlights from the course and an introduction to the seven-week focus group concept.

We have invited others to assist in the teaching. Also, students have been blessed and excited to hear testimonies from recent focus group graduates.

Every effort is made to create an upbeat atmosphere (music, balloons, visual aids, play money, video inserts) and a seminar handout is provided.

These seminars are great, but they can only introduce the material in the book and course. They should never be viewed as a substitute for focus group participation.

X. FINAL TIPS TO LEADERS AND LITS

1. Have fun with your group. Be creative with visual aids, sound effects, balloons, posters, etc. Your group should look forward to each session.

2. God will bless you for sowing into the lives of others. Lean on the Holy Spirit.

3. Get comfortable with the scripture verses used in this course. Include reading and praying the Word in your preparation time, in each class session, and each leaders' meeting.

4. Spiritual warfare is important. Kick the devil out: before, during and after all weekly meetings.

5. **Study the material well so you can teach without just reading the lessons. Please do not bore your group! Use appropriate examples, not rabbit trails; and stay on schedule.**

6. Get very comfortable with examples 1 and 2, so you can easily explain what Bob and Mary Jones did in all cases.

7. Be on the lookout for future LITs and course leaders. Nourish them and mention them in your weekly reports. Pray for them.

8. **Leaders and LITs of focus groups are definitely not expected to be financial experts. This course does not even require a high school diploma. Do not allow the devil to make you feel inadequate. Stick to the weekly lesson material and you will do well.**

XI. THANKS TO LEADERS AND LITS

We are excited about your commitment to lead or help lead a Financial Freedom in 7 Weeks Plus focus group. You are sowing into the legacy of many future generations. Spread the news of this course to others and encourage them to enroll in future courses.

We thank you for your commitment and feel sure that, as you teach this course with all your hearts, God will look down, smile and say: "Well done good and faithful servants."

XII. REPORTS

God is not the author of confusion and we all need some measure of accountability. For this course, the reports are simple, but important.

1. **A Focus Group Registration Form** is completed no later than week one. It is simply a list of every focus group member with accurate contact information that is easy to read, so it can be photocopied clearly. You will need this for contacts as the course progresses.

   One copy of the completed form (printed or typed) goes to the church or ministry coordinator and both the leaders and LITs should retain a copy. (We recommend that each member of the leadership team have his own copy.)

   A blank copy of the registration form is provided in this section. Please copy the form as needed or prepare your own (customized) form in conjunction with your church or ministry coordinator.

   Please remember, your church or ministry coordinator may be simultaneously overseeing several focus groups, so make their job easier with timely, easy-to-read reports.

2. **A Financial Freedom Weekly Report** is used to report highlights of each focus group session. The report is <u>confidential</u> but should provide enough information so the church or ministry coordinator can get a "feel" for each participant's progress and can pray for specific areas of need.

   This report also has a section (on the first page) which is used for a brief report of what took place at the (separate) weekly leadership meeting. This adds accountability to your leadership commitment.

   The weekly report has a section for recording the total weekly offering. The offering should be counted, verified, and signed by one of the leaders and one of the LITs.

   The weekly report and offerings (checks) should be promptly mailed or delivered to the church or ministry coordinator.

   The leaders and LITs should retain a copy of the signed weekly report. It should be kept <u>confidential</u>.

   The weekly report should be completed as soon as the weekly focus group dismisses.

   For their own records, many leaders also make a photocopy of all the offering checks.

   A sample of the ***Financial Freedom Weekly Report*** is provided in this chapter.

3. **A Final Report to the church or ministry coordinator.** Accountability is a key element of the stewardship principle. Therefore, it is strongly recommended that the leadership team prepare a brief letter, approximately 60 to 75 days after the seventh and final weekly session, to the sponsoring church or ministry coordinator. No special form is needed. The sole purpose of this (letter style) report is to list all group members, including LITs, who faithfully completed the course and their 30 to 45 day review session. The letter should also list any focus group participants who have <u>not</u> completed the review.

   It would also be appropriate to indicate how course completion (graduation) certificates were presented.

FOCUS GROUP REGISTRATION FORM

(Please Print or Type)
(Page 1 of 2)

Week One Meeting Date: ______________
Scheduled Time: Start: _______ End: _____

Group Leaders: ____
Leaders in Training (LITs): ____________________________________
Address for Meeting:

____

____

City: ____________________, State: ___________, Zip Code: _________

Directions to Meeting Place:

____

____

____

____

Group Members (For married couples, print both names; include all leaders)

Leaders Names: ____
Address: ____
City: ____________________, State: ___________, Zip Code: _________
Home Phone: __________________ Work Phone: ___________________
E-mail: _______________ Cell Phone: _________________ Fees Paid?: ____

LITs Names: ____
Address: ____
City: ____________________, State: ___________, Zip Code: _________
Home Phone: __________________ Work Phone: ___________________
E-mail: _______________ Cell Phone: _________________ Fees Paid?: ____

Names: ____
Address: ____
City: ____________________, State: ___________, Zip Code: _________
Home Phone: __________________ Work Phone: ___________________
E-mail: _______________ Cell Phone: _________________ Fees Paid?: ____

Focus Group Registration Form (Page 2 of 2)

Names: ____
Address: ____
City: ____________________, State: __________, Zip Code: ________
Home Phone: __________________ Work Phone: __________________
E-mail: ______________ Cell Phone: __________________ Fees Paid?: ___

Names: ____
Address: ____
City: ____________________, State: __________, Zip Code: ________
Home Phone: __________________ Work Phone: __________________
E-mail: ______________ Cell Phone: __________________ Fees Paid?: ___

Names: ____
Address: ____
City: ____________________, State: __________, Zip Code: ________
Home Phone: __________________ Work Phone: __________________
E-mail: ______________ Cell Phone: __________________ Fees Paid?: ___

Names: ____
Address: ____
City: ____________________, State: __________, Zip Code: ________
Home Phone: __________________ Work Phone: __________________
E-mail: ______________ Cell Phone: __________________ Fees Paid?: ___

Names: ____
Address: ____
City: ____________________, State: __________, Zip Code: ________
Home Phone: __________________ Work Phone: __________________
E-mail: ______________ Cell Phone: __________________ Fees Paid?: ___

Names: ____
Address: ____
City: ____________________, State: __________, Zip Code: ________
Home Phone: __________________ Work Phone: __________________
E-mail: ______________ Cell Phone: __________________ Fees Paid?: ___

FINANCIAL FREEDOM WEEKLY REPORT
FOR WEEK # __________

(Please Print or Type)

(Page 1 of 3)

WEEKLY LEADERSHIP MEETING REPORT SECTION

Leaders-Please only use this box to report on what happened in the weekly leadership meeting of the Focus Group Leaders & LITs.

City: ______________________ State: ____________________

Meeting Date: _________________ Start Time: ______________ End Time: __________

Group Leaders: ____

Leaders in Training (LITs): ____

Comments from Leadership Meeting (Prayers, Needs, Lessons, & Homework):

____

____

____

____

____

____

____

____

____

____

____

____

____

____

____

____

____

____

WEEKLY FOCUS GROUP MEETING REPORT (Page 2 of 3)

Leaders – Use the following report space for brief, printed comments regarding the progress of each individual or couple. Include comments on Leaders, by LITs, and on LITs, by Leaders.

Meeting Date: ______________ Start Time: _________ End Time: ________

Focus Group Members:

Please assess the progress of each individual or couple, including leadership *Indicate Attendance*

Comments	***Him***	***Her***
#1 Names:		
#2 Names:		
#3 Names:		
#4 Names:		
#5 Names:		
#6 Names:		
#7 Names:		
#8 Names:		
#9 Names:		
#10 Names:		
#11 Names:		
#12 Names:		

GROUP LEADERS PROGRESS (Comments by LITs):

Attendance	
Him	Her
___	___

____

____

____

LEADERS IN TRAINING PROGRESS (Comments by Leaders):

Attendance	
Him	Her
___	___

____

____

____

LEADERS COMMENTS REGARDING THE FOCUS GROUP SESSION:

____

____

____

____

WEEKLY OFFERING REPORT

Offering (Checks Only) .... Total: $________

Offering dedicated to: ______________________________________

Offering Counted By:

Group Leader Signature (One): ____________________ Date: _________

LIT Signature (One): __________________________ Date: _________

EXAMPLE (Page 1 of 3)
FINANCIAL FREEDOM WEEKLY REPORT
FOR WEEK # *One*
(Please Print or Type)

WEEKLY LEADERSHIP MEETING REPORT SECTION

Leaders-Please only use this box to report on what happened in the weekly leadership meeting of the Focus Group Leaders & LITs.

City: San Antonio State: TX
Meeting Date: 5/10/02 Start Time: 7 PM End Time: 8:45 PM
Group Leaders: Bill & Maureen Sitter
Leaders in Training (LITs): Bob & Mary Jones

Comments from Leadership Meeting (Prayers, Needs, Lessons, & Homework):
The 2 leadership couples prayed for our new Focus Group which starts in 5 days. We did spiritual warfare for each person who committed to our group. We agreed on who would call each participant as a reminder. We reviewed the Focus Group Leaders' Instructions section of the course manual and the Leaders previewed the Week 1 Lesson. LITs will be ready to help with introductions, set up for the class and, in the future, to lead the homework sharing time.

WEEKLY FOCUS GROUP MEETING REPORT (EXAMPLE)

Leaders – Use the following report space for brief, printed comments regarding the progress of each individual or couple. Include comments on Leaders, by LITs, and on LITs, by Leaders.

Meeting Date: 5/15/02 Start Time: 7 PM End Time: 9:30 PM

Focus Group Members:

Please assess the progress of each individual or couple, including leadership *Indicate Attendance*

Comments	*Him*	*Her*
#1 Names: Tom & Barbara Smith	Yes	Yes
They really need this course and are believing for a breakthrough.		
#2 Names: John & Mary Doe	Yes	Yes
They are in deep stress over past due bills. But are prepared to change habits & learn.		
#3 Names: Mike & JoAnn Difficulty	Yes	Yes
They barely made it to class. Big argument on pending bankruptcy. But praise God, they are committed to 7-week course.		
#4 Names: Larry & Louise Just Get Bye	Yes	Late
She had to work late. They really need help. Leaders prayed for them after class. They have hope in God.		
#5 Names: Dan & Debra Niceman	Yes	No
She just got called out of town at the last minute. Dan says they have little debt and want to learn to lead. He will teach Debra this week's lesson & they'll do homework together.		
#6 Names: John & Ann Greatpotential	Yes	Yes
They have a great attitude and want God's best for their family. Seem open to learning good stewardship. May be future LITs. Leaders will monitor potential as weeks progress.		
#7 Names:		
#8 Names:		
#9 Names:		

EXAMPLE CONTINUED (Page 3 of 3)

GROUP LEADERS PROGRESS (Comments by LITs):

Attendance	
Him	Her
Yes	Yes

Bill & Maureen Sitter:

LITs feel course is in good hands and they look forward to mentoring by Leaders. Maureen's visual aids are great! Group felt comfortable and liked the music. It helped to have praise song words typed, large print, for all.

LEADERS IN TRAINING PROGRESS (Comments by Leaders):

Attendance	
Him	Her
Yes	Yes

Bob & Mary Jones:

Leaders see great potential. They need mentoring and really seek to leave a Godly financial legacy. We see a friendship bond forming.

LEADERS COMMENTS REGARDING THIS FOCUS GROUP SESSION:

Overall, a very good start to this 7-week journey. Leadership team will call each couple before next week's session, to encourage and reinforce commitment.

WEEKLY OFFERING REPORT

Offering (Checks Only)................................ Total: $ 75.00

Offering dedicated to: Sponsoring Church Benevolence Fund

Offering Counted By:

Group Leader Signature (One): *Maureen Sitter* Date: 5-15-02

LIT Signature (One): *Bob Jones* Date: 5-15-02

(FOR EXAMPLE PURPOSES)

CERTIFICATE
OF
GRADUATION

John & Jane Doe

Have Completed the
Financial Freedom in 7 Weeks Plus Course
and the Review Session and
Are Hereby Awarded this Certificate

Date Completed:

Focus Group Leaders:

CHAPTER 11

"Study and be eager and do your utmost to present yourself to God approved, (tested by trial), a workman who has no cause to be ashamed, correctly analyzing and accurately dividing – rightly handling and skillfully teaching – the Word of Truth."
2 Timothy 2:15 (Amplified)

Additional References

CHAPTER 11
ADDITIONAL REFERENCES

There are many excellent Christian and secular resources in the area of finances. The following list is only the tip of the finance reference iceberg, and we encourage you to aggressively seek out and study good material. Your church and area Christian bookstores are a great place to start. **We exhort you to weigh all advice carefully, using God's Word as the final authority.**

1. The Bible. It may be helpful to read multiple translations. There are far more than 1,000 applicable scriptures concerning finances, some scholars place the number at over 2,000.

2. Crown Financial Ministries. This is the new name for the combination of Larry Burkett's Christian Financial Concepts Ministry and Howard Dayton's Crown Ministries. This organization has provided excellent Christian financial resources for 25 years. Their resource catalog features an incredible assortment of training materials for ages three and up, including books, audio and video tapes, budgeting workbooks for teens and adults, board games, a three-compartment bank for children, group study materials, and budgeting and cash control software. This website features an online budget guide, mortgage calculator, credit card payment calculator, and a lease versus purchase calculator. Phone 1-866-424-4000. Website: www.crown.org

3. Ron Blue has published an excellent variety of Christian study materials. The Authors of this course are especially thankful for his (now out of print) Master Your Money Workbook, by Thomas Nelson Publishers.

4. Marriage Ministries International is an international ministry which provides a wonderful "Married for Life" course. Although not a finance course, it shows couples how to pray, to work together, and to do spiritual warfare as a one flesh team. These powerful tools are very helpful in dealing with financial stress. Website: www.marriage.org

5. Pastor Rick Godwin of Eagles Nest Christian Fellowship (soon to be Summit Christian Center of San Antonio) provides an excellent four tape audio message: "Money and the Bible" and two new tapes entitled: "The Steward's Risk and Reward" and "First Fruits."
Phone 1-800-675-3297. Website: www.rickgodwin.org

6. Alan Vincent produced two powerful tape series which clearly present God's instructions on money, prosperity, and much more. Alan also identifies Free Masonry as a powerful demonic force which attacks in the area of finances. We urge you to obtain "Prosperity" and "Money Talks" by contacting Outpouring Ministries, 8308 Fredericksburg Rd., San Antonio, TX 78229. 210-614-9330.
E-mail: outpouringmin@aol.com

7. Billy Graham is widely acclaimed as one of the world's most powerful evangelists. We commend readers of this book to the following paperbacks on Salvation and the Holy Spirit. How to be Born Again and The Holy Spirit. Both are published by Word Publishing and are available in Christian bookstores.

8. T.D. Jakes, Sr. provides a powerful pamphlet entitled But I Can't Afford To Tithe. Phone 918-523-5590 or www.alburypublishing.com

9. Kenneth Copeland Ministries provides excellent tapes and books dealing with finances. A popular 1974 book, now re-printed, is The Laws of Prosperity published by KCP Publications. Website: www.kcm.org

10. Mary Hunt has written a number of popular books, including The Complete Cheapskate and How to Debt Proof Your Kids published by Broadman & Holdman. She also produces a monthly newsletter entitled The *Cheapskate Monthly*. Phone: 1-800-550-3502. Website: www.cheapskatemonthly.com

11. The Prayer of Jabez and Secrets of the Vine are two powerful, inspirational books authored by Bruce Wilkinson and published by Multnomah Publishers, Inc. Website: www.prayerofjabez.com

12. Terry Savage provides current practical financial advice in her book The Savage Truth on Money, published by John Wiley & Sons, Inc. You may have seen her on Christian TV. Website: www.terrysavage.com

13. Marilyn Hickey Ministries offers an informative pamphlet on the subject of tithes, offerings, and alms: *God's Plan for Blessing You!* Phone: 303-770-0400. Website: www.mhmin.org

14. Dr. Edward L. Haygood of Agape Christian Fellowship in Los Angeles, CA, produced a helpful pamphlet entitled: *Why the Tithe?* Published by Harrison House.

15. Wilson J. Humber wrote a good paperback entitled Dollars and Sense... Making the most of what you have, published by Navpress. We thank him and others for the "spending plan" concept versus the "budget" concept.

16. John Ankerberg and John Weldon wrote: The Secret Teachings of the Masonic Lodge. This book provides a Christian perspective on Free Masonry and is published by Moody Press. The reader of this work will understand why Free Masonry is included in the list of occult activities, in chapter nine which is entitled: "Breaking Curses, Blockages & Strongholds That Control Our Finances".

17. Robert Kiyosaki and Sharon Lechter C.P.A. authored a very popular paradigm-changing book entitled Rich Dad Poor Dad, and other recent books, published by TechPress. They also provide two (expensive but very educational) board games trademarked Cash flow 101 and Cash flow 202. Phone 1-800-308-3585. Website: www.cashflowtech.com

18. Craig Hill and Earl Pitts wrote a paperback, Wealth, Riches and Money, published by Family Foundation. Craig and Jan Hill's ministry, Family Foundations International, can be contacted at 303-797-1139. Website: www.familyfi.org

19. David Bach authored a book entitled Smart Couples Finish Rich, published by Broadway. Although not a Christian-oriented book, it contains some excellent practical advice. Website: www.Finishrich.com

20. The Fellowship of Companies for Christ International (FCCI) released an excellent 3 tape, audiotape set, entitled: *Financial Freedom God's Way*. Phone: 405-917-1681. Website: www.fcci.org

21. Money Management Software. There are many PC-based software programs designed to help you control and keep track of spending. There are also debt-reduction software programs. Among the more popular budgeting software offerings are: *Quicken* and *QuickBooks Pro*, by Intuit; *Money Matters Basic* and *Money Matters Deluxe* from Crown Financial Ministries; and Microsoft's *Microsoft Money* program.

22. Bible Memory Challenge Ministries is dedicated to providing easy to read, laminated, pocket- sized scripture cards. In addition to many existing flashcard sets that bless families, a brand new companion set for this book is being produced — "Financial Freedom in 7 Weeks Plus." To order, call 1-800-257-6694 or visit their website: www.bibleflashcard.com

23. WWW.DEBTFREELEGACY.COM As this book Financial Freedom in 7 Weeks Plus goes to press, the authors have reserved this website. We invite you to join us in prayer that God will allow us to use this website to provide more tools to help people get truly financially free and to pass on the following legacy for generations to come. Psalm 25:10 *"All the ways of the Lord are loving and faithful for those who keep the demands of his covenant. For the sake of your name, O Lord, forgive my iniquity, though it is great. Who, then, is the man that fears the Lord? He will instruct him in the way chosen for him. He will spend his days in prosperity, and his descendants will inherit the land." (NIV)*

Note: We are grateful to God for His Word, to these authors, and to every other person who has, or who will, contribute sound financial teaching to the Body of Christ.

CHAPTER 12

"He who ignores discipline comes to poverty and shame,
but whoever heeds correction is honored."
Proverbs 13:18 (NIV)

"If you therefore have not been faithful in the use of unrighteous mammon (money) who will entrust the true riches to you?....No servant can serve two masters....you cannot serve God and Mammon."
Quoted from Luke 16 verses 11 and 13 (NAS)

Financial Example #1

PROJECTED INCOME AND BIBLICAL GIVING

(Example #1 - Before Course)

NAME(S): Bob and Mary Jones **Date: June 30, 2000**

Projected Income

	Amount Paid Monthly	Mo. x 12 =Subtotal for Yr.	Amount Paid Other Than Monthly	Total Annual Amount	Total Annual Amt. Div. by 12 = Avg. Mo. Amt.
Sources:					
Gross wages: husband	$4,000	$48,000		$48,000	$4,000
Gross wages: wife					
Dividends					
Interest					
Rents (cash flow)					
Business Income/"Increase"					
Pensions & annuities					
Other					
TOTAL GROSS INCOME:	**$4,000**	**$48,000**		**$48,000**	**$4,000**

Projected Giving

	Organization	Amount Paid Monthly	Mo. x 12 =Subtotal for Yr.	Amount Paid Other than Monthly	Total Annual Amount	Total Annual Amt. Div. by 12 = Avg. Mo. Amt.
10% Tithe	Church	$350	$4,200		$4,200	$350
Freewill Offerings	Missions	$10	$120		$120	$10
Alms						
Other	Misc. Charities			$600	$600	$50
Other	United Way	$5	$60		$60	$5
Other						
TOTAL GIVING:		**$365**	**$4,380**	**$600**	**$4,980**	**$415**

Once the income is determined, the next step is to determine where it goes. Begin with giving. Project your giving for the year by considering each organization you support. This can be from pledges, percentages of income, past giving, or specific giving goals. You may want to check your actual giving to date and then project what you plan to give for the rest of the year.

NOTE ON USING THIS FORM: This form will help you arrive at an average monthly amount which is crucial for your spending plan and cash flow management. Record the monthly amount in the first column and then multiply by 12 months for a yearly subtotal. In the third column, record amounts that do not occur every month. Add columns 2 and 3 together to get the total annual amount for column 4. Finally, divide the total annual amount by 12 to get the average monthly amount. Do this for each line item.

LIST YOUR ASSETS

TYPES OF ASSETS (Example #1)		
1. Liquid Assets (Easily Converted to Cash)		
Cash on Hand	$200	
Checking Account Balance	$1,800	
Money market funds		
CDs (% interest rate)		
Savings (% interest rate)	$5,000	
Stocks & Bonds		
Life insurance cash values	$3,500	
Other (Describe)		
TOTAL Liquid Assets:		**$10,500**
2. Non-liquid Assets		
Home (market value)	$75,000	
Land (market value)	$25,000	
Net Worth (Value) of Business		
Real Estate investments (Not Home)		
Jet Ski, Camper, RV, Boats, etc.	$10,000	
Automobiles at market value	$20,000	
Furniture & personal property (conservative market value)	$10,000	
Valuable Collections (stamps, coins,etc.)	$3,000	
Retirement Funds Balance	$20,000	
Funds due from others (Receivables)		
Other (Describe)		
Other (Describe)		
TOTAL Non-liquid Assets		**$163,000**
3. Total Assets (1 & 2)		**$173,500**
Name(s): Bob & Mary Jones (Example #1)		
Date of Completion: June 30, 2000		

DEBT REPAYMENT SCHEDULE

NAME(S): **Bob and Mary Jones (Example #1)**
DATE: **June 30, 2000**

	LENDER	$ BALANCE	$ MONTHLY PAYMENT	INT. %	REMAINING PAYMENTS	PAY-OFF DATE
1	Credit Card A	4,000	67	18.0	300	6/30/2025
2	Credit Card B	2,000	33	18.0	300	6/30/2025
3	Car Loan	7,000	307	12.0	36	6/30/2003
4	Parent's Loan	3,000	50	0.0	60	6/30/2005
5						
6						
7						
8						
9						
10						
11						
12						
13						
14						
15						
TOTAL:		**$16,000**	**$457**			

NOTE ON USING DEBT REPAYMENT SCHEDULE:
This form should include all debts with the exception of a primary home mortgage. The mortgage obligation is a debt and must be included as a liability when you complete the ***List Your Liabilities*** form. However, the mortgage payment is not included on this form because it will be included in the monthly housing expense category when you complete the ***Estimated Monthly Living Expenses*** form.

LIST YOUR LIABILITIES
(Example #1)

LENDER (CREDITOR):	BALANCE DUE:	INTEREST RATE %	PAYMENT SCHEDULE	
			PER MONTH:	UNTIL (MO./YR.):
1. Credit Card A	$4,000	18.00%	$67	6/30/2025
2. Credit Card B	$2,000	18.00%	$33	6/30/2025
3. Car Loan	$7,000	12.00%	$307	6/30/2003
4. Mortgage	$80,000	9.00%	$675	6/30/2025
5. Parent's Loan	$3,000	0.00%	$50	6/30/2005
6.				
7.				
8.				
9.				
10.				
11.				
12.				
13.				
14.				
15.				
16.				
17.				
18.				
19.				
20.				
21.				
22.				
23.				
TOTALS:	$96,000		$1,132.00	

NAME(S): Bob & Mary Jones (Example #1)

DATE COMPLETED: June 30, 2000

Note: This form should include all debts previously listed on the "Debt Repayment Schedule", and should also include the home mortgage.

BALANCE SHEET AND NET WORTH STATEMENT
(Example #1)

A. Assets

Liquid Assets:	$10,500
Non-liquid Assets:	$163,000

Total Assets: **$173,500**

B. Less: Total Liabilities: (-) **(96,000)**

C. Net Worth: (Total Assets - Total Liabilities) **$77,500**

Name(s): Bob & Mary Jones (Example #1)

Date Completed: June 30, 2000

Comments:

Note on using this form: *Complete this form using data from your, recently completed,* ***List Your Assets*** *and* ***List Your Liabilities*** *forms. Then, subtract* ***total liabilities*** *from* ***total assets****, and record your NET WORTH.*

ESTIMATED MONTHLY LIVING EXPENSES

(3 Page Form - Example #1)

EXAMPLE #1 (Page 1 of 3)	Amount Paid Monthly	Mo. x 12 = Subtotal for Yr.	Amount Paid Other Than Monthly	Total Annual Amount	Total Annual Amt. Div. by 12 = Avg. Mo. Amt.
A. Housing					
Mortgage or Rent Payment	$675	$8,100		$8,100	$675
Insurance for Home			$500	$500	$42
Property taxes (not in House Pmt.)			$1,500	$1,500	$125
Electricity	$60	$720		$720	$60
Heating	$50	$600		$600	$50
Water	$25	$300		$300	$25
Garbage Collection					
Telephone	$50	$600		$600	$50
Cleaning Services					
Repairs/maintenance	$35	$420		$420	$35
Improvements & Furnishings					
Supplies for Home	$10	$120		$120	$10
Other					
TOTAL HOUSING EXPENSES	**$905**	**$10,860**	**$2,000**	**$12,860**	**$1,072**
B. Food	**$500**	**$6,000**		**$6,000**	**$500**
C. Clothing					
Husband	$25	$300		$300	$25
Wife	$35	$420		$420	$35
Children	$50	$600		$600	$50
TOTAL CLOTHING	**$110**	**$1,320**		**$1,320**	**$110**
D. Transportation					
Auto Insurance			$600	$600	$50
Gas & Oil & Filters	$200	$2,400		$2,400	$200
Repairs/Maintenance	$24	$288		$288	$24
Parking	$12	$144		$144	$12
Bus/Train/Subway					
Other					
TOTAL TRANSPORTATION	**$236**	**$2,832**	**$600**	**$3,432**	**$286**

Living Expenses Form (Pg. 2 of 3) Example #1	Amount Paid Monthly	Mo. x 12 = Subtotal for Yr.	Amount Paid Other Than Monthly	Total Annual Amount	Total Annual Amt. Div. by 12 = Avg. Mo. Amt.
E. Entertainment/Recreation:					
Dining Out	$50	$600		$600	$50
Childcare	$15	$180		$180	$15
Newspapers/cable/magazines	$20	$240		$240	$20
Vacation			$2,500	$2,500	$208
Club Dues/Fees					
Classes/Courses/Activities					
Other	$15	$180		$180	$15
TOTAL ENTERTAINMENT:	**$100**	**$1,200**	**$2,500**	**$3,700**	**$308**
F. Medical Expenses					
Medical/Health Insurance	$50	$600		$600	$50
Doctors	$50	$600		$600	$50
Dentists	$10	$120		$120	$10
Drugs	$10	$120		$120	$10
TOTAL MEDICAL:	**$120**	**$1,440**		**$1,440**	**$120**
G. Insurance					
Life (All Family Members)	$135	$1,620		$1,620	$135
Disability					
Other					
TOTAL INSURANCE:	**$135**	**$1,620**		**$1,620**	**$135**
H. Children:					
School lunches	$35	$420		$420	$35
Allowances	$30	$360		$360	$30
School Tuition					
Lessons/Special Fees/Dues	$25	$300		$300	$25
Other					
TOTAL CHILDREN:	**$90**	**$1,080**		**$1,080**	**$90**
I. Gifts/Occasions:					
Christmas			$650	$650	$54
Birthdays			$200	$200	$17
Anniversary			$50	$50	$4
Holidays other than Christmas					
Other			$50	$50	$5
TOTAL GIFTS:			**$950**	**$950**	**$80**

Living Expenses Form (Pg. 3 of 3) Example #1	Amount Paid Monthly	Mo. x 12 = Subtotal for Yr.	Amount Paid Other Than Monthly	Total Annual Amount	Total Annual Amt. Div. by 12 = Avg. Mo. Amt.
J. Miscellaneous					
Toiletries	$20	$240		$240	$20
Husband: lunches, etc.	$55	$660		$660	$55
Wife: lunches, etc.	$35	$420		$420	$35
Dry cleaning/laundry	$35	$420		$420	$35
Pet care (medical/tags/food)					
Beauty/barber	$30	$360		$360	$30
Other					
Other					
TOTAL MISCELLANEOUS:	**$175**	**$2,100**		**$2,100**	**$175**
TOTAL LIVING EXPENSES	**$2,371**	**$28,452**	**$6,050**	**$34,502**	**$2,876**

Name(s): Bob & Mary Jones (Example #1)

Date Completed: June 30, 2000

Conclusions or Comments: This was Bob & Mary's first time to estimate monthly living expenses. They were surprised at some categories and will adjust in Example #2.

NOTE ON USING THIS FORM: This form will help you arrive at an average monthly amount which is crucial for your spending plan and cash flow management. Record the monthly amount in the first column and then multiply by 12 months for a yearly subtotal. In the third column, record amounts that do not occur every month. Add columns 2 and 3 together to get the total annual amount for column 4. Finally, divide the total annual amount by 12 to get the average monthly amount. Do this for each line item (A-J). Add the ten monthly average expense categories (A-J) to arrive at your estimated monthly total living expenses.

Several expenses do not occur monthly, but must be planned for, such as: auto insurance, most gift categories, and home or auto repairs. It is important that these items be placed in the column labeled "Amount Paid Other Than Monthly". In Chapter 7, you will learn how to reserve for these in a "Freedom Account".

Please use pencil and no decimal points. Remember, these are your **best estimates** for an average month. You will learn to adjust and correct, as you use this form several times.

MONTHLY CASH FLOW ANALYSIS

Name(s): Bob & Mary Jones (Example #1) **Date: June 30, 2000**

Gross Income:		**$4,000**
Less Priority Expenses:		
A. Giving (tithes, offerings & alms)	$415	
B. Taxes (Payroll Records)	$750	
C. Debt (Total Repayments)	$457	
Total Priority Expenses: (-).		**($1,622)**
NET SPENDABLE INCOME: (Gross income less A, B, & C =)		**$2,378**
Monthly Living Expenses:		
A. Housing	$1,072	
B. Food	$500	
C. Clothing	$110	
D. Transportation	$286	
E. Entertainment/recreation	$308	
F. Medical	$120	
G. Insurance	$135	
H. Children	$90	
I. Gifts	$80	
J. Miscellaneous	$175	
TOTAL MONTHLY LIVING EXPENSES:		**$2,876**
Monthly Cash Flow Margin: (Net Spendable Income Minus Total (A-J) Living Expenses)		**($498)**
Your Commitments for Monthly Positive Cash Flow Margin:		
A. Savings	$	
B. Retirement	$	
C. Extra Debt Payment	$	
D. Additional Giving	$	
Total Commitments for + Cash Flow:		**$**
Uncommitted Monthly Cash Flow Margin:		**$**

Comments: THERE IS A SERIOUS NEGATIVE MONTHLY CASH FLOW MARGIN PROBLEM. IMMEDIATE CORRECTIVE ACTION IS NEEDED TO AVOID FURTHER DEBT AND TO REDUCE EXPENSES.

CHAPTER 13

"Everyone who comes to Me, and hears My words, and acts upon them, I will show you whom he is like: he is like a man building a house, who dug deep and laid a foundation upon the rock; and when a flood rose, the torrent burst against that house and could not shake it, because it had been well built."
Luke 6:47-48 (NAS)

Financial Example #2

PROJECTED INCOME AND BIBLICAL GIVING

(Example #2 - After Course)

NAME(S):Bob and Mary Jones **Date: August 31, 2001**

Projected Income

	Amount Paid Monthly	Mo. x 12 =Subtotal for Yr.	Amount Paid Other Than Monthly	Total Annual Amount	Total Annual Amt. Div. by 12 = Avg. Mo. Amt.
Sources:					
Gross wages: husband	$4,000	$48,000		$48,000	$4,000
Gross wages: wife					
Dividends					
Interest					
Rents (cash flow)					
Business Income/"Increase"					
Pensions & annuities					
Other					
TOTAL GROSS INCOME:	**$4,000**	**$48,000**		**$48,000**	**$4,000**

Projected Giving

	Organization	Amount Paid Monthly	Mo. x 12 =Subtotal for Yr.	Amount Paid Other than Monthly	Total Annual Amount	Total Annual Amt. Div. by 12 = Avg. Mo. Amt.
10% Tithe	Church	$400	$4,800		$4,800	$400
Freewill Offerings	Missions	$5	$60		$60	$5
Alms	Benevolence	$5	$60		$60	$5
Other	United Way	$5	$60		$60	$5
Other						
Other						
TOTAL GIVING:		**$415**	**$4,980**		**$4,980**	**$415**

Once the income is determined, the next step is to determine where it goes. Begin with giving. Project your giving for the year by considering each organization you support. This can be from pledges, percentages of income, past giving, or specific giving goals. You may want to check your actual giving to date and then project what you plan to give for the rest of the year.

NOTE ON USING THIS FORM: This form will help you arrive at an average monthly amount which is crucial for your spending plan and cash flow management. Record the monthly amount in the first column and then multiply by 12 months for a yearly subtotal. In the third column, record amounts that do not occur every month. Add columns 2 and 3 together to get the total annual amount for column 4. Finally, divide the total annual amount by 12 to get the average monthly amount. Do this for each line item.

LIST YOUR ASSETS

TYPES OF ASSETS (Example #2)		
1 . Liquid Assets (Easily Converted to Cash)		
Cash on Hand	$200	
Checking Account Balance	$1,800	
Money market funds		
CDs (% interest rate)		
Savings (% interest rate)	$5,500	
Stocks & Bonds		
Life insurance cash values	$0	
Other (Describe)		
TOTAL Liquid Assets:		**$7,500**
2. Non-liquid Assets		
Home (market value)	$75,000	
Land (market value)	$25,000	
Net Worth (Value) of Business		
Real Estate investments (Not Home)		
Jet Ski, Camper, RV, Boats, etc. (Sold)	$0	
Automobiles at market value	$20,000	
Furniture & personal property (conservative market value)	$10,000	
Valuable Collections (stamps, coins,etc.) (Sold)	$0	
Retirement Funds Balance	$20,000	
Funds due from others (Receivables)		
Other (Describe)		
Other (Describe)		
TOTAL Non-liquid Assets		**$150,000**
3. Total Assets (1 & 2)		**$157,500**
Name(s): Bob & Mary Jones (Example #2)		
Date of Completion: August 31, 2001		

DEBT REPAYMENT SCHEDULE

NAME(S): **Bob and Mary Jones (Example #2)**
DATE: **August 31, 2001**

	LENDER	$ BALANCE	$ MONTHLY PAYMENT	INT. %	REMAINING PAYMENTS	PAY-OFF DATE
1	Credit Card A	$0				
2	Credit Card B	$0				
3	Car Loan	$0				
4	Parent's Loan	$0				
5						
6						
7						
8						
9						
10						
11						
12						
13						
14						
15						
TOTAL:		$0	$0			

NOTE ON USING DEBT REPAYMENT SCHEDULE:
This form should include all debts with the exception of a primary home mortgage. The mortgage obligation is a debt and must be included as a liability when you complete the ***List Your Liabilities*** form. However, the mortgage payment is not included on this form because it will be included in the monthly housing expense category when you complete the ***Estimated Monthly Living Expenses*** form.

LIST YOUR LIABILITIES

(Example #2)

LENDER (CREDITOR):	BALANCE DUE:	INTEREST RATE %	PAYMENT SCHEDULE	
			PER MONTH:	UNTIL (MO./YR.):
1. Credit Card A	$0			
2. Credit Card B	$0			
3. Car Loan	$0			
4. Mortgage **	$80,000	9.00%	$675	6/30/2025
5. Parent's Loan	$0			
6.				
7.				
8.				
9.				
10.				
11.				
12.				
13.				
14.				
15.				
16.				
17.				
18.				
19.				
20.				
21.				
22.				
23.				
TOTALS:	$80,000		$675.00	

NAME(S): Bob & Mary Jones (Example #2)

DATE COMPLETED: August 31, 2001

****Note: For simplicity, we left the mortgage balance at $80,000. In reality, the balance would be slightly lower, due to one year of principal payments.**

Note: This form should include all debts previously listed on the "Debt Repayment Schedule", and should also include the home mortgage.

BALANCE SHEET AND NET WORTH STATEMENT
(Example #2)

A. Assets

Liquid Assets:	$7,500	
Non-liquid Assets:	$150,000	
Total Assets:		**$157,500**
B. Less: Total Liabilities: (-)		**(80,000)**
C. Net Worth: (Total Assets - Total Liabilities)		**$77,500**

Name(s): Bob & Mary Jones (Example #2)

Date Completed: August 31, 2001

Comments:

Note on Using this Form: *Complete this form using data from your, recently completed,* ***List Your Assets*** *&* ***List Your Liabilities*** *Forms. Then, subtract* ***total liabilities*** *from* ***total assets*** *& Record your NET WORTH.*

ESTIMATED MONTHLY LIVING EXPENSES

(3 Page Form - Example #2)

EXAMPLE #2 (Page 1 of 3)	Amount Paid Monthly	Mo. x 12 = Subtotal for Yr.	Amount Paid Other Than Monthly	Total Annual Amount	Total Annual Amt. Div. by 12 = Avg. Mo. Amt.
A. Housing					
Mortgage or Rent Payment	$675	$8,100		$8,100	$675
Insurance for Home			$500	$500	$42
Property taxes (not in House Pmt.)			$1,500	$1,500	$125
Electricity	$60	$720		$720	$60
Heating	$50	$600		$600	$50
Water	$25	$300		$300	$25
Garbage Collection					
Telephone	$40	$480		$480	$40
Cleaning Services					
Repairs/maintenance	$25	$300		$300	$25
Improvements & Furnishings					
Supplies for Home	$10	$120		$120	$10
Other					
TOTAL HOUSING EXPENSES	**$885**	**$10,620**	**$2,000**	**$12,620**	**$1,052**
B. Food	**$425**	**$5,100**		**$5,100**	**$425**
C. Clothing					
Husband	$20	$240		$240	$20
Wife	$30	$360		$360	$30
Children	$45	$540		$540	$45
TOTAL CLOTHING	**$95**	**$1,140**		**$1,140**	**$95**
D. Transportation					
Auto Insurance			$600	$600	$50
Gas & Oil & Filters	$100	$1,200		$1,200	$100
Repairs/Maintenance	$12	$144		$144	$12
Parking	$12	$144		$144	$12
Bus/Train/Subway					
Other					
TOTAL TRANSPORTATION	**$124**	**$1,488**	**$600**	**$2,088**	**$174**

Living Expenses Form (Pg. 2 of 3) Example #2	Amount Paid Monthly	Mo. x 12 = Subtotal for Yr.	Amount Paid Other Than Monthly	Total Annual Amount	Total Annual Amt. Div. by 12 = Avg. Mo. Amt.
E. Entertainment/Recreation:					
Dining Out	$25	$300		$300	$25
Childcare	$5	$60		$60	$5
Newspapers/cable/magazines	$10	$120		$120	$10
Vacation			$720	$720	$60
Club Dues/Fees					
Classes/Courses/Activities					
Other	$10	$120		$120	$10
TOTAL ENTERTAINMENT:	**$50**	**$600**	**$720**	**$1,320**	**$110**
F. Medical Expenses					
Medical/Health Insurance	$50	$600		$600	$50
Doctors	$50	$600		$600	$50
Dentists	$10	$120		$120	$10
Drugs	$10	$120		$120	$10
TOTAL MEDICAL:	**$120**	**$1,440**		**$1,440**	**$120**
G. Insurance					
Life (All Family Members)	$35	$420		$420	$35
Disability					
Other					
TOTAL INSURANCE:	**$35**	**$420**		**$420**	**$35**
H. Children:					
School lunches	$35	$420		$420	$35
Allowances	$30	$360		$360	$30
School Tuition					
Lessons/Special Fees/Dues	$25	$300		$300	$25
Other					
TOTAL CHILDREN:	**$90**	**$1,080**		**$1,080**	**$90**
I. Gifts/Occasions:					
Christmas			$360	$360	$30
Birthdays			$120	$120	$10
Anniversary			$50	$50	$4
Holidays other than Christmas					
Other			$24	$24	$2
TOTAL GIFTS:			**$554**	**$554**	**$46**

Living Expenses Form (Pg. 3 of 3) Example #2	Amount Paid Monthly	Mo. x 12 = Subtotal for Yr.	Amount Paid Other Than Monthly	Total Annual Amount	Total Annual Amt. Div. by 12 = Avg. Mo. Amt.
J. Miscellaneous					
Toiletries	$15	$180		$180	$15
Husband: lunches, etc.	$35	$420		$420	$35
Wife: lunches, etc.	$20	$240		$240	$20
Dry cleaning/laundry	$20	$240		$240	$20
Pet care (medical/tags/food)					
Beauty/barber	$20	$240		$240	$20
Other					
Other					
TOTAL MISCELLANEOUS:	**$110**	**$1,320**		**$1,320**	**$110**
TOTAL LIVING EXPENSES	**$1,934**	**$23,208**	**$3,874**	**$27,082**	**$2,257**

Name(s): Bob & Mary Jones (Example #2)

Date Completed: August 31, 2001

Conclusions or Comments:

NOTE ON USING THIS FORM: This form will help you arrive at an average monthly amount which is crucial for your spending plan and cash flow management. Record the monthly amount in the first column and then multiply by 12 months for a yearly subtotal. In the third column, record amounts that do not occur every month. Add columns 2 and 3 together to get the total annual amount for column 4. Finally, divide the total annual amount by 12 to get the average monthly amount. Do this for each line item (A-J). Add the ten monthly average expense categories (A-J) to arrive at your estimated monthly total living expenses.

Several expenses do not occur monthly, but must be planned for, such as: auto insurance, most gift categories, and home or auto repairs. It is important that these items be placed in the column labeled "Amount Paid Other Than Monthly". In Chapter 7, you will learn how to reserve for these in a "Freedom Account".

Please use pencil and no decimal points. Remember, these are your **best estimates** for an average month. You will learn to adjust and correct, as you use this form several times.

MONTHLY CASH FLOW ANALYSIS

Name(s): Bob & Mary Jones (Example #2)		**Date: August 31, 2001**
Gross Income:		**$4,000**
Less Priority Expenses:		
A. Giving (Tithes & Offerings)	$415	
B. Taxes (Payroll Records)	$750	
C. Debt (Repayments)	$0	
Total Priority Expenses: (-)		**($1,165)**
NET SPENDABLE INCOME: (Gross income less A, B, & C =)		**$2,835**
Monthly Living Expenses:		
A. Housing	$1,052	
B. Food	$425	
C. Clothing	$95	
D. Transportation	$174	
E. Entertainment/recreation	$110	
F. Medical	$120	
G. Insurance	$35	
H. Children	$90	
I. Gifts	$46	
J. Miscellaneous	$110	
TOTAL MONTHLY LIVING EXPENSES:		**$2,257**
MONTHLY Cash Flow Margin: (Net Spendable Income Minus Total A-J Living Expenses)		**$578**
Your Commitments for Monthly Positive Cash Flow Margin:		
A. Savings	$100	
B. Retirement	$100	
C. Extra Debt Payment - on mortgage	$100	
D. Additional Giving	$50	
Total Commitments for + Cash Flow:		**$350**
Uncommitted Monthly Cash Flow Margin:		**$228**

Comments: Now that high interest debt has been eliminated, this family has a balanced spending plan and is en route to paying off the mortgage. They have $228 per month in uncommitted cash flow and have the freedom to re-work their spending plan as needed.

CHAPTER 14

"Be sure you know the condition of your flocks, give careful attention to your herds; for riches do not endure forever, and a crown is not secure for all generations."
Proverbs 27:23-24 (NIV)

Cash Flow Control Example

MONTHLY CASH FLOW CONTROL FORM (CF-1)

Financial Freedom Plan: "Keeping Track of God's Money"

EXAMPLE A: One Year After Course Completion

Based on Data From Prior Example #2 Spending Plan.

Name(s): Bob & Mary Jones **Date Completed:** 8/31/01 **For Month:** August **Year:** 2001

Projected/Pla			Actual This Month							Comparison		
			Week 1	Week 2	Week 3	Week 4	Week 5	Monthly Total		Mo Plan	Mo Actual	Plus/ Minus ( )
Monthly Gross Inc.-Cash Flow Form	4,000	---	1,000	1,000	1,000	1,000	0	4,000		4,000	4,000	0
Less Total Giving-Cash Flow Form	-415	---	-115	-100	-100	-100	0	-415		-415	-415	0
Less Taxes-Cash Flow Form	-750	---	-188	-187	-188	-187	0	-750		-750	-750	0
Less Debt Repayment-Cash Flow Form	0	---	0	0	0	0	0	0		0	0	0
Net Spendable Inc.-Cash Flow Form	**2,835**	**Total**	697	713	712	713	0	2,835	**Total:**	2,835	2,835	0

LIV. EXPENSE	1	2	3	4	5	6	7	8	9	10	11	12	13	14	15	16	17	18	19	20	21	22	23	24	25	26	27	28	29	30	31	Actual Total	Month Plan	Diff.
A-J: (See Living Expenses Form)																																		
A-Housing					735					50					25					40			25					10				885	1,052	167
B-Food	100						125											100								100						425	425	0
C-Clothing			20					30								40																90	95	5
D-Trans.		12					25							25							25				40			25		32		184	174	-10
E-Ent./Rec.	10				10						5				15				48											10		98	110	12
F-Med.Ex.									30								50								50							130	120	-10
G-Insurance							35																									35	35	0
H-Children	5		8				5			8				5			8	25			7			8				5			8	92	90	-2
I-Gifts/Spec. Occ.				20								15																				35	46	11
J-Misc.		18						20					5				25					21				11			6			106	110	4
Total (A-J):	115	30	28	20	745	0	190	50	30	58	5	15	5	30	40	40	83	125	48	40	32	21	25	8	90	111	0	40	6	42	8	2,080	2,257	177

RECAP MONTHLY DATA

Actual Net Spendable Income:	$	2,835
Less Actual (A-J) Living Expenses:	(	2,080)
Actual Cash Flow Margin this Month:	$	755
Planned CF From Monthly CF Analysis Form:	$	578
Temporary Surplus or Deficit ( ) this Month	$	177

After completing this form, proceed to form CF-2 to display & track your uses of positive cash flow.

Note: If CF is Negative or Zero, then the Form CF-2 will **not Yet** apply; proceed to annual summary form (CF-3).

Comments/Action Needed: Bob & Mary actually have $177 more cash flow than an average month per their plan. This $177 temporary surplus will be deposited into their special "Freedom Account" checking account, which will be used when they need to pay bills for planned expenses, like insurance, that do not occur every month.

Advice on Using Form: *Only use a very sharp pencil; no decimals, round-up to nearest dollar; use a minus sign or brackets ( ) to indicate minus numbers; fill in all possible blanks; recheck math, and if possible use a calculator with adding machine tape.*

TRACKING USE OF MONTHLY POSITIVE CASH FLOW MARGIN (FORM CF-2)

"Keeping Track of God's Cash Flow"

Name(s): Bob & Mary Jones **Date Completed:** 8/31/01 **For Month:** August **Year:** 2001

EXAMPLE B: One Year After Completion Based on Data From Bob & Mary's CF-1 Form.

Actual Net Spendable Income:	$2,835
Less Actual (A-J) Living Expenses:	($2,080)
Actual Cash Flow Margin this Month:	$755
Planned CF From Monthly CF Analysis Form:	$578
Temporary Surplus or Deficit ( ) this Month:	$177

Below, Record Daily Transactions & Totals:

Uses For Positive Cash Flow Margin

	1	2	3	4	5	6	7	8	9	10	11	12	13	14	15	16	17	18	19	20	21	22	23	24	25	26	27	28	29	30	31	Actual Tot.
"Freedom Acct."																														177		177
Ex. Debt Repay.					100																											100
Savings																														100		100
Extra Giving															50																	50
Retirement																														100		100
Money Market																														228		228
Other (Explain):																																
TOTALS:	0	0	0	0	100	0	0	0	0	0	0	0	0	0	50	0	0	0	0	0	0	0	0	0	0	0	0	0	0	605	0	755

Step 1: Add each daily column to get a daily total.

Step 2: When the month is complete add the daily (1-31) totals across & record in actual total space.

Step 3: Also, when month is complete, add across for each category (example "Freedom Account") and record total in appropriate total space for that category.

Step 4: Add the monthly totals down. The total must equal step 2 total.

Step 5: To check your calculations, the actual total monthly cash flow must equal the Actual Cash Flow Margin value in the box at the top of this form.

Step 6: Now proceed to Form CF-3: Yearly Cash Flow Summary.

Comments/Action Needed: Bob & Mary waited until near the end of the month to use most of their positive cash flow; this gave them some extra reserve funds during the month. The $177 temporary surplus was deposited into their special "Freedom Account" checking account for non-monthly, but planned, expenses.

YEARLY CASH FLOW SUMMARY (FORM CF-3)	**EXAMPLE C:** One Year After Course Completion Based on Data From Bob & Mary's CF-1 & CF-2 Forms.

"Keeping Track of God's Money Annually"

Actual Summary by Month (From Monthly Cash Flow Control Forms: CF-1 & CF-2)

Name(s): Bob & Mary Jones **Date Completed:** 8/31/01 **Year:** 200

		Jan.	Feb.	Mar.	April	May	June	July	Aug.	Sept.	Oct.	Nov.	Dec.	Year Total	Year Plan	Diff.
	Monthly Income								4,000							
	Less Giving								-415							
	Less Taxes								-750							
	Less Debt Repay.								0							
1	*Equals-Net Spend.*								2,835							
	Living Exps. (A-J)															
	A-Housing								885							
	B-Food								425							
	C-Clothing								90							
	D-Transportation								184							
	E-Ent./Rec.								98							
	F-Med. Expenses								130							
	G-Insurance								35							
	H-Children								92							
	I-Gifts/Spec. Occ.								35							
	J-Miscellaneous								106							
2	***Sub Total (A-J):***								2,080							
	Cash Flow Uses:															
	"Freedom Account"								177							
	Ex. Debt Repayment								100							
	Savings								100							
	Extra Giving								50							
	Retirement								100							
	Money Market								228							
	Other (Explain):								0							
3	**Sub Tot. C.F. Uses:**								755							
4	**TOTAL: 2 + 3 =4**								2,835							
	4 Should = 1															

Comments/Action Needed: This is just an example. A family can start their plan in any month. Do not put off starting; any month is a great time to begin!

Advice on using this Form: Use a very sharp pencil & have a calculator & eraser handy. Round all values to nearest whole dollar; no decimals.

CHAPTER 15

"The plans of the diligent lead to profit as surely as haste leads to poverty."
Proverbs 21:5 (NIV)

"Jabez cried to the God of Israel, saying, Oh that you would bless me and enlarge my border, and that Your hand might be with me, and You would keep me from evil so it might not hurt me! And God granted his request."
1 Chronicles 4:10 (Amplified)

Blank Forms

SPECIAL NOTE – RESTRICTED FORM COPY PERMISSION

Owners of this book are granted permission to photocopy these blank forms (only) and only for personal use.

PROJECTED INCOME AND BIBLICAL GIVING

NAME(S):____________________________ Date: ________________

Projected Income

INCOME SOURCES:	Amount Paid Monthly	Mo. x 12 =Subtotal for Yr.	Amount Paid Other Than Monthly	Total Annual Amount	Total Annual Amt. Div. by 12 = Avg. Mo. Amt.
Gross wages: husband					
Gross wages: wife					
Dividends					
Interest					
Rents (Income Less Expenses)					
Business Income/"Increase"					
Retirement Funds					
Other					
TOTAL GROSS INCOME:	$	$	$	$	$

Projected Giving

	Organization	Amount Paid Monthly	Mo. x 12 =Subtotal for Yr.	Amount Paid Other than Monthly	Total Annual Amount	Total Annual Amt. Div. by 12 = Avg. Mo. Amt.
10% Tithe						
Freewill Offerings						
Alms (Poor)						
Other Charities						
Other Charities						
Other Giving						
TOTAL GIVING:		$	$	$	$	$

Once the income is determined, the next step is to determine where it goes. Begin with giving. Project your giving for the year by considering each organization you support. This can be from specific giving goals, percentages of income, or past giving records. You may want to check your actual giving to date and then project what you plan to give for the rest of the year.

NOTE ON USING THIS FORM: This form will help you arrive at an average monthly amount which is crucial for your spending plan and cash flow management. Record the monthly amount in the first column and then multiply by 12 months for a yearly subtotal. In the third column, record amounts that do not occur every month. Add columns 2 and 3 together to get the total annual amount for column 4. Finally, divide the total annual amount by 12 to get the average monthly amount. Do this for each line item.

FINANCIAL VISION AND FAITH GOALS

This Form may be used for 1 yr. up to 5 yr. Goals (Page 1 of 4)

Name(s):____________________ Date Goal Form Completed: __________

By(month & year): ________________ we see the following faith goals being accomplished.

BIBLICAL GIVING GOALS:

We will pay our 10% tithe plus give & sow __________% of our increase for offerings & alms.

We will be making additional gifts each year of __________ to ____________________

First Action Step:

First Action Step By (Month & Year):

SAVING GOALS:

Type of Savings Account (Do Not Include Investments)	*Amount*	*Annual Return*
	$	%
	$	%
TOTAL AMOUNT	$	

First Action Step:

First Action Step By (Month & Year):

EDUCATION FUND GOALS:

A college or special education fund will exist for each of our children/grandchildren:

Child	*Type of College*	*Approximate Annual Cost*	*Approximate Total Cost*	*Goal Amount*
		$	$	$
		$	$	$
		$	$	$
		$	$	$

First Action Step:

First Action Step By (Month & Year):

FINANCIAL VISION AND FAITH GOALS

(Page 2 of 4)

DEBT REPAYMENT GOALS:

We will have paid off the following debts:

Creditors	*Total Owed*
____________	$ ____________
____________	$ ____________
____________	$ ____________
____________	$ ____________
____________	$ ____________
____________	$ ____________
____________	$ ____________

First Action Step:

First Action Step By (Month & Year):

MAJOR PURCHASES:

We will have made the following major purchases/expenditures: (new home, car, vacations, etc.)

Purchase/Expenditure	*Goal Amount*
____________	$ ____________
____________	$ ____________
____________	$ ____________
____________	$ ____________
____________	$ ____________
____________	$ ____________

First Action Step:

First Action Step By (Month & Year):

LIFESTYLE GOALS:

For the Next ______ Years, My (Our) intention(s) is (are) to achieve one of the following lifestyles:

Check One:

________ Maintain Present Level (Giving, Saving & Spending).

________ Enlarge Spending Plan (Giving, Saving & Spending).

________ Cut Back on Lifestyle and Spending Plan.

Following is a brief explanation of the strategy to achieve the Lifestyle selection checked above: ________________________________

First Action Step:

First Action Step By (Month & Year):

FINANCIAL VISION AND FAITH GOALS

START A BUSINESS:

I (We) will have started our own business which will require an approximate investment of: $ ______________

Describe Your Business: ______________________________

____

____

First Action Step: ______________________________

First Action Step By (Month & Year): ______________________________

____

____

INVESTMENT GOALS:

I (We) will have the following investments (Stocks, Bonds, Mutual Funds, Real Estate, Savings, Etc.):

Type of Investment	***Amount Invested***	***Annual Return***
	$	$
	$	$
	$	$
	$	$
	$	$
	$	$
Total Goal:	$	

First Action Step: ______________________________

First Action Step By (Month & Year): ______________________________

OTHER GOALS: (list, explain & estimate values if applicable)

____

____

____

____

First Action Step: ______________________________

First Action Step By (Month & Year): ______________________________

____

____

____

FINANCIAL VISION AND FAITH GOALS

ESTATE PLANNING:

I (We) would like to pass on to my spouse (children) the following estate (describe basics):

First Action Step:

First Action Step By (Month & Year):

CONGRATULATIONS:

Once Godly goals are established, you are ahead of 95% of the people in the world.

The very next step is to begin taking your First Action Steps to accomplish the goals that God has given you. These may be very small steps. For example, a savings plan goal may start by your opening a savings account with a $5 deposit. It may seem small, but in reality it is a huge action step.....so don't delay.

MOVE IN FAITH:

You need to move in faith. You prayed and set these goals knowing that God has a wonderful plan for you (see Jeremiah 29:11). God has the resources. You need to supply the faith and the diligence to be a good and faithful steward. Then let God be God, He is your pilot and your provider.

REVIEW/REVISE ANNUALLY:

Make a commitment to review your goals at least once a year; maybe at the start of the New Year. Thank God for progress and for Breakthrough! Set new goals, or revise; these are your goals.

Married Couples: Be sure to do your goal setting, and goals review, as a one flesh couple.

DEBT REPAYMENT SCHEDULE

NAME(S): ______________________

DATE: ______________________

	LENDER	$ BALANCE	$ MONTHLY PAYMENT	INT. %	REMAINING PAYMENTS	PAY-OFF DATE
1						
2						
3						
4						
5						
6						
7						
8						
9						
10						
11						
12						
13						
14						
15						
TOTAL:						

NOTE ON USING DEBT REPAYMENT SCHEDULE:

This form should include all debts with the exception of a primary home mortgage. The mortgage obligation is a debt and must be included as a liability when you complete the ***List Your Liabilities*** form. However, the mortgage payment is not included on this form because it will be included in the monthly housing expense category when you complete the ***Estimated Monthly Living Expenses*** form. **If your list of debts exceeds the 15 spaces given, make extra pages. Do not despair, you are on the road to Financial Freedom.**

LIST YOUR ASSETS

TYPES OF ASSETS	
1. Liquid Assets (Easily Converted to Cash)	
Cash on Hand	
Checking Account Balance	
Money market funds	
CDs (% interest rate)	
Savings (% interest rate)	
Stocks & Bonds	
Life insurance cash values	
Other (Describe)	
TOTAL Liquid Assets:	$
2. Non-liquid Assets	
Home (market value)	
Land (market value)	
Net Worth (Value) of Business	
Real Estate investments (Not Home)	
Jet Ski, Camper, RV, Boats, etc.	
Automobiles at market value	
Furniture & personal property (conservative market value)	
Valuable Collections (stamps, coins,etc.)	
Retirement Funds Balance	
Funds due from others (Receivables)	
Other (Describe)	
Other (Describe)	
TOTAL Non-liquid Assets	$
3. Total Assets (1 & 2)	$
Name(s):	
Date of Completion:	

LIST YOUR LIABILITIES

LENDER (CREDITOR):	BALANCE DUE:	INTEREST RATE %	PAYMENT SCHEDULE PER MONTH:	UNTIL (MO./YR.):
1.	$		$	
2.				
3.				
4.				
5.				
6.				
7.				
8.				
9.				
10.				
11.				
12.				
13.				
14.				
15.				
16.				
17.				
18.				
19.				
20.				
21.				
22.				
23.				
TOTALS:	$		$	

NAME(S):

DATE COMPLETED:

Note: This form should include all debts previously listed on the "Debt Repayment Schedule", and should also include the home mortgage.

BALANCE SHEET AND NET WORTH STATEMENT

A. Assets

Liquid Assets: $ ________

Non-liquid Assets: $ ________

Total Assets: $ ________

B. Less: Total Liabilities: (-) $ ________

C. Net Worth: (Total Assets - Total Liabilities) $ ________

Name(s):

Date Completed:

Comments:

Note on Using this Form: *Complete this form using data from your, recently completed,* ***List Your Assets*** *&* ***List Your Liabilities*** *Forms. Then, subtract* ***total liabilities*** *from* ***total assets*** *& Record your NET WORTH.*

ESTIMATED MONTHLY LIVING EXPENSES (3 Page Form)

Living Expenses Form (Page 1 of 3)	Amount Paid Monthly	Mo. x 12 = Subtotal for Yr.	Amount Paid Other Than Monthly	Total Annual Amount	Total Annual Amt. Div. by 12 = Avg. Mo. Amt.
A. Housing					
Mortgage or Rent Payment					
Insurance for Home					
Property taxes (not in House Pmt.)					
Electricity					
Heating					
Water					
Garbage Collection					
Telephone					
Cleaning Services					
Repairs/maintenance					
Improvements & Furnishings					
Supplies for Home					
Other					
TOTAL HOUSING EXPENSES	$	$	$	$	$
B. Food	$	$	$	$	$
C. Clothing					
Husband					
Wife					
Children					
TOTAL CLOTHING	$	$	$	$	$
D. Transportation					
Auto Insurance					
Gas & Oil & Filters					
Repairs/Maintenance					
Parking					
Bus/Train/Subway					
Other					
TOTAL TRANSPORTATION	$	$	$	$	$

Living Expenses Form (Pg. 2 of 3)	Amount Paid Monthly	Mo. x 12 = Subtotal for Yr.	Amount Paid Other Than Monthly	Total Annual Amount	Total Annual Amt. Div. by 12 = Avg. Mo. Amt.
E. Entertainment/Recreation:					
Dining Out					
Childcare					
Newspapers/cable/magazines					
Vacation					
Club Dues/Fees					
Classes/Courses/Activities					
Other					
TOTAL ENTERTAINMENT:	$	$	$	$	$
F. Medical Expenses					
Medical/Health Insurance					
Doctors					
Dentists					
Drugs					
TOTAL MEDICAL:	$	$	$	$	$
G. Insurance					
Life (All Family Members)					
Disability					
Other					
TOTAL INSURANCE:	$	$	$	$	$
H. Children:					
School lunches					
Allowances					
School Tuition					
Lessons/Special Fees/Dues					
Other					
TOTAL CHILDREN:	$	$	$	$	$
I. Gifts/Occasions:					
Christmas					
Birthdays					
Anniversary					
Holidays other than Christmas					
Other					
TOTAL GIFTS:	$	$	$	$	$

Living Expenses Form (Pg. 3 of 3)	Amount Paid Monthly	Mo. x 12 = Subtotal for Yr.	Amount Paid Other Than Monthly	Total Annual Amount	Total Annual Amt. Div. by 12 = Avg. Mo. Amt.
J. Miscellaneous					
Toiletries					
Husband: lunches, etc.					
Wife: lunches, etc.					
Dry cleaning/laundry					
Pet care (medical/tags/food)					
Beauty/barber					
Other					
Other					
TOTAL MISCELLANEOUS:	$	$	$	$	$
TOTAL LIVING EXPENSES	$	$	$	$	$

Name(s):

Date Completed:

Conclusions or Comments:

NOTE ON USING THIS FORM: This form will help you arrive at an average monthly amount which is crucial for your spending plan and cash flow management. Record the monthly amount in the first column and then multiply by 12 months for a yearly subtotal. In the third column, record amounts that do not occur every month. Add columns 2 and 3 together to get the total annual amount for column 4. Finally, divide the total annual amount by 12 to get the average monthly amount. Do this for each line item (A-J). Add the ten monthly average expense categories (A-J) to arrive at your estimated monthly total living expenses.

Several expenses do not occur monthly, but must be planned for, such as: auto insurance, most gift categories, and home or auto repairs. It is important that these items be placed in the column labeled "Amount Paid Other Than Monthly". In Chapter 7, you will learn how to reserve for these in a "Freedom Account".

Please use pencil and no decimal points. Remember, these are your **best estimates** for an average month. You will learn to adjust and correct, as you use this form several times.

MONTHLY CASH FLOW ANALYSIS

Name(s): **Date:**

Gross Income: . . . . **$** ____________

Less Priority Expenses:

A. Giving (Tithes & Offerings) $ ____________

B. Taxes (Payroll Records) $ ____________

C. Debt (Total Repayments) $ ____________

Total Priority Expenses: (-) . . . . **$ (** ____________ **)**

NET SPENDABLE INCOME:
(Gross income less A, B, & C =) **$** ____________

Monthly Living Expenses:

A. Housing ____________
B. Food ____________
C. Clothing ____________
D. Transportation ____________
E. Entertainment/recreation ____________
F. Medical ____________
G. Insurance ____________
H. Children ____________
I. Gifts ____________
J. Miscellaneous ____________

TOTAL MONTHLY LIVING EXPENSES: **$** ____________

Monthly Cash Flow Margin: **$** ____________
(Net Spendable Income Minus Total A-J Living Expenses)

Your Commitments For Monthly Positive Cash Flow Margin:

A. Savings $ ____________
B. Retirement $ ____________
C. Extra Debt Payments $ ____________
D. Additional Giving $ ____________

Total Commitments for + Cash Flow: **$** ____________

Uncommitted Monthly Cash Flow Margin: **$** ____________

Comments: (What will you change?):

MONTHLY CASH FLOW CONTROL FORM (CF-1)

Financial Freedom Plan: "Keeping Track of God's Money"

Name(s): ____________________ **Date Completed:** ________ **For Month:** ________ **Year:** ________

Projected/Plan			Actual This Month							Comparison		
			Week 1	Week 2	Week 3	Week 4	Week 5	Monthly Total		Mo Plan	Mo Actual	Plus/ Minus ( )
Monthly Gross Income-Cash Flow Form		---										
Less Total Giving-Cash Flow Form		---							----------			
Less Taxes-Cash Flow Form		---							----------			
Less Debt Repayment-Cash Flow Form		---							----------			
Net Spendable Income-Cash Flow Form		Total							Total:			

LIV. EXPENSE	1	2	3	4	5	6	7	8	9	10	11	12	13	14	15	16	17	18	19	20	21	22	23	24	25	26	27	28	29	30	31	Actual Total	Month Plan	Diff.
A-J: (See Living Expenses Form)																																		
A-Housing																																		
B-Food																																		
C-Clothing																																		
D-Trans.																																		
E-Ent./Rec.																																		
F-Med.Ex.																																		
G-Insurance																																		
H-Children																																		
I-Gifts/Spec. Occ.																																		
J-Misc.																																		
Total (A-J):																																		

RECAP MONTHLY DATA

Actual Net Spendable Income:	$ ________
Less Actual (A-J) Living Expenses:	(________)
Actual Cash Flow Margin this Month:	$ ________
Planned CF From Monthly CF Analysis Form:	$ ________
Temporary Surplus or Deficit ( ) this Month:	$ ________

After completing this form, proceed to form CF-2 to display & track your uses of positive cash flow.

Note: If CF is Negative or Zero, then the Form CF-2 will **not Yet** apply; proceed to annual summary form (CF-3).

Comments/Action Needed:

Advice on Using Form: *Only use a very sharp pencil; no decimals, round-up to nearest dollar; use brackets ( ) to indicate minus numbers; fill in all possible blanks; recheck math, and if possible use a calculator with adding machine tape.*

TRACKING USE OF MONTHLY POSITIVE CASH FLOW MARGIN (FORM CF-2)

"Keeping Track of God's Cash Flow"

Name(s): ____________________ **Date Completed:** __________ **For Month:** __________ **Year:** _______

From Form CF-1 you determined your monthly cash flow margin. Only if it is positive, use the box to the right to repeat the "Recap Monthly Data" numbers for CF-1. →

Actual Net Spendable Income:	______
Less Actual (A-J) Living Expenses:	______
Actual Cash Flow Margin this Month:	______
Planned CF From Monthly CF Analysis Form:	______
Temporary Surplus or Deficit ( ) this Month:	______

Below, Record Daily Transactions & Totals:

Uses For Positive Cash Flow Margin

	1	2	3	4	5	6	7	8	9	10	11	12	13	14	15	16	17	18	19	20	21	22	23	24	25	26	27	28	29	30	31	Actual Tot.
"Freedom Acct."																																
Ex. Debt Repay.																																
Savings																																
Extra Giving																																
Retirement																																
Money Market																																
Other (Explain):																																
TOTALS:																																

Step 1: Add each daily column to get a daily total.

Step 2: When the month is complete add the daily (1-31) totals across & record in actual total space.

Step 3: Also, when month is complete, add across for each category (example "Freedom Account") and record total in appropriate total space for that category.

Step 4: Add the monthly totals down. The total must equal step 2 total.

Step 5: To check your calculations, the actual total monthly cash flow must equal the Actual Cash Flow Margin value in the box at the top of this form.

Step 6: Now proceed to Form CF-3: Yearly Cash Flow Summary.

Comments/Action Needed:

YEARLY CASH FLOW SUMMARY (FORM CF-3)

"Keeping Track of God's Money Annually"

Actual Summary by Month (From Monthly Cash Flow Control Forms: CF-1 & CF-2)

Name(s): ________________ **Date Completed:** ________ **Year:** ____

		Jan.	Feb.	Mar.	April	May	June	July	Aug.	Sept.	Oct.	Nov.	Dec.	Year Total	Year Plan	Diff.
	Monthly Income															
	Less Giving															
	Less Taxes															
	Less Debt Repay.															
1	*Equals-Net Spend.*															
	Living Exps. (A-J)															
	A-Housing															
	B-Food															
	C-Clothing															
	D-Transportation															
	E-Ent./Rec.															
	F-Med. Expenses															
	G-Insurance															
	H-Children															
	I-Gifts/Spec. Occ.															
	J-Miscellaneous															
2	***Sub Total (A-J):***															
	Cash Flow Uses:															
	"Freedom Account"															
	Ex. Debt Repayment															
	Saving															
	Extra Giving															
	Retirement															
	Money Market															
	Other (Explain):															
3	**Sub Tot. C.F. Uses:**															
4	**TOTAL: 2 + 3 =4**															
	4 Should = 1															

Comments/Action Needed:

Advice on using this Form: Use a very sharp pencil & have a calculator & eraser handy. Round all values to nearest whole dollar; no decimals.

NOTES

NOTES

NOTES

NOTES

To Order This Book
Please Visit Our Website For Instructions
www.debtfreelegacy.com

Contact Authors @
Bill and Maureen Sitter
23995 Bat Cave Road, Suite #200
San Antonio, Texas 78266
Toll Free: 1-800-392-9410
Fax: 210-651-5562
E-mail: bill@jordansitter.com
Website: www.debtfreelegacy.com

To Order This Book
Please Visit Our Website For Instructions
www.debtfreelegacy.com

Contact Authors @
Bill and Maureen Sitter
23995 Bat Cave Road, Suite #200
San Antonio, Texas 78266
Toll Free: 1-800-392-9410
Fax: 210-651-5562
E-mail: bill@jordansitter.com
Website: www.debtfreelegacy.com